Deception in High Places

There is a companion website for this book – www.deceptioninhighplaces.com – on which you can find the text of some of the key documents cited in this book, as well as how to find out more about the arms trade and corruption.

Deception in High Places

A History of Bribery in Britain's Arms Trade

Nicholas Gilby

PlutoPress
www.plutobooks.com

First published 2014 by Pluto Press
345 Archway Road, London N6 5AA

www.plutobooks.com

Distributed in the United States of America exclusively by
Palgrave Macmillan, a division of St. Martin's Press LLC,
175 Fifth Avenue, New York, NY 10010

British Library Cataloguing in Publication Data
A catalogue record for this book is available from the British Library

ISBN	978 0 7453 3427 1	Hardback
ISBN	978 0 7453 3426 4	Paperback
ISBN	978 1 7837 1129 1	PDF eBook
ISBN	978 1 7837 1131 4	Kindle eBook
ISBN	978 1 7837 1130 7	EPUB eBook

Library of Congress Cataloging in Publication Data applied for

10   9   8   7   6   5   4   3   2   1

Typeset from disk by Stanford DTP Services, Northampton, England
Cover design by Melanie Patrick
Simultaneously printed digitally by CPI Antony Rowe, Chippenham, UK
and Edwards Bros in the United States of America

Contents

List of Figures and Illustrations   vi
Acknowledgements   vii
Preface   ix

1   The Chancer: Negotiating BAE's First Saudi Deals
(1963–66)   1

2   Hand in Glove: Whitehall's Involvement in Bribery
Schemes (1968–73)   21

3   The 'Deniable Fiddle': Dealing with the Saudi Arabian
National Guard (1968–72)   40

4   The 'Special Relationship': Britain and the Shah of Iran
(1970–78)   56

5   Parting Ways: British and American Corruption Scandals
(1975–76)   72

6   At Arm's Length: How the British Government Avoided
Taking Action against Corruption (1976–78)   92

7   Thwarted: How International Action against Corruption
was Stopped in its Tracks (1975–80)   110

8   'Business as Usual' (1980–2001)   129

9   An Investigation Interrupted: The SFO and BAE Systems
(2004–10)   154

Conclusion   179

Notes   186
Index   225

List of Figures and Illustrations

Figures

1.1 Key figures of the Saudi Royal Family (1962–80) 2
8.1 Some Saudi royals connected to the Al Yamamah arms deal 133

Illustrations

1 A British Aircraft Corporation Thunderbird Mark 1 missile 6
2 A British Aircraft Corporation Lightning Mark 55, in Royal
Saudi Air Force colours 8
3 Geoffrey Edwards, agent for the British Aircraft Corporation,
Associated Electrical Industries and Airwork in Saudi Arabia
in the 1960s 10
4 Sir Lester Suffield, Head of Defence Sales in the Ministry
of Defence, 1969–76 29
5 British Prime Minister Harold Wilson welcomes
King Feisal of Saudi
Arabia to Downing Street, May 1967 34
6 King Abdullah of Saudi Arabia meeting British Prime
Minister Tony Blair at Downing Street, 1998 41
7 The Shah of Iran, pictured in 1971 57
8 Sir Frank Cooper, Permanent Secretary, Ministry of
Defence, 1976–82 100
9 A British Aerospace Tornado Air Defence Variant fighter 135
10 A British Aerospace Tornado Interdictor/Strike
fighter-bomber 135
11 Saudi Minister of Defence and Aviation Prince Sultan
and British Defence Secretary Michael Heseltine signing
the first Al Yamamah Memorandum of Understanding in
London, September 1985 136
12 A prototype Eurofighter Typhoon fighter 166

Acknowledgements

For long periods I thought this book would never be published. I would like to thank my family, friends and some (former) colleagues for their encouragement. To those who may have thought I was wasting my time, thank you for being too polite to say so.

I would like to thank Helen Angle, Graham Kelly and Dr Sally Malam for granting me a sabbatical in 2006 to start the research in earnest. I am also grateful to the unfailingly helpful staff of the institutions which have given me access to their collections: The National Archives, the Institution of Engineering and Technology, the British Library, Cambridge University Library and the Churchill Archives Centre at Churchill College, Cambridge. I am grateful to Dr Clare Chambers and Dr Phil Parvin for their generous hospitality in Cambridge. Peter Gardiner very kindly allowed me access to his private archive documenting BAE's programme of benefits for Prince Turki bin Nasser, and Richard Brooks kindly gave me his documents about SIMEC.

Material from the Vickers Archive is produced by permission from the Vickers Archive held at the Cambridge University Library, and I am also grateful to the Syndics of Cambridge University Library for permitting me to publish quotations from the Vickers Archive. Material from the Caldecote Papers is produced by permission of the Institution of Engineering and Technology. The OECD Publishing Division and SEC Historical Society have also kindly given permission for me to quote from their documents.

It took me a long time to find a publisher who was prepared to publish this book. I am enormously grateful to David Castle and Anne Beech at Pluto Press for awarding me a contract, and for their patience during the contract negotiations. I greatly appreciate the patience and professionalism of all at Pluto who have helped the book through the publishing process. I would also like to thank my former agent, Leslie Gardiner, for her efforts on my behalf, and Laurie Flynn for introducing me to her.

The Trust for Research and Education on the Arms Trade supported me financially during my sabbatical. It also paid for the illustrations, and, along with the Joseph Rowntree Charitable Trust, contributed to the cost of the libel check this book has undergone. The support of their trustees, and of Celia McKeon of Joseph Rowntree Charitable Trust, has been wonderful and indispensable. I am indebted to Henry McLaughlin of Campaign Against Arms Trade for his advice on funding applications.

I would like to thank Andrew Feinstein, Nick Hildyard, Dr Sue Hawley, Dr Anna Stavrianakis and Professor Mark Phythian for being so generous with their time and advice over the years. Andreas Cebulla kindly agreed to be a 'lay' reader of the draft manuscript.

I enjoyed hugely working with all those at Campaign Against Arms Trade who were involved in the 'Control BAE' campaign, which aimed to reopen the Serious Fraud Office's investigation into the Al Yamamah arms deal. In particular, Mike Lewis and Symon Hill both did outstanding work. We were extremely fortunate to have a first-class team of lawyers representing us during the Judicial Review (winning a famous victory in the High Court) and the satellite litigation: Jamie Beagent and Richard Stein of Leigh Day & Co., Ben Jaffey of Blackstone Chambers, Lord Pannick, Anthony Peto QC, Dinah Rose QC and Philippe Sands QC.

During that time and since, I worked closely with a number of journalists, and would like to thank in particular Rob Evans and Peter Marshall for their support and encouragement.

Important parts of the story told in this book would have remained an official secret without my victory over the Foreign and Commonwealth Office in an Information Tribunal. I owe an enormous debt of thanks to Jamie Beagent and Rachel Logan for their assistance; Phil Michaels for his encouragement and feedback on my legal submissions; Carne Ross of Independent Diplomat, and the late Joe Roeber for agreeing to testify on my behalf. Most importantly, Tom Hickman of Blackstone Chambers was incredibly supportive and provided invaluable shrewd tactical advice. Khawar Qureshi QC very kindly agreed to represent me in the closed hearings as my 'special advocate'. For legal advice on libel issues I am greatly indebted to Dr Glen Reynolds, and Tamsin Allen and Athalie Matthews of Bindmans.

Lastly, I would like to thank Ann Feltham and Ian Prichard of Campaign Against Arms Trade, both of whom have been outstandingly supportive of my work over very many years, and who have been a pleasure to work with.

Finally, any errors in the book are, of course, entirely my responsibility.

Preface

> No area of the corruption story is as full of intrigue and shrouded in
> secrecy than international trade in arms and weapons systems.

So writes a co-founder of Transparency International, Frank Vogl, in
his book *Waging War on Corruption*.[1] In this book you can peer behind
the veil of secrecy and see the intrigues of the political elites of several
countries, into what author and former South African politician
Andrew Feinstein has called a 'shadow world'. I will show you how
bribery schemes run by British and American arms companies work.

What is bribery? The three international anti-corruption
agreements – the OECD Convention on Combating Bribery of Foreign
Public Officials in International Business Transactions, the UN
Convention against Corruption, and the Council of Europe's Criminal
Law Convention on Corruption – define a bribe. This is an 'undue
advantage', which may be of a monetary or non-monetary nature,
tangible or intangible.[2] In this book I use the word 'bribery' to mean the
passing, or the intention of passing, an undue advantage to a decision-
maker, directly or indirectly, in return for the award of a commercial
contract. However, whether bribery is illegal depends on the law at the
time in the country of the bribe giver and the bribe receiver.

Corruption is not defined by these international agreements, as it
manifests itself in a large number of ways.[3] Transparency International
defines it as 'the abuse of entrusted power for private gain',[4] and this is
what I mean by corruption. However, the word 'entrusted' is not always
apt, for in many countries mentioned in this book, those abusing their
power have not been 'entrusted' with it by the consent of their people.

Transparency International further distinguishes between 'grand',
'petty' and 'political' corruption. In this book I mostly describe
'grand corruption', in other words 'acts committed at a high level of
government that distort policies or the central functioning of the state,
enabling leaders to benefit at the expense of the public good'. Typically,
huge sums are involved.

Some behaviour can be characterised as corrupt, but is not
necessarily illegal. As will become clear, most of the actions of British

companies described in this book were not illegal under English law at the time. Further, many of those involved might not think of their own behaviour as 'corrupt'. You can be the judge of that.

In 2010 one of Britain's biggest companies, BAE Systems, was fined $400 million in America because its actions[5] 'impeded U.S. efforts to ensure international trade is free of corruption'. It remains one of the largest ever fines imposed on a company investigated for corruption anywhere. But what prompted the American investigation was the high profile failure of a British investigation of the company's most important contract – Al Yamamah – Britain's biggest ever arms deal. For in 2006 BAE's customer – the Saudi Government – successfully pressurised the British Government into ending a major corruption investigation into the deal. In this book you can read the whole story.

It is a story that goes back 50 years, and involves dubious deals every step of the way. I will describe how British arms companies have tried to bribe to get contracts – sometimes successfully, sometimes not – not only in Saudi Arabia, but also in Lebanon, Iran, Kuwait, and other countries. Implicated in these bribery schemes are some of the most powerful people in these countries at the time.

The arms trade has been a significant part of international trade and relations between Governments for several centuries. Having expanded rapidly during the Cold War, declined afterwards,[6] but revived after the 11 September 2001 terrorist attacks in America,[7] it is currently worth tens of billions of pounds a year. Its importance is due to its role in enabling Governments to equip themselves for war cost-effectively, support allies and deter enemies, and in permitting the development of ever more technologically sophisticated weapons.[8] However, since at least the time of the First World War, which prompted public concern about 'merchants of death',[9] the international arms trade has been the subject of controversy. Today the legal and illegal international arms trade facilitates massacres and human rights abuses around the world. While the Russians supply tyrannies such as Assad's Syria and Khamenei's Iran, Britain has recently supplied Gaddafi's Libya and the Americans Mubarak's Egypt. The many legitimate reasons to be concerned about the international arms trade (its effects on security, human rights, development, and so on) recently found expression in the successful campaign to agree an Arms Trade Treaty at the UN.

Corruption has been particularly rife in the arms trade for decades. In his excellent book *The Arms Bazaar*, first published in 1977,[10] Anthony Sampson explained why this was so 100 years ago:[11]

> The great majority of orders were from governments, where the decision could well depend on one or two individuals, whose support was therefore essential. The advantage of buying one warship or gun, as opposed to another, were often uncertain, and arguments could thus easily be swayed. The orders were often very large, so that a single decision was more critical for an arms company. And the sales were usually conducted in secrecy, for reasons of national security. Moreover as the commission increased, officials might well favour bigger orders, beyond the capacity or needs of their country, to ensure that their share would be greater.

This still holds true today. The late Joe Roeber, whose book, *The Hidden Market: Corruption in the International Arms Trade* was sadly never published, argued a few years ago[12] that the arms industry was 'hard-wired' for corruption, because the international arms market was over-supplied. Further, in many countries purchasing decisions are often made by an unaccountable political elite. Not only are different weapons systems difficult to compare, each contract is complex and contains unique requirements. As Roeber said, 'an unknowable price can accommodate any amount of covert payments'.

Today, arms trade corruption still enriches the political elites in many countries. Indeed, for some, whose tenure at the top may be insecure or short, a big arms deal is the best chance they may ever have to get rich.

Arms trade corruption is, typically, grand corruption: a crime of the establishment, and that is what makes it an important issue.

The effects of grand corruption are profound. The UN Convention against Corruption argues the 'illicit acquisition of personal wealth can be particularly damaging to democratic institutions, national economies and the rule of law' and refers to 'the seriousness of problems and threats posed by corruption to the stability and security of societies'. The grand corruption I describe in this book affects many countries such as developing African countries and the oil-rich states of the Middle East, but also democracies such as South Africa.

In this book I also describe how the Governments of Britain and America – two countries rightly known for their relatively high standards of integrity in public life and strong commitment to the rule of law – reacted to bribery schemes in arms deals over the last 50 years. Politicians and officials in Britain and America knew some arms companies paid bribes, and sometimes knew the details. When deciding what to do, they faced a range of competing considerations – stopping improper behaviour, securing lucrative exports, and maintaining good relations with foreign governments. They had only a limited ability to influence the behaviour of the bribe payers and receivers and usually every option carried a significant penalty. I want to explain the dilemmas decision-makers faced.

That corruption is common in international trade is widely accepted. But, paradoxically, there is little hard evidence in the public domain. Corruption is a secret conspiracy entered into by consenting adults and hence documents detailing it rarely become available. There are few open corporate archives. As secret conspiracies are difficult to uncover, there are few prosecutions. Further, bribe payers and receivers tend to be rich and/or powerful, and the fear of libel action can deter public discussion of specific cases. But, to understand how to stop corruption, we need to understand how bribery schemes work.

I do not argue that British and American companies are worse than those from other major exporting countries. The examples in this book focus on Britain and America for a number of reasons. Firstly, Britain and America are relatively open societies where historical and legal documents can be obtained quite easily. Secondly, both countries have been important participants in the international arms trade for many decades. Thirdly, I do not have the time, resources, or language skills to study the historical documents of other major arms trade participants such as Russia or France.

To write this book I have relied entirely on documents which are in the public domain. I have not stolen anyone's secrets, nor do I have any 'insider' sources. Where, on occasion, the details of well publicised allegations are omitted, this is because I do not have access to the documents.

My main sources are the historical documents of the British Government, kept at The National Archives. The legal international arms trade is very heavily supervised by Governments, and Government officials tend to know more about the detail of arms deals than they do about international trade in other sectors. Much of their insider knowledge is preserved in Government documents.

I have also used a small number of collections of private papers. The papers of Lord Caldecote, who once directed the British Aircraft Corporation's dealings in Saudi Arabia, are now available for public inspection at the Institution of Engineering and Technology in London. They throw considerable light on how what is now BAE won its first deals in Saudi Arabia in the 1960s. The Vickers Archive, maintained by Cambridge University Library, contains papers showing how Vickers went about trying to sell a submarine in Saudi Arabia during that decade. Lastly, some of the papers of Peter Gardiner, who ran BAE's programme of benefits for the Saudi Prince who controlled the Al Yamamah deal, are available to inspect at the offices of Campaign Against Arms Trade in London.

I have also relied extensively on papers disclosed following legal proceedings. Firstly, the Judicial Review of the Serious Fraud Office's decision to terminate its corruption investigation into BAE's dealings in Saudi Arabia meant many important recent Government documents entered the public domain. Secondly, because many of the historical documents about the bribery around the Saudi Arabian National Guard deal (described in Chapter 3) and Geoffrey Edwards's litigation against Associated Electrical Industries (described in Chapter 5) were withheld by the British Government, I used the Freedom of Information Act to obtain them. I met strong resistance from the Foreign and Commonwealth Office, who employed a leading QC and another barrister to put their case at an Information Tribunal, though I was unrepresented. The then Ambassador to Riyadh, William Patey, also gave evidence. I was very fortunate to prevail in this ground-breaking case,[13] and as a result was able to obtain many more documents.

I have relied on four main sources about American arms deals and the advent of the Foreign Corrupt Practices Act. The first is a collection of historical documents made available on the internet by the Securities and Exchange Commission Historical Society (see www.sechistorical.org). The second is a collection of diplomatic cables made available on the internet by the National Archives and Records Administration (see www.aad.archives.gov/aad/series-description.jsp?s=4073&cat=all&bc=sl). The third are the documents published during the hearings of Senator Frank Church's Committee in the mid 1970s. Lastly, I have also used publicly available documents from American legal proceedings.

Allow me to anticipate three criticisms of this book. Firstly, it is irrelevant to today's world, because it is history. Secondly, that the book is unreliable, because it presents a partial picture, based on incomplete information. Thirdly, that the book is an over-simplified account of the events described.

Firstly, corruption in international trade has a basic character that is the same now as it ever was. Company A wishes to be awarded a contract by decision-maker B. Thus, in a successful bribery scheme Company A needs to transmit money or other benefits to decision-maker B. To be effective this transaction needs to be concealed. This is best done by an intermediary or chain of intermediaries receiving money or other benefits from Company A and passing them to decision-maker B (with the intermediaries pocketing some of the money as a recompense for their time and trouble). Though bribery schemes can be complex, they necessarily have this basic character. The unchanging dynamic of corruption in international trade means we can today still learn worthwhile lessons from historical examples.

Secondly, evidence about corruption is bound to be partial. Secret activities are naturally difficult to uncover and investigate, even for law enforcement agencies. Bribery schemes in international trade cross jurisdictions. Further, those involved frequently use shell companies in offshore jurisdictions, where often it is impossible for anyone to tell who really controls a company, to maintain secrecy. For example, the Serious Fraud Office's investigation of BAE took six years to complete, and involved the investigation of entities in Switzerland and other offshore secrecy jurisdictions.

Evidence from corporate records is usually superior to Government records, particularly as corporate documents sometimes detail who the intended beneficiaries are. However, as we will see, often companies keep very poor or no records of corrupt transactions, to ensure they do not come to light.

The British Government declassifies a mass of historical documents every year, but this is not the full story. Firstly, not all Government records are preserved. Secondly, officials do not always record everything they know (for example, the diplomat who saw the list of 'influential Saudis' bribed by Geoffrey Edwards in the 1960s did not record their names). Lastly, almost no information from the Secret

Intelligence Service (SIS) or the Government Communications Headquarters (GCHQ) is declassified.[14] Officials were not, for the most part, directly involved in making corrupt payments, and much of what they recorded was hearsay. However, because of their access to senior executives and because the culture of Whitehall prizes accuracy, much of this information is likely to be very reliable.

It is only on some occasions I can prove money from Company A reached decision-maker B (on some occasions of course, a deal being negotiated was never finalised). However, this problem is also one encountered by law enforcement agencies, as well those who in the 1970s investigated the questionable practices of the Lockheed Aircraft Corporation in America and British Leyland in Britain. The report of Lockheed's Special Review Committee explains eloquently:[15]

> The most vexing and frustrating problem with which the Committee and its lawyers and accountants have had to wrestle is how much of the commissions paid in respect of sales in any country was kept by the consultant, and how much, if any, was passed along as improper payments to government or customer officials.

I agree with their conclusion:[16] 'The Committee believes that in many instances the most significant aspect of a particular payment was its intended disposition in Lockheed's eyes – rather than its actual ultimate destination.'

I cannot be sure I have uncovered all the available evidence of arms trade corruption in British Government files since the mid 1960s because of the constraints on my time in the past nine years. Further research may be able to paint a fuller picture. I have focused on countries which were Britain's major arms customers, and/or where there was good reason to believe corruption was likely.

For almost all the examples in this book, it is highly unlikely any new evidence about them will ever emerge. If you believe that one should not conclude behaviour is corrupt based on partial information, that is tantamount to saying corruption does not exist. Moreover, it is self-evidently reasonable to draw conclusions about the past based on incomplete information. That is what history is.

Lastly, the book is not a full account of the events described. That is partly because the publisher asked me to write 70,000 words, and partly because I wanted the book to remain accessible to the general reader. However, I have taken great care to state the essential facts, and so the account is not, I believe, misleading.

In the interests of transparency, I have retained the original drafting and spelling in the documents wherever possible. I have eschewed the use of acronyms, where possible, to make life easier for the reader. Thus I use 'Britain' to refer to the UK, and 'America' to refer to the USA. Lastly, to give the reader a better sense of the size of the sums involved in the deals described in the book, I have calculated what they would be worth in 'today's money' using GDP deflators published by the British and American Governments (downloaded on 23 June 2013 and 24 June 2013 respectively).

The book is structured broadly chronologically, but also thematically to maintain coherence, so that on occasion I introduce a new part of the story by going back into the past, or by recapping.

The book begins by introducing one common thread that runs through it – Britain's arms trade with Saudi Arabia – a remarkable (and corrupt) relationship that has endured unbroken for around 50 years. Chapter 2 looks at the British Government's involvement in bribery schemes, and official attitudes, during the 1960s and 1970s. I then describe in Chapters 3 and 4 the bribery schemes used by British arms companies in the 1970s in the two countries that were Britain's biggest customers – Saudi Arabia and Iran.

From this point on I compare developments in Britain and America. In Chapter 5 I compare the behaviour of the British companies with two of America's largest arms companies – Lockheed and the Northrop Corporation. In particular I describe two arms trade corruption scandals – one in America and one in Britain – and explain why they led to new anti-corruption laws in America but not in Britain. Chapters 6 and 7 look at British Government efforts – firstly at home, secondly on the international stage – to avoid taking effective action against corruption. In Chapter 8 I describe how British arms companies – in particular BAE – went about winning deals in the 1980s and 1990s. Chapter 9 describes the corruption investigation of BAE and its ramifications.

1

The Chancer: Negotiating BAE's
First Saudi Deals (1963–66)

Fifty years ago, Saudi Arabia was for businessmen with a pioneer spirit. Britain's Ambassador remembered when it was untouched by the modern world, known by diplomats as a land of 'sandy wastes and rocky wilderness'.[1] Just after the Second World War, he recalled, Jedda, halfway down the Arabian peninsula on the Red Sea coast and nowadays Saudi Arabia's second largest city, sat behind 'an ancient wall sheltering the cluster of tall coral houses'. Water 'came from a rusty "condenser" which reluctantly took the salt from the sea water, the finished product being delivered to us in old petrol tins by sweating porters'. Riyadh, the capital, was a place of 'mud houses and forts and...crenellated towers', only reached 'by desert track...[in] five days by car'.

The discovery of oil in 1938 changed the country. By the early 1960s, Jedda was 'sleepily emerging into the twentieth century'.[2] It now had 'broad roads, tree-lined avenues, modern villas, flats and offices which have herded back the old town into an untidy heap in the middle'.[3] Riyadh had 'wide avenues, flanked by modern buildings housing the various Ministries'. The Saudis kept alive centuries-old traditions with 'flowing robes...endless cups of bitter coffee and their fierce bedouin retainers'.

Ibn Saud, after whom Saudi Arabia takes its name, conquered Arabia's desert tribes in the first decades of the twentieth century. His sons have ruled Saudi Arabia since his death.

The Saudi Princes saw the kingdom as their 'fief'.[4] As one British Ambassador put it:[5]

I doubt if there are any among them, not even King Faisal himself, who have seriously questioned the inherent right of the [Saudi Royal Family] to regard Saudi Arabia as a family business, or to regard the promotion

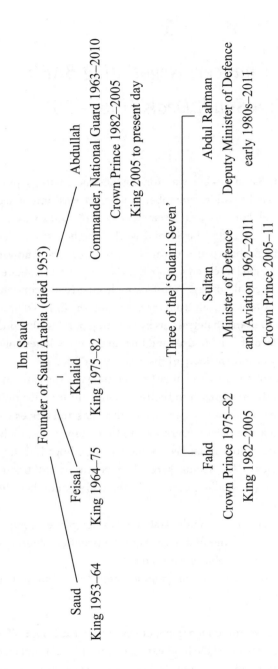

Ibn Saud
Founder of Saudi Arabia (died 1953)

Saud
King 1953–64

Feisal
King 1964–75

Khalid
King 1975–82

Abdullah
Commander, National Guard 1963–2010
Crown Prince 1982–2005
King 2005 to present day

Three of the 'Sudairi Seven'

Fahd
Crown Prince 1975–82
King 1982–2005

Sultan
Minister of Defence
and Aviation 1962–2011
Crown Prince 2005–11

Abdul Rahman
Deputy Minister of Defence
early 1980s–2011

Figure 1.1 Key figures of the Saudi Royal Family (1962–80)

of the interests of the family business as taking priority over everything else.

After Ibn Saud's death in 1953, the Saudis lived lavishly on oil money, spending their new riches on 'pleasure, palaces and Cadillacs'.[6] The rule of the new King, Saud, 'a man of the utmost folly',[7] left the country almost bankrupt by 1958.[8]

Years of austerity began. King Saud's (half-)brothers forced him to give real power to his younger half-brother, Feisal. Feisal cut back Princely allowances by two-thirds over six years. In Riyadh visitors noticed palatial houses abandoned half-built.[9] To maintain their lifestyles the Princes needed new sources of income.

At the same time, Saudi Arabia, with few educated people, could not develop without help from foreign companies. But the country was not an easy place with which to do business.

In 1963, there were only six British businessmen in Saudi Arabia.[10] Few could face dealing with the 'truly massive incompetence' of the Government bureaucracy.[11] Saudi officials were[12] 'more often than not inefficient, idle and corrupt' whose working day lasted, London was told,[13] an average of 45 minutes. Doing business was made even harder by 'the inefficiency of the mails, the telegraph office and Saudi Arabian Airlines'.[14]

Saudi Arabia was ready for a big arms deal. In 1962 in neighbouring Yemen, Army officers inspired by the Egyptian leader General Nasser overthrew the ruling Imam. Nasser hated Arabian sheikhs, blaming them for the Arab world's backwardness. He sent troops to prevent the Imam returning to power. The Saudi Princes took fright because they 'suddenly found themselves confronted with a Power on their borders...devoted to the overthrow of monarchical régimes'.[15] They now wanted modern weapons. With Saudi oil revenues growing at over 10 per cent per year,[16] they could afford them. The senior Princes could also use bribes from arms deals to restore and increase their incomes.

Geoffrey Edwards

To win a major deal in Saudi Arabia, British arms companies needed a business agent to work in the shadows. Then, as now, many companies looking for a deal in a country where they were not already well established, used agents. Agents could fulfil a number of legitimate roles. One British Ministry of Defence official pointed out they could[17]

> lobby officers and officials…find out about the availability of funds and perhaps suggest to people that availabilities might be created; they sniff out the activities of our competitors and they sing the virtues of our equipment and our services.

However, often they were also central to bribery schemes.

Even today, it is often impractical for a company to monitor the activities of its agents abroad closely, and it certainly was in Saudi Arabia in the 1960s. So, rather than paying for their time, most companies paid agents a 'commission' – a percentage of the final selling price – as an incentive to work hard. These were, in effect, 'no win, no fee' arrangements.

British arms companies needed a chancer, someone who knew the territory, willing to endure the hardships and able to deal with Princes. That man was Geoffrey Edwards. In 1961, aged 40,[18] he left St Aubin, Jersey,[19] and rented a house in Jedda.[20] Edwards, a heavy drinker[21], was likely to find this trying. While diplomats could smuggle alcohol into this dry Muslim country in the diplomatic bag, unfortunately, an agent of the British Aircraft Corporation warned[22], businessmen caught carrying alcohol would be 'sent out of the country on the next aircraft' and 'they DO search your bags'.

In Saudi Arabia, the King and his (half-)brothers made all the important decisions. Straight away, Edwards got chummy with the senior Princes – 'the only real way', said British diplomats,[23] 'of doing business in the country'. He developed a close relationship with the Minister of Defence, Prince Mohammed bin Saud[24] and his successor from 1962, Prince Sultan.[25] British companies seeking contracts in Saudi Arabia learned about Edwards's excellent contacts, and a number hired him.[26]

Edwards and the Thunderbird Missile Deal

In early 1963, the senior Princes were afraid of bombing by Egyptian aircraft based in Yemen. They toyed with stationing a mobile missile system, for shooting down aircraft, around Riyadh, Jedda and Taif (a resort in the mountains near Jedda, where the Saudi Royal Family rested during the hottest summer months).[27]

At that time, the British Aircraft Corporation (BAC – now called BAE Systems) manufactured a mobile missile system called Thunderbird, used by the British Army. Edwards approached BAC claiming[28] he was 'the sole person charged with a responsibility for the procurement of certain major items of defence equipment [including Thunderbird missiles] by Prince Sultaan [sic], Minister of Defence, and Prince Abdul Rahman'. Abdul Rahman was a 'major businessman',[29] the brother of Sultan, and[30] 'a power behind the scenes'. On a visit to London he met BAC salesman Alec Sanson and 'confirmed all that Geoffrey Edwards had told us'.[31]

Associated Electrical Industries (AEI), makers of radars used by the Thunderbird system, confirmed to BAC[32] 'that Edwards had in fact established himself in a most exceptional position with…the Finance and Defence Ministries'. At the end of July 1963, Edwards arranged a meeting for Sanson at Sultan's house in Saudi Arabia with Sultan and Abdul Rahman.[33] Suitably impressed, BAC decided to work with Edwards. To be at the heart of the deal, Edwards needed BAC's backing, and so BAC agreed to write a letter to Sultan, telling him:[34]

> Mr. Edwards has our complete trust and confidence not only in the transmission of documents [about Thunderbird and other equipment] between your Ministry and this Corporation, but also as regards the arranging of such guarantees and other financial matters as may be necessary in Saudi Arabia in connection with such transactions.

Personality politics dominated Saudi decision-making. One British Ambassador sneered:[35]

> I doubt if, even on important subjects, there is any systematic marshalling of information and argument, much less preparation of policy papers: [Feisal] absorbs in discussion with his advisers an undigested and unassessed pot-pourri of facts and opinions…and forms his own opinion. This system – or lack of it – leaves him heavily dependent on his advisers for his knowledge of facts.

The Saudi Royal Family was full of what one Ambassador called[36] 'complex jealousies'. But, Feisal was setting 'a personal example in various ways.'[37] He was, thought British diplomats,[38] 'by far the most impressive of all the Royal Family' and 'reputed to be above corruption. He indulges in none of the vices and excesses practised by most of his brothers.' He lived modestly, driving himself to his office every morning unescorted.[39]

However, his example was ignored by many of his subjects and (half-)brothers. Diplomats in Jedda told London[40] 'the level of business morality' was 'not particularly high, even by Middle East standards' because of the 'backstairs fixing going on'.

BAC soon learned about Edwards's methods. In December 1963, Sanson told Lord Caldecote, the BAC Director responsible for Saudi Arabia, that a deal for 100 Thunderbird missiles would be worth around £18 million (worth about £280 million today). Sanson said that, officially, the agent's commission would be a modest 2 per cent.

1.   A British Aircraft Corporation Thunderbird Mark 1 missile.

© Nicholas Gilby. Picture courtesy of the Midland Air Museum.

However, Sanson's memo to Caldecote[41] suggests that BAC considered that other payments might be necessary. Sanson listed other promised payments, concealed in the price quoted, 'which have to be recognised by B.A.C. in the event that the sale is successful'.

The first entry on his list reads '(3a) 5% on the total value of the contract due to Prince Abdul Rahman – (Brother of Prince Sultaan [sic] – Minister of Defence and Prince Fahid [sic] – Minister of the Interior). This amounts to £900,000' (worth about £14 million today). The second entry was 'a "sweetening" payment made by G. Edwards to the Defence Sub committee' of officials. Their cut was £8,000 (worth about £125,000 today). Third was £80,000 (worth about £1.25 million today) earmarked as 'a payment to certain Defence Committee members'. Last was 'Prince Fahid [sic]', the Minister of the Interior, in line for a 'possible' £4,000 (worth about £62,500 today). He was a brother of Abdul Rahman and Sultan, and King from 1982 to 2005. Overall, these promised payments made up 5.75 per cent of the contract price.

Sanson proposed that BAC should not make these under-the-table payments directly. A 'Gross Commission' should be given to Edwards who would 'meet all disbursements'. Any money left over would be his reward. Sanson suggested paying the commissions once a Letter of Intent to buy Thunderbird missiles (with accompanying down payment) had been received from the Saudi bureaucracy. Almost half of the money due under the Letter of Intent (£2 million) would then be paid out by Edwards in kick-backs (£992,000).

Two months later, in February 1964, Caldecote told Foreign Office Minister, Lord Carrington, that Edwards was 'a "buccaneer" rather than a gentleman'.[42] Another BAC salesman, Gordon Duguid, confided to British Ambassador Sir Colin Crowe that 'he did not find Mr. Edwards' methods of business very agreeable'.[43] But, said Caldecote, 'he was the type of man needed if B.A.C. were to do business effectively in Saudi Arabia'.[44] Crowe 'confirmed [Duguid's] own impressions that the country was completely corrupt, particularly due to the fact that the system lent itself completely to corruption'.[45] Eleven days later, BAC formally appointed Edwards as their agent.[46]

BAC promised Edwards[47] that if he sold the Saudis any Thunderbird missiles, Lightning fighter jets, Jet Provost training aircraft, Canberra bombers, or Vigilant anti-tank weapons, his personal cut (above and beyond the pay-offs he might have to make) would be 1.5 per cent of the contract price. The agreement would be reviewed annually. BAC wanted to know about pay-offs, and so Edwards was not to 'incur any obligation or liability on behalf of the Corporation without our prior approval in writing'.

The Saudis postponed a final decision on Thunderbird missiles,[48] because BAC could not deliver any missiles until 1966.[49] They now had a more ambitious plan – to buy an air defence system.

Edwards and the Saudi Arabian Air Defence Scheme

From 1963 to 1965, Edwards devoted himself to selling the British offer. This was made by a consortium of three British companies – BAC, AEI and Airwork. Forty modern Lightning fighter jets, made by BAC, would defend Saudi skies. Saudi pilots would train on 25 Jet Provost aircraft, also sold by BAC. Nine radar stations, supplied by AEI, would enable the Saudis to guide the Lightning aircraft towards their targets. Airwork would provide training, logistics and other support. The price of what became the Saudi Arabian Air Defence scheme was £118 million[50] (worth about £1.6 billion today). In the late 1960s, the

2.   A British Aircraft Corporation Lightning Mark 55, in Royal Saudi Air Force colours, one of 40 Lightnings sold to the Saudis in late 1965. The 34 Lightning Mark 53s sold cost £775,000, of which £48,500 was paid in 'agency fees'.

© Nicholas Gilby. Picture courtesy of the Midland Air Museum.

British Ambassador in Jedda called it the 'greatest of all British overseas defence contracts'.[51]

By the summer of 1964 Edwards was the agent for the three companies.[52] Their rivals were the American companies Lockheed Aircraft Corporation (now called Lockheed Martin) and Northrop Corporation (now called Northrop Grumman), and the French company Dassault.

AEI hired Edwards three days after he was appointed as the BAC agent,[53] promising him 7.5 per cent of AEI's final contract price. In April 1963 Edwards agreed with Abdul Rahman[54] that, in return for 'giving or continuing to give his assistance' to AEI's attempts to sell radars to Saudi Arabia, Abdul Rahman would receive 3 per cent of the installed cost of the equipment. In November 1963 AEI wrote to the Prince[55] acknowledging his 'joint interest with [Edwards] in this matter. We would confirm that the earned commission will be paid immediately when due'. Airwork agreed[56] to pay Edwards 5 per cent of their contract price.

Edwards knew that if he made it worthwhile for the senior Princes to back the British consortium, he could win a deal. After all, as Sultan himself said to BAC,[57] 'one aeroplane was like any other aeroplane to them'. Duguid informed Ambassador Crowe[58] of 'Mr. Edwards' contacts and the necessity for sweetening members of the Defence Committee'. Crowe told London 'I had the impression that B.A.C. wish to use Mr. Edwards as the channel through which they would funnel whatever douceurs might be found necessary'. Edwards boasted to BAC:[59] 'my partnership with Prince Abdul Rahman Bin Abdul Azziz is invaluable and you know to some extent how well this works with his brother the Minister of Defence'.

A committee of Saudi colonels evaluated the competing aircraft. Edwards informed BAC and the British Government that the committee had finally recommended 40 Lightning aircraft, AEI radar and Thunderbird missiles.[60]

BAC now drew up a 'Letter of Intention to Purchase' for the Saudis to sign. BAC asked the Saudis to put down a 10 per cent deposit. If either side pulled out later, the deposit would be repaid by BAC.[61]

However, Duguid told BAC's Legal Department,[62] 'Edwards yesterday warned me that as soon as this 10% is paid over the various Saudi officials who have been promised backsheesh will expect to receive a pro rata payment'. Duguid asked his colleagues whether BAC would deduct the bribes paid from the Saudi Government's deposit

3.   'A "buccaneer" rather than a gentleman': Geoffrey Edwards (back left), agent for the British Aircraft Corporation, Associated Electrical Industries and Airwork in Saudi Arabia in the 1960s. One British diplomat was shown documents that 'disclosed details of payments' Edwards 'made to a number of influential Saudis' to win a huge arms deal for the three companies.

Picture courtesy of the *Jersey Evening Post*.

if the deal did not go ahead (asking for bribes to be refunded is, one imagines, tricky).

BAC's lawyers were squeamish about what they called 'kick-backs'.[63] They advised 'BAC should not be seen to be making such payments and certainly this would be the effect of claiming them as deductible if and when we are called upon to repay to the Saudi Government their preliminary downpayment...such an action would be quite unacceptable'. So BAC's management decided[64] 'no special commissions would be payable until the final Purchase Agreement is signed by both parties'.

The French and the Americans had not given up. Northrop tried to hire Edwards in March 1964, but were rebuffed.[65] BAC forwarded British diplomats a report Edwards wrote that mentioned his arrangement with the French agent to knock Dassault out of contention.[66]

Edwards's main problem was maintaining his credibility in Saudi eyes. He needed to ensure his role as 'fixer' was beyond challenge. In August 1964 he wrote to Duguid[67] (in his capacity as a BAC representative), reminding him of their 'underlying gentlemens' [sic] agreement' because 'very little has been written between us'.

He complained the blundering intervention of Edgar Carr, another BAC agent in the Middle East, could scupper his plans if the Saudis did not see him as BAC's key man. Edwards said he

> was asked in Riyadh last Tuesday to give my personal written guarantee that I will make all payment due when the final stages of our contract are reached and subsequently through the course of the contract period. I did not hesitate to do this, although I have nothing more than my written commission agreement with you.

The reason these assurances to leading Saudis were important, Edwards explained, was greed, for 'Saudi Arabia has never yet bought anything that they really need'. A decision would be made only 'after examination of all factors relating to themselves'. And Edwards could satisfy Saudi greed. He went on:

> I must emphasise this particular point because if they suspect for one moment that my importance to this deal has in any way been reduced in the eyes of your Corporation, they will feel that obligations already made by me will not be honoured and I thank God that I was in Riyadh in the last few days in order to confirm my position. I agree that the Lightning is the best aircraft for them and so is all the other equipment that we have offered, but do not imagine, for one moment, that these grounds are sufficient for them to place the order with us.

He then set out his pitch to continue as BAC's main agent. Firstly, he claimed credit for creating 'the thought for the defence system and therefore the business'. Secondly, he pointed out, he had already incurred about £45,000 (worth about £675,000 today) in expenses, and 'refused all American competitors' offers out of loyalty to the British companies and our country'. Lastly, he reminded Duguid of his 'invaluable partnership' with Abdul Rahman, the Defence Minister's brother. Edwards continued to work for the British companies.

The Americans were formidable competition. They were the main suppliers of military equipment to Saudi Arabia at the time. They had an enormous interest in Saudi Arabia because of the Arabian American Oil Company (ARAMCO). Owned by four American oil companies, ARAMCO had the exclusive right to drill in Saudi Arabia's huge Eastern Province oil fields. The State Department fretted[68] that a British or French arms deal would be a 'significant set-back for our long-term position of primacy in Saudi Arabia'. The American companies also had, said one of BAC senior manager,[69] 'large quantities of money... available as baksheesh'.

Lockheed's sales campaign began in earnest in December 1964. Their agent, Adnan Khashoggi,[70] a renowned playboy and fixer, was close to Sultan. Edwards was unfazed. In his situation report in early 1965, passed by BAC to diplomats in London, he asserted:[71]

> I am confident of the eventual outcome and would ask you to remember that I know all these people intimately and would also assure you that my own commercial instinct would not allow me to carry on with my present expenditure in excess of £1,000 per month [worth about £15,000 today] if I were not confident of the end result.

BAC salesman Glen Hobday was flustered. He moaned:[72]

> Lockheed unfortunately seem to be still spending money to buy their way in...This type of approach to business is most difficult to counter and there is no real solution to it except to 'join them'.

By March 1965, senior American generals had visited Saudi Arabia to lobby Feisal and Sultan on behalf of the American companies.[73] Now Edwards asked BAC for more money.

Hobday kept Lord Caldecote and other BAC directors closely informed of developments. As required in his agency agreement, Edwards told Hobday exactly what he was doing. Hobday assured his bosses[74] that Edwards's friends and associates were 'some very influential Saudis indeed...Edwards has also made the right contacts'.

Edwards had, 'to [Hobday's] knowledge, made personal arrangements with the right people so that they will benefit from the deal'.

A month later, in April 1965, Hobday provided BAC with more detail.[75] Further special commissions of £720,000 (worth about £10.75 million today) had been requested. He told BAC 'I am of the opinion that this is the last and final escalation of commissions.' In return, Hobday asked Edwards to obtain a Saudi down payment of 10 per cent when the Letter of Intent was signed, and a further 25 per cent on contract signature. Hobday explained that 'down payments of reasonable magnitude are required if the special commissions [Edwards] requires on signature of the contract are to be paid'. He wrote to Edwards promising him the requested further special commissions.

A few months later, the British and American Governments agreed to offer the Saudis a joint deal. The Pentagon's chief arms salesman, Henry Kuss, told Edwards,[76] the 'U.S. Government are prepared to refrain from competing with the U.K. in the sale of military aircraft to Saudi Arabia', as long as the American company Raytheon could sell Hawk surface-to-air missiles as part of the British deal.

On 7 December 1965, Sultan signed a Letter of Intent, promising to buy a British air defence system. The price was just over £103 million (worth about £1.5 billion today). The British Government learned this included commissions of £7.8 million (worth about £112 million today) – 7.5 per cent of the price.[77] Contracts for BAC, AEI and Airwork would be signed later, after the completion of surveys in Saudi Arabia to agree the final requirement.

This was the start of BAE's relationship with Saudi Arabia, which has continued uninterrupted for almost half a century. From the start, the company made pay-offs to top Saudis, and the British Government knew.

BAE never intended you to know this story, of course. They have not made these documents public. But Lord Caldecote kept among his personal papers 15 files relating to the Saudi Arabian Air Defence scheme. His family gave these papers to the archives of the Institution of Engineering and Technology, behind the Savoy Hotel in Central London. When I read them I was astonished to find they were completely uncensored.

Back in 1965, Edwards had triumphed, with help from Abdul Rahman. As the Prince's lawyers later explained,[78] the Prince 'gave assistance...and thereby [AEI] obtained the proposed contract'.

The deal was good business for the senior Princes. In his budget for 1965–66, Feisal had set aside the equivalent of around £14 million (worth about £200 million today) in allowances for the large number of Princes in the Royal Family.[79] So £7.8 million of commissions, mostly paid to a small circle of senior figures, were worth over half of the Saudi Royal Family's official income. One Ambassador later observed,[80] 'though corruption is long established in Saudi Arabia, the pattern of large commissions on arms sales as a major source of enrichment…was probably set by the Air Defence Scheme'.

The British Government and the Saudi Arabian Air Defence Scheme

In the official world of Whitehall, strenuous efforts had been made to secure the deal. John Stonehouse, the Parliamentary Secretary at Roy Jenkins's Ministry of Aviation in Harold Wilson's Labour Government, told industrialists in 1964[81] that

> The old idea that Ministers and civil servants should keep at arm's length from the squalid commercial world is a nonsense. Selling Britain's products is a noble task…this Government is behind you all the way in promoting British aircraft overseas; you must regard all of us in the Ministry as an extension of your own selling organisation.

Stonehouse recalled[82] that

> within weeks of taking office [in October 1964] I heard of a fantastic opportunity for British industry in the sale of an air defence system to the oil rich Saudi Arabia. The information was brought to me by a tall, overweight ex-RAF Group Captain…Geoffrey Edwards was not a mystic imbued with moral fervour about the Arab cause. He was involved for the money; and the money involved was huge: no less than two and a half per cent to five per cent on orders which could total hundreds of millions of pounds.

The British Government had already assured the Saudis[83] that 'B.A.C. are a highly reputable firm' and that they had 'no reason to doubt that the British Aircraft Corporation and its associated companies will do their utmost to meet their obligations'. The new Defence Secretary,

Denis Healey, wrote to Sultan telling him[84] Whitehall would 'do everything we can to keep the firms up to the mark'.

During the sales campaign Stonehouse visited Saudi Arabia several times[85]. He was under no illusions. He wrote[86] that

> most people in Government frowned upon Geoffrey Edwards as an arms salesman grasping after his fat commissions. I did not. In an area such as Arabia much of the commission would any way have to be spent in bribes and, anyhow what was the point of adopting a 'holier-than-thou' attitude when Britain's factories sorely needed that business and our balance of payments needed the foreign currency.

He understood that Edwards 'had to pay out vast sums to all sorts of contact men, including huge amounts for the Royal Family'.[87]

Jenkins told Wilson[88] the deal was 'a great triumph for John Stonehouse, who has been tireless in his efforts to persuade the Saudis to buy British'. Wilson agreed. He said[89] 'this is a great achievement. Please give him, and all who worked with him, my heartiest congratulations. His salesmanship is a great inspiration to all of us.' Wilson made Stonehouse a Privy Council member for 'services to export'.[90]

The available British Government documents suggest that, although Whitehall threw its full weight behind the consortium's sales campaign in Saudi Arabia, officials and Ministers knew few details about the commissions. Those arrangements were left to Edwards.

Seven months later, Edwards and BAC finally secured the sale of 46 Thunderbird missiles to the Saudis.[91] Edwards's commission was 7.5 per cent.[92] Hobday, who had managed Edwards's negotiation of the Saudi Arabian Air Defence deal in 1965, was awarded an Order of the British Empire in the 1969 New Year Honours.

Britain's Bribery Laws in the Mid 1960s

In the mid 1960s, the only one of Britain's corruption laws relevant to overseas bribery was the Prevention of Corruption Act 1906. The Act made it illegal to 'corruptly give', 'agree to give', or 'offer', any gift to any agent as an inducement or reward for doing or forbearing to do any act in relation to his principal's affairs or business, or for showing or forbearing to show favour or disfavour to any person in relation to his principal's affairs or business.

The Act was reviewed by the Government Law Officers in 1978.[93] They concluded with certainty that, for the law to be broken, the offer, agreement or payment of a bribe would have to take place in England and Wales. They thought, but with less certainty, that if only the offer or agreement took place in England and Wales (and the actual payment was made abroad), it would only be illegal if the agreement was between the payer and the recipient (in other words, without involving an intermediary). The prosecution would also have to show that the offer, agreement or bribe was made 'corruptly', and in other words was not permissible in the bribe recipient's country.

In this context Edwards offered and paid the bribes to the Saudis. The available documents I have seen suggest BAC made no offer, agreement or payment directly to any Saudi decision-maker. The recipients ('influential Saudis'[94]) were the 'agents' and in the Saudi context the 'principal' was the King (Feisal).

Feisal banned commissions in arms deals to any agent or representative in Saudi Arabia on 20 October 1968. It is not clear whether there had been any previous similar decree. Hence it cannot be said beyond reasonable doubt any offer, agreement or gift Edwards made was made 'corruptly', because these actions took place before October 1968.

Edwards was from Jersey and lived in Saudi Arabia, as did the bribe recipients. Hence his actions took place outside the jurisdiction of England and Wales.

BAC, of course, was based in England and Wales, and correspondence about bribery took place there. However, the Law Officers thought, though not with certainty, that

an agreement in England or Wales made between two company directors or employees that they, or their company or employer, will make abroad a corrupt gift or corrupt offer to give to an agent is not an offence triable in England and Wales.

Vickers's Business Methods in Saudi Arabia

Edwards's methods were typical for British and American companies at that time. In the late 1960s Vickers was a major British arms company. A 'tentative enquiry for one Submarine by a source reputedly close to the Saudi Government'[95] was followed up by the Chairman of Vickers's Shipbuilding Group, Leonard Redshaw.

Redshaw appointed a Lebanese company as the agent for Vickers and gave it six months to win a deal.[96] A London-based company, Wingetac Trading Ltd, was appointed as go-between.[97]

Around two weeks later, Wingetac told Redshaw[98] that 'the next stage forward was to line up with yourselves various commissions to parties with "fingers in the pie", including a hefty 10% cloaked under "Saudi Arabian Interests"', and sent him draft letters promising commissions. Once the letters were signed by Redshaw and reached the recipients, Redshaw was assured, 'the matter of your discussing the submarine, and arranging the contract therefor, will be but the question of only a few weeks'.

Wingetac said[99] that five separate commission arrangements were required. But Redshaw wanted to pay Wingetac one commission only, and for them to take care of the other pay-offs. Wingetac replied[100] that this was impossible because

> no one Arab trusts the other therefore individual commission arrangements simply have to be made. Equally our agents forcibly inform us effectively: our principals are the buyers, if the suppliers do not conform with commission instructions given to them by the principals then we cannot operate.

If Redshaw did not follow instructions 'the project might go elsewhere'. But if he did, he was promised[101] 'no opposition to our proposal. Also we will not be faced by any counter proposal.' The letters were duly drafted.

Redshaw's boss at head office queried these distasteful arrangements. One of the partners in Wingetac wrote to him, confirming the commissions were for 'Saudi Arabian Officials', saying:[102]

> I have done this type of business with Middle Eastern countries since the end of the [Second World War], and it is customary to include in any transaction commissions for responsible Officials in relevant Government Departments...I should have thought that Vickers, who have been supplying arms to various countries for many many years, must be familiar with this practice...it would be more than regrettable if Britain at this particular stage would lose an order running into

several million pounds for the sake of moral principles which may not be acceptable here but which are customary in the Middle East.

Redshaw knew the commissions would end up in Swiss bank accounts. He told the person in Switzerland handling them[103] that the agreed 12.5 per cent would be 'placed to your respective Orders with Banks of your choices in Switzerland in currencies to be mutually agreed between yourself and my Company'.

There the paper trail runs cold. However, a British Naval Intelligence Summary of 1973, listing the Order of Battle of the Royal Saudi Arabian Navy, strongly suggests the sale never happened.[104]

American companies like Lockheed behaved in a similar way. In Turkey, for instance, Lockheed appointed a businessman in Ankara as their agent to sell the F-104 Starfighter aircraft. One Lockheed executive worried[105] there was '*little indication that [the agent] is offering really significant inducement at decision-making levels*'. Lockheed's proposed reworded agreement would ensure[106] the agent had 'a thoroughly adequate amount with which to buy real influence'.

Just as Lord Caldecote at BAC had full knowledge about commissions and their purpose, so did Lockheed's senior management. One Lockheed auditor recalled company President Carl Kotchian describing payments made to an agent. Kotchian explained:[107]

These payments are made in connection with our marketing effort. This man [the Lockheed agent in Japan] has connections…in the rest of the world generally speaking you must practice this kind of thing in order to sell airplanes. You must have a man who has connections and give him money.

Lockheed also maintained a Swiss bank account,[108] in the name of a Swiss lawyer.[109] Lockheed paid money to the lawyer intending that it would reach the Dutch Prince Bernhard[110] who had enormous influence over Dutch military procurement.

The Creation of the Ministry of Defence's Arms Sales Unit

Meanwhile British Government officials were becoming much more heavily involved in selling arms. For, in the mid 1960s, the British

Government decided to embark on a big arms sales drive. Although Britain had ended the Second World War dominating the international arms market along with the Americans, it faced increasing competition from the Soviet Union and France.[111] The arms industry, like other parts of Britain's manufacturing base, was in decline.

The Americans had set up an arms sales organisation within the Pentagon in 1961 under Kuss, increasing American arms sales fourfold in just three years.[112] Prominent British industrialists such as Lord Nelson, the Joint Deputy Chairman of BAC, complained to the British Defence Secretary that the British arms industry was falling behind. The British Government, desperate for more exports, wanted to bolster a traditional industrial strength.

A leading businessman, Sir Donald Stokes, was brought in by Healey in 1965 to recommend changes in Whitehall to 'increase exports of U.K. arms'.[113] Stokes was forthright, telling the Air Force Minister,[114] 'a great many arms sales were made not because anyone wanted the arms, but because of the commission involved en route'. A week later, at a meeting with the Ministry of Defence's Permanent Secretary,[115] 'Sir Donald Stokes…indicated that it was often necessary to offer bribes to make sales.'

Stokes's final report[116] said the Government's objective should be 'not merely to maintain our arms exports at their present level… but to increase them substantially'. He recognised, however, the political difficulties with paying commissions, and recommended the Government should follow standard commercial practice and hire agents to do the dirty work. Stokes wrote coyly:[117]

> good commercial agents will be of the greatest value to the [Ministry of Defence]'s own overseas sales staff; apart from providing an additional source of information, they are better placed than an official to dispense the less orthodox inducements.

On his recommendation, a Defence Sales Organisation (DSO) was set up inside the Ministry of Defence. Healey told Parliament it would seek to secure Britain's 'rightful share' of a £1 billion (worth about £14.3 billion today) international arms market.[118]

The Permanent Secretary at the Foreign Office sent a circular to all British Ambassadors,[119] saying 'we must exploit markets wherever this is possible…where no positive reason exists for not selling arms…

we should do all that we can to sell them'. He told the diplomats, 'the efforts of [the Head of Defence Sales] Mr. Raymond Brown and his Office of Defence Sales need all the assistance which we can give them'.

But this begged a question. Should British Government officials get directly involved in bribery? Where should the line be drawn?

2

Hand in Glove: Whitehall's Involvement in Bribery Schemes (1968–73)

On 1 July 1966, the Defence Sales Organisation (DSO) was created within the Ministry of Defence to market British arms aggressively overseas, led by Raymond Brown from Racal. DSO officials used Britain's network of diplomats and military officers (known as Attachés) overseas to gather information, and support and promote British firms and equipment. In this respect the role of the DSO, which today is called the Defence & Security Organisation within UK Trade & Investment, has changed little in almost 50 years.

Whitehall's Attitudes Towards Bribery

Stokes's recommendation that the DSO should employ agents to pay 'commissions' chimed perfectly with the attitude and behaviour of senior Ministry of Defence officials, such as Harold Hubert, the Director of Sales. He became Director of Army Sales in the DSO.

Hubert was no stranger to shady deals. In 1965 he sold rifles and ammunition to Geoffrey Edwards,[1] who shipped them to Saudi Arabia. When London suggested[2] 'any sweetening of the Saudis is a matter for Edwards and not the Ministry of Defence', one diplomat in Jedda replied that he had[3] 'grounds for believing that certain [Saudi] military officers received bribes in consideration of passing the rifles as satisfactory'.

Indeed, diplomats wanted to keep well away from bribery. In the summer of 1964, Hubert had informed Britain's Embassy in Tehran[4] that he wanted to sell arms 'through a suitable local agent'. The Embassy protested[5] 'about the encouragement of graft' and the plan was dropped. Hubert was unrepentant, declaring[6] he was 'not keen to educate the Persians in virtuous ways. My task is to sell British equipment.'

Undeterred, in the spring of 1965 he appointed a Lebanese company, Near East Resources, as the Ministry of Defence's sales agent in Iran (where they were asked to sell 'through the back door'[7]), and Lebanon, Jordan, and Iraq too,[8] because of their 'influence in high places'.[9] The diplomats were livid and worried the company might besmirch the good name of the British Government.[10] One sneered that putting arms sales 'in the hands of a Lebanese businessman...is really appalling'.[11] So the Ministry of Defence decided to use Near East Resources in Lebanon and Jordan only.[12]

Once the DSO was created diplomats became more uncertain about whether the Government should be involved in arms trade corruption. One asked the Foreign Office from Caracas[13] whether the Government were 'prepared, through an agent, to enter into a Government-to-Government contract in the negotiation of which there will have been an element of bribery and which will itself reflect this bribery (though in a concealed form)'. In Venezuela 'the question of bribery would almost certainly arise', yet the Ambassador had ordered Embassy staff not to get involved. The diplomat warned that 'demand [for arms] can also originate from others, from Presidents down to junior officers, entirely for reasons of personal financial gain; and this type of demand can be stimulated by an agent who can dangle the carrot of such financial gain'. Hubert interjected dismissively[14]

I am completely mystified by just what your problem is...people who deal with the arms trade, even if they are sitting in a Government office, live day by day with this sort of activity, and equally day by day they carry out transactions knowing that at some point bribery is involved. Obviously I and my colleagues in this office do not ourselves engage in it but we believe that various people who are somewhere along the chain of our transactions do. They do not tell us what they are doing and we do not enquire. We are interested in the end result.

The diplomats in London told the Embassy in Caracas[15] they 'accept[ed] the proposition that an agent acting in a Government-to-Government deal (or of course firm-to-Government) should get his commission and that the price [Her Majesty's Government] charge must reflect this cost'. Three months later the Treasury agreed[16] the DSO could use agents who were 'persons or firms of repute' to 'promote exports where it is clear that the market could not be exploited without their help' and be 'remunerated on a basis which reflects the services rendered and can be defended as fair and reasonable'.

The difficulty was, as Hubert had told the Embassy in Caracas, that agents could perform legitimate services in return for their commission, such as keeping an eye on competitor companies, finding out about whether funds were available for arms purchases, and promoting the equipment and services offered by British arms companies. However, as Hubert had suggested, there was a high risk that commissions would also be used by agents to pay bribes, and many British officials and arms company executives assumed, knew or intended that agents used their commission in this way.

The Defence Sales Organisation's Business Agents

In 1968 a DSO official told colleagues[17] 'all firms which really want to export have representatives (where business is big)'. The Attachés could not perform this role for they were 'on the wrong side of a very formal fence; nor can they get mixed up in the push and pull behind the scenes'. The official asked: 'is it considered that there a taste of impropriety about employing agents?...no such connotation exists in principle when firms do it'.

The DSO soon hired agents, and not just in the Middle East. In the Netherlands, the DSO promised £50,000[18] (worth about £675,000 today) to an agent 'to help with the promotion of the Chieftain Tank for sale to Holland because of the influence it was considered he could bring to bear in influential quarters'.[19] But the deal never came off.

In Jordan the DSO appointed Shehadah Twal in late 1969.[20] Twal was promised a 2.5 per cent fee, and told to 'keep the Department fully informed of any sales promotion'. The Defence Attaché in Amman told the DSO[21] Twal was 'previously hand in glove with [Major General] Sherif Nasser and I expect him to remain so'. Nasser was King Hussein's uncle and Commander-in-Chief of the Jordanian Army. Hubert's deputy claimed,[22] 'Sherif Nasser is known as "Mr. 15 per cent" so far as Services equipment is concerned. Unless we can keep in with him and offer acceptable terms, it is unlikely that we can hope for any serious business.' Brown told Defence Secretary Denis Healey[23] Twal had been hired because of 'the need to have individuals at the Departments' disposal to ensure that those able to influence where orders may go are appropriately recompensed by the agents'. In November 1970 the DSO sold 16 Centurion tanks to Jordan. As Twal was incurring 'considerable expenditure on sales promotion and entertainment',[24] he was paid a commission of £6,600 in 1971 (worth about £69,000 today).[25]

There was one obvious problem with the DSO employing agents and paying commissions. As is the case today, corruption in arms deals almost always involved bribing influential and powerful people in the buyer country. In many countries, even where corruption was rife, it was often officially banned. This is because the rulers knew that their subjects would not like them enriching themselves, even this was expected or suspected. The public exposure of bribery could cause a scandal. And if the British Government was involved, that could seriously affect Britain's relations with that country's government.

This problem had been spelt out clearly by diplomats in Tehran, who told London[26] 'it is the declared policy of the Shah [the ruler of Iran] and his Government to stamp [corruption] out'. The Ambassador opposed Hubert appointing an agent, because it 'could well be politically embarrassing. In this sort of country the dividing line between a legitimate commission and graft is never an easy one to draw.' The British Government might 'be accused of lending ourselves to attempts at graft'.

Bribery could also be politically toxic because of the internal politics within a customer government. If some well-connected people were paid off, and their rivals were not, then the agent's actions could make Britain's relations with some highly influential people very difficult.

The DSO faced this problem in Saudi Arabia, when failing to sell the Saudis a Navy in the late 1960s. A British Naval Officer, Commander Gaunt, visited Saudi Arabia several times to advise the Saudis. He was given 'personal proof'[27] that 'a number of senior Saudi officers are only concerned with the financial gain which they personally can make out of the deal'. He told his colleagues[28] of four competing factions of commercial agents, whom he claimed were trying to sell their influence with top Saudis.

A Dirty Deal in Lebanon

In Lebanon, by attempting to use bribery to secure a deal, the DSO did get mixed up in the country's internal politics. This was a problem because, a Foreign and Commonwealth Office 'country assessment sheet' explained,[29] 'any outside intervention in Lebanese affairs is normally resented and is open to misinterpretation'.

British officials expected dubious commercial practices in Lebanon. One Ambassador wrote[30] that 'in this highly competitive market, economic forces (in which bribery must be included) are normally overriding'. Another quoted an old saying of the souks:[31] 'always count your fingers after shaking hands with a Lebanese'.

In 1969, William Brandt's Sons and Company Ltd, a City merchant bank, and a defence consultant, Peter Burnand, were asked to propose a package of arms for the Lebanese Army.[32] The Lebanese would borrow money from Brandt's to pay for the deal.[33]

The DSO helped Burnand put together his offer, made to the Lebanese in April 1970.[34] According to the Ambassador,[35] the prices had been 'calculated on the assumption that the money available to the Lebanese for arms purchases will be the £8m. of the Brandt's loan [worth about £98 million today], minus a (rather swingeing) £2.2m. [worth about £27 million today] to be devoted to agents' commissions and other rake-offs by middle men'.

Burnand's agent in Lebanon was a prominent businessman, Abdullah Habre. Habre was an active supporter of Camile Chamoun,[36] who was the leader of the National Liberal Party and a former Lebanese President. One diplomat explained[37] that 'the Chamounists are the most right-wing of the Lebanese Christian political groups, and generally regarded as a pro-British faction in the Lebanon'. Chamoun was a strong supporter of Prime Minister Saeb Salam.

The purpose of the commissions was spelt out in an internal memo by a Brandt's employee. He wrote:[38]

the commission built into Burnand's proposal represents, in the main, sums of money which will be paid by Habre, in the event of the transaction reaching fruition, to various prominent political personalities who in turn will use these resources to support Chamoun's interests in the forthcoming [1972] elections.

Although I have seen no evidence that the British Government was actively trying to influence the outcome of these elections, the commission arrangements were politically convenient.

Burnand spoke to Colonel Antony Cawston, the British Defence Attaché in Beirut, and was 'frank about Abdulla Habre's fixing operations'.[39] The DSO's involvement was essential as 'the deal has little chance of going through unless [Burnand] and Habre are associated with any Ministry of Defence negotiators in order to reassure the official Lebanese concerned that they will get their cut'. A few days later, Hubert visited Beirut to see for himself. He reported[40] that Habre 'is apparently influential. He seems to have taken immense trouble to influence the Prime Minister [Saeb Salam], other key figures supporting him, and also certain people who would otherwise oppose the deal.'

The package being put forward by Burnand included equipment from the British companies Alvis, the British Aircraft Corporation (BAC), Daimler, Shorts, and Vickers. Each of these companies employed Near East Resources as their agents in Lebanon.[41] Its Managing Director, Sulayman Alamuddin, was said[42] to be 'a close personal and family friend of Hubert'.

But there was a major political obstacle. Salam was[43] 'a long standing personal enemy of Najeeb Allamudim' (Sulayman's older brother) and thus 'it is in the interest of Allamudim to prevent Burnand's deal succeeding at all costs, as the commission payable [to Habre] will be employed to help to keep their opponents in power'.

Hubert wrote that Near East Resources[44]

do not seem to have access to the top politicians. In particular they had no inkling of Abdulla Habre's activities in spite of the breadth of his operations. Nevertheless they have the agencies [with Alvis, BAC, Daimler, Shorts and Vickers] and the commissions with the result that a double set of backhanders has to be included in the prices.

Moreover, Near East Resources's commissions would be wasted as 'there are no means of applying these funds to the people who have seemed to be the more effective'.

Hubert told Brandt's[45] that 'if our prices are set too high, as they must be with the inclusion of the enormous cut for the Habre team, we run a great risk of never getting to the starting line, let alone winning the competitive race'. He proposed[46] Near East Resources 'establish collaboration with [Burnand's man] Abdullah Habre'. Hubert told Brandt's[47] that the DSO and the diplomats thought that if 'the size of the mark up could possibly cause a scandal, the decision might well be taken that it was not worth taking the risk'. Habre failed to deliver a deal. Cawston informed London[48] that 'the Prime Minister [Salam] has spoken openly of having been offered financial inducements by Habre, and Habre's efforts are thereby almost completely discredited'. Burnand reduced the commission from the original 13 per cent to 10 per cent in 1971,[49] but Hubert complained[50] the British price remained 'uncompetitive'.

The situation changed when, in 1971, President Suleiman Frangié told the British Ambassador he wanted a Government-to-Government deal. Hubert and Cawston decided to dump Brandt's and Burnand, and submit a proposal through a company called Millbank Technical Services (MTS).[51]

MTS (of which more later) was a subsidiary of the Crown Agents and had quasi-Governmental status. The company was set up in 1967 so that the Crown Agents (who provided financial, professional and commercial services for British colonies) could deliver export contracts and offer customers credit via Britain's Export Credits Guarantee Department.[52] Soon after it was founded, the DSO used MTS[53] as 'a quasi-official body to act as a trust worthy intermediary'.

Understandably, Brandt's and Burnand took their exclusion from MTS's offer badly, but Hubert and his colleagues refused to provide them exclusive backing[54] because Habre was discredited. Further, Hubert explained,[55] the new Lebanese Defence Minister, Dr Elias Saba, insisted on excluding agents and middlemen from arms deals.

After the DSO made an offer through MTS, a middleman named Chidiac visited Hubert in London.[56] Cawston informed Hubert[57] 'Chidiac certainly has influence with Chamoun and has good contacts at [General Head Quarters]'. At a meeting Chidiac told Hubert[58] he 'is operating not just to support Chamoun but has close contacts with President and [The Commander-in-Chief of the Lebanese Armed Forces, General] Ghanems son is in his firm'. Subsequently Chamoun told Cawston[59] he was Chidiac's friend and that Chidiac had 'some pull at [General Head Quarters]'.

Hubert explained to Cawston[60] that Chidiac would want 5 per cent commission or less, enabling MTS to offer a more competitive price than Brandt's and Burnand. However, on a subsequent visit to Beirut, the new Head of Defence Sales, Lester Suffield 'seriously offended Chamoun'. As the Chargé d'affaires at the Embassy explained:[61]

...Chamoun has played a prominent part in the preliminary negotiations and in ensuring that we got full consideration for our wares. When I called on him myself at one point I formed the clear impression that he was looking for some benefit as a result of his efforts: this would probably take the shape of a contribution to his party funds in preparation for the election next year. Although Chamoun is not a member of the Government, he is one of its principal supporters and his influence is very great...He may still be in a position to increase our share of the cake, but he could certainly damage our prospects if he continues in his present mood.

2. Suffield was told by the Lebanese Minister of Defence [Dr Saba] that he should have no truck with any 'fixers', and Suffield concluded that Chamoun was just one of several such. He therefore refused to see Chamoun as arranged, and the latter has sulked...

3. ...Chamoun is in Paris until 27 September...while we must give due weight to Dr Saba's wishes, we must remember that he is not a fixture... Chamoun should be told that we are grateful for his efforts (I believe that Suffield's failure to make even this gesture has particularly rankled) and assured that he is not shut out. The implication would be that MTS or the manufacturers would sweeten him later when contracts had been arranged. I suggest that someone senior either from [the DSO] or from MTS should go to Paris as soon as possible to re-assure Chamoun.

Britain's new Ambassador to Lebanon, Paul Wright, told London[62] that because of Suffield's blunder, '(i) Chamoun may well (and in my view probably will) have to be taken care of, and (ii) in spite of what Saba said to Suffield, we may find in the end that the same applies to him or to other important Lebanese'. Wright asked Suffield[63] 'to get Chamoun to come clean in two respects: first, as to what and how much he actually wants: second, that Chidiac is in fact his man'.

An MTS Manager, Basil Dove, went to Chamoun's weekend retreat in the mountains outside Beirut. He then[64]

broached the question of the number of persons who were alleging in London that they had seen Chamoun and were conveying the impression that they were to be instrumental in finalising whatever arrangements might be necessary in the interests of the sale of British arms. Chamoun acknowledged that he had had many visitors, but that he wished suitable arrangements to be concluded through his friend Mr.

4.   Sir Lester Suffield, Head of Defence Sales in the Ministry of Defence, 1969–76. He authorised Government facilitation of bribery schemes in Kuwait, Lebanon, and Saudi Arabia, as well as commissions on huge deals with Iran.

Picture by PA/PA Archive/Press Association Images.

Chalabi, the Iraqi banker resident in Beirut…Chamoun went on to say that Chidiac himself had been most helpful in recent months and should be recompensed for his pains through Chalabi. Chidiac should be told that 'he need not worry and that everything would be all right'.

Dove arranged a follow-up meeting with Chamoun in London where he hoped to 'have an opportunity of more detailed discussions as to the "nuts and bolts" of the arrangement with Chalabi'.

Although the DSO were now offering the Lebanese British equipment through MTS rather than Brandt's and Burnand, the previous problem remained. MTS would have to pay commission to Chamoun, but the British companies involved would owe commission to their agent Alamuddin, Salam's enemy. The only difference was that Chamoun's commission would be less than Habre's.

The position of an agent in an arms deal is an insecure one. The agent and his clients stand to receive enormous, and possibly life-changing, sums of money in return for the successful exertion of influence. But the covert, politically sensitive nature of the dealings creates perpetual insecurity. A change in the political climate can see agents and their clients being cut out of a deal with, unless they are powerful, no chance of redress. It must be rather galling to have vast sums 'unfairly' snatched from one's grasp at the last moment.

The Lebanese agents were worried they would be cut out of the deal. One day Chidiac turned up at the British Embassy in Beirut and said:[65]

...Chamoun would handle everything direct himself.

3. The implication of this, according to Chidiac, is that Chamoun is now convinced that a substantial deal is within sight and wishes to get out of his obligations to a [sic] third parties. Chidiac is very concerned since a number of Army officers[,] officials and other useful intermediaries have been kept sweet and if they now see no prospect of further recompense they may turn sour. Chidiac said he was therefore thinking in terms of a formula whereby Chamoun should be offered commission of up to 1 per cent and he, Chidiac, would take an additional 1–2 per cent commission to be used to keep his string of intermediaries sweet. Chidiac said that as Chamoun was not aware of the total amount of the commission likely to be available, an arrangement of this sort should be feasible.

Around three weeks later, Burnand and Habre confided in the Embassy. Cawston reported to London[66] that 'both were obviously worried about Brandts prospects' now they knew of the MTS offer. They alleged that Chamoun had not supported Brandts and that he had specified a percentage for someone else...This had been a shock to Habr[e] who had been called to London to hear this news. Habr[e] followed Chamoun to Paris and there confronted him with these two reported statements. According to Habr[e] Chamoun denied both and said he had always supported Brandts and had menttioned [sic] no one else's name to the British.

Three days later, Alamuddin visited Ambassador Wright. He was worried that the MTS quote was too high. He told Wright[67]

> that if, when firm prices had been quoted by MTS, it looked as if there might be a danger of our losing the orders, he would be compelled to quote prices for Vickers and Alvis equipment independently these would be lower than the MTS prices.

Ambassador Wright warned London:[68]

> if [President] Frangié hears of money being paid to Chamoun in circumstances which make it look as if [Her Majesty's Government] are interfering in the elections to be held probably in March/April 1972, he would call the whole thing off. I would not put it past Alamuddine to blow the gaff himself in order to cut out MTS [and, with Brandt's and Burnand also out of the running, win the whole deal for himself]...I am therefore concerned to avert any risk that [Her Majesty's Government] may be accused of interference by their connexion with Chamoun, not to mention losing the arms contract.

Wright pointed out that, having recommended MTS to the Lebanese, the British Government could 'hardly disclaim knowledge of, nor I think responsibility for, their actions'. Rather than abandoning Chamoun, he suggested that

> MTS could formally appoint Chalabi (so far as we know Chamoun's present chosen intermediary) and pay him the commission in return for 'handling' services etc...we would then be in a position to say that naturally MTS need a representative on the spot and have to pay him something. The Lebanese might see through this but they would not be able to bring any charges against us that we could not plausibly refute.

London agreed. A few weeks later, Cawston told Hubert[69] that Chalabi

tells me that Chamoun is perturbed by the possibility of gettin [sic] less than five per cent because part of the five per cent was destined for the Prime Minister [Salam] who is in turn annoyed that the matter is not firm. If this is true then this commission would be well spent.

Despite these manoeuvres behind the scenes, the Lebanese did not buy British. And in the meantime a scandal erupted in Lebanon which made the British 'commission' arrangements much riskier.

The French company Thomson Houston had a contract to sell Crotale surface-to-air missiles to the Lebanese armed forces. The British Embassy in Beirut informed London[70] that behind this deal

undoubtedly lies the spectre of corruption. There is little doubt that a number of important people have been taking a big rake-off from the deal and the prospect of personal profit probably weighed more heavily than defence needs at the time the decision to order Crotale missiles was taken.

A political storm ensued. The diplomats told London that one agent accused, Mrs Lily Saad, was jailed.[71]

Nor did the British escape unscathed. The Commander-in-Chief of the Lebanese Armed Forces, General Ghanem, told Cawston he was convinced that 'substantial commissions had been arranged by the British'. Wright now suggested to Suffield[72] that they

put the record right with the Lebanese, especially in view of the publicity which is now being given to similar charges against the French. Lebanese suspicions about the British have not yet appeared in the press but they may still do so at any time with consequent harm to our reputation…the one weakness in our position is of course the previous arrangement with Chamoun, which I suspect is behind the present problem.

The answer was to withdraw the MTS offer. As it was over one year since MTS had made arrangements with Chamoun and Chalabi, Wright concluded 'I do not think it will matter greatly if Chamoun is now left out. His influence is not as great as it was and I now feel that the disadvantages of any further connection with him will outweigh any advantages'. He recommended[73] 'we should also rigidly eschew further attempts to influence the Lebanese by the payment of commissions... it was at least as important to emerge smelling as sweet as possible as it was to secure any orders'.

However, Lebanese bribe requests continued to discomfort Whitehall. In 1973, Hawker Siddeley tried to sell two Hunter aircraft to the Lebanese Ministry of Defence. The Embassy in Beirut told London an intermediary had said[74] 'the Minister of Defence requires a percentage commission. This information was accompanied by the usual threats of "no commission – no deal" and as having an effect on future sales of British equipment.'

King Feisal Bans Bribery in Saudi Arms Deals

As Governments in the Middle East began to ban bribery, getting caught could land the British Government in big trouble. They had a narrow escape in Lebanon. One year before Brandt's and Burnand's first proposal, an arms deal scandal led to a ban on bribery in such deals in Saudi Arabia, making British efforts to sell arms to the country much more complicated than they had been in Geoffrey Edwards's heyday.

In the early 1960s, the Saudis had expressed interest in buying armoured vehicles from Alvis for their Army.[75] The DSO's dealings with a number of agents on Alvis's behalf, including Edwards, came to nothing,[76] and in February 1968 the French newspaper *Le Monde* reported a Saudi purchase of 220 Panhard armoured cars.[77]

King Feisal found out how the French obtained this contract. In May 1968 London heard this scandal was 'a particularly nasty one' and that Feisal had ordered an inquiry.[78] Raymond Brown, then Head of Defence Sales, was told by the Saudi Ambassador to London, Abdurrahman Al-Helaissi,[79] that the 'King is seriously concerned over Panhard contract and is expected to thke [sic] strong action'.

On 20 October 1968 Feisal banned commissions. The Embassy in Jedda sent London a news report claiming[80] 'the Saudi Arabian Government has recently issued a circular letter to all aircraft companies and military equipment production organizations asking them to refrain forthwith from paying any kind of commissions or remunerations to any agent or representative in Saudi Arabia'. The

5.   British Prime Minister Harold Wilson welcomes King Feisal of Saudi Arabia to Downing Street, May 1967. In October 1968, Feisal banned commissions on arms deals with his Kingdom.

Source: S&G/S&G Barratts/EMPICS Archive.

Picture courtesy of Press Association Images.

circular from the Saudi Ministry of Finance[81] stipulated that 'all contracts must contain a declaration from the contractor that he has not paid any commission to any middleman or broker for the sake of concluding the contract'.

Now, any British company caught paying commissions could expect to be shut out of Saudi Arabia permanently. If the British Government was associated with commissions paid by British arms companies then, given the highly personal nature of Feisal's rule, serious damage to Britain's relations with Saudi Arabia would inevitably follow.

Vickers and King Feisal's Ban on Bribery

Rather awkwardly, Feisal issued his decree at a crucial point in the attempt by the British company Vickers to sell tanks to the Saudi Army, with heavy British Government support.

In 1967, the Saudis had asked Vickers[82] for 175 tanks, radio sets, spares, training and maintenance workshops costing £33,842,825[83] (worth about £455 million today). Vickers informed the DSO that they would pay 10 per cent commission on each tank and the training and workshop equipment.[84]

The Defence Attaché at the Embassy in Jedda, Colin Fitzpatrick, recommended[85] that Vickers appoint Zaid Sudairi, nephew of the Defence Minister Prince Sultan, as their agent. But instead, Vickers used Ali Ali Reza, a member of one of Saudi Arabia's major commercial families. The agreed commission rate was 7.5 per cent (worth £2,538,212 or about £32.5 million today).[86] The Ali Reza family, said one Vickers salesman,[87] 'were not anxious to be known to be Armaments Agents within Saudi Arabia'.

Sir Leslie Rowan, the Chairman of Vickers, asked the British Government to support his sales visit to Saudi Arabia in October 1968. Diplomats in London wanted to, saying[88] 'if Vickers were to go in, particularly at this level, with no more than half-hearted Embassy support, or even with none at all, it would seriously prejudice their chances and give the competition [the French[89]] a gratuitous advantage'.

On 16 October, Fitzpatrick discussed the 'stage management' of the visit with General Makki Tounisi, the Director of Operations in the Saudi Army. Fitzpatrick told Vickers[90] that 'Saudi military opinion appears to be that although they do not really want or need tanks now, they are prepared to be quote persuaded unquote to the contrary'. He reported:

> my conclusion is that if a firm understanding is reached with Tounisi before the visit [of Rowan] takes place, that the amount of quote squeeze unquote available to him will be around three point five per cent of contract if one is signed, then he will fix military committee to approve Vickers tank.

The bribe requested was thus £1,184,499 (worth about £15 million today). Four days after Fitzpatrick and Tounisi met, Feisal banned commissions on arms deals.

Vickers Director Jim Robbie spoke to Ali Ali Reza on the telephone the day after Feisal's decree had been issued. He informed his colleagues:[91]

I told Ali Alireza that we regarded any question of commission as his problem and his alone, but if this request by the General [Tounisi] meant that the 7½% which we had included was insufficient, we should know immediately. His advice was that we should include a little bit more. (We have, in fact, already got a fair negotiating margin in our price). *Alireza emphasised the point, however, that we must not at any time disclose to anyone in Saudi Arabia that we are employing agents.*

One week after this call, Rowan met Feisal, accompanied by British Ambassador Willie Morris. Morris told London[92] that Feisal warned Rowan 'against agents and middlemen trying to make illegitimate gains…he was not just thinking of commercial agents but of Government servants who claimed to be able to influence decisions'.

Back in London, Donal McCarthy was the Head of the Arabian Department in the Foreign and Commonwealth Office, and responsible for Britain's relations with Saudi Arabia. He watched the unfolding drama with alarm. One day after Fitzpatrick's telegram about Tounisi's bribe request arrived in London, he wrote to Morris.[93]

He opened, 'I realise that getting big contracts in Saudi Arabia requires a judicious element of bribery', but admitted to being 'slightly shaken' by Tounisi's bribe request. McCarthy could 'visualise circumstances in which, with the Panhard representatives's assistance, "Le Figaro" might find itself in a position to carry the headline "British Military Attache bribes Saudi General for tank deal"'. Acknowledging it was 'difficult to draw lines in these matters' he said Fitzpatrick should not get involved. For

that is really what the Saudi agent is for. And, though I cannot speak for British firms, my impression is that most big British firms would prefer to know nothing about it and would expect the local agent to find the cut out of his percentage. The Ali Rezas may reasonably be supposed to know their way through this one.

He concluded, 'altogether I should prefer to see this sort of thing conveyed through channels other than the Foreign Office telegraphic system'.

Morris replied a fortnight later in a letter[94] entitled 'The Fiddle Factor in Saudi Defence Contracts'. He explained that Tounisi had discussed the 'squeeze' with an interpreter. Fitzpatrick 'allowed himself to listen, but entered into no discussion, showing that whatever it might have to do with Vickers, it had nothing to do with him'. Morris agreed that 'we should avoid getting involved in the fiddling; but if we are to give British firms the help they need, we cannot close our eyes and ears, even if we keep our mouths tight shut'. He finished 'I meant, by way of precaution, to suggest to Stephenson of Vickers when he was here that he destroy any written record of our message; but I failed to do so. Perhaps you could arrange for this to be put to him?' A subordinate asked if he should do so, but was told 'No. Let this drop.'

The interpreter was a Palestinian, Hassan Gabr, who according to Vickers salesman retired Colonel Bernard Heath[95] was the 'head interpreter on Sultan's Staff and consequently knows a lot about what is going on'.

Heath told colleagues[96] Gabr was concerned Vickers had rebuffed

> Prince Fahd's offer to act for us in swinging the tank deal in our favour. He said that time was short and that the French had powerful people acting for them. He said that Fahd was still in London and still ready to co-operate. We repeated that we preferred not to use agents in deference to the King's wishes, but he insisted that everyone else used agents and that no deal would go through unless Sultan and the Army Officers got a cut.

Heath suggested:

> the Alirezas must have pressure put on them to investigate the claims of Hassan Gabr and Prince Fahd, and they must come out with a clear recommendation as to their value in getting the order through. If necessary any commission paid to these people must come out of the Alirezas' commission.

Vickers ignored Feisal's decree but could not work out who the most effective agents were. And so, in December 1971, the Saudis bought 200 AMX-30 tanks.[97] The Defence Attaché in Jedda had, more than one year before, told London[98] that it was 'rumoured that the French are again paying an extremely high commission (28%)', far above the rather meagre 7.5 per cent offered by Vickers.

Thus the dilemma faced by Vickers and other British companies was acute. Some of Feisal's (half-)brothers and others in the Council of Ministers wanted to continue with the old ways and encouraged the companies to ignore Feisal's decree. They were of course, the very people who would recommend to Feisal what equipment to buy.

As Morris told the new Head of Defence Sales, Lester Suffield,[99] the world of arms sales in Saudi Arabia was 'a jungle inhabited by beasts of prey in which one must move with caution and uncertainty. The magnates are (justifiably) suspicious of one another and their agents; alliances and rivalries amongst both are constantly shifting'. To keep track, in January 1969 Morris started 'a compendium of information which might be called "Who pays whom in Saudi Arabia"'.[100] He kept a file on corruption in his office.[101]

So the DSO was not shy about dealing with agents, and indeed had some on their books. Events in Saudi Arabia in the late 1960s and Lebanon in the early 1970s illustrated the risks involved in getting mixed up in bribery. In Lebanon, nimble footwork had enabled the British to pull back from the brink, and avoid the odium attached to the French. In Saudi Arabia, officials, while doing all they could to help the British companies find their way through the jungle, had not become directly involved.

But these deals, while significant, were not the 'mega-deals' worth billions in today's money. In the last half of the 1960s, oil production in the Middle East was increasing by around 10 per cent every year. By 1970 the Middle East was producing almost 67 per cent more oil than it had in 1965.[102] Absolute rulers in the Middle East now had vast sums to spend on arms deals. And, not surprisingly, those in positions of power and influence, and their hangers-on, were now even keener to get their cut.

So when, around this time, the Saudis and the Iranians both gave Britain the chance to win a mega-deal, the question of how to deal with corruption became much more difficult, especially when they requested the respectability of a Government-to-Government contract.

The two main mega-deals in prospect were with the Saudi Arabian National Guard and the Iranian Ministry of War. To win them, Britain would have to deal directly with two of the most important people in the Middle East.

In Saudi Arabia the customer was Prince Abdullah, the National Guard commander. Highly influential then as a member of the Council of Ministers, he is now, over 40 years later, the Saudi King. In Iran the customer was the ruler, His Imperial Majesty Mohammed Reza Shah

Pahlavi, the 'King of Kings'. The Shah dominated Iran in the 1970s, but in 1979 he was forced to flee the country following the Islamic revolution, and died in exile one year later.

So, with the temptation of two mega-deals in front of British Government officials, where would the line be drawn?

3

The 'Deniable Fiddle': Dealing with the Saudi Arabian National Guard (1968–72)

Prince Abdullah became King of Saudi Arabia in 2005. His father, Ibn Saud, had children by many different women, and hence Abdullah has a large number of half-brothers.

Some of them, the so-called 'Sudairi Seven', have controlled the Saudi Ministry of Defence and Aviation and the regular Armed Forces since 1962. They include Prince Sultan (Defence Minister from 1962 until his death in 2011) and Prince Abdul Rahman (Geoffrey Edwards's main contact when he won the air defence system contract in the 1960s).

In 1963 Abdullah became Commander of the Saudi Arabian National Guard, Saudi Arabia's second army. According to a British Cabinet Committee paper,[1] the Saudi Royal Family maintained two armies, because they were 'well aware that the regular army has in other Arab countries proved to be the main source of danger to established régimes'. Thus King Saud had built up a 'so-called "White" Army of Beduin tribesmen into a guard for the royal house'. Abdullah has therefore been a very important figure for over 50 years.

Corruption was rife in arms deals with Sultan's Ministry of Defence and Aviation. King Feisal's irritation with this corruption led to his decree banning agents and commissions in October 1968.

By contrast, before 1968, arms deals with the National Guard were relatively clean. The Embassy in Jedda explained to London:[2] 'Prince Abdulla intends to do business on a government-to-government basis and will not employ commercial agents'. An official quipped, 'too bad for G. Edwards!'.

British Officials Facilitate a 'Deniable Fiddle'

However, one month after Feisal's decree, in November 1968, a Lebanese fixer claimed to the British Defence Attaché in

6.   King Abdullah of Saudi Arabia (left) meeting British
Prime Minister Tony Blair (right) at Downing Street, 1998.
Abdullah commanded the Saudi Arabian National Guard
from 1963 to 2010, and became King in 2005.

Picture by Adam Butler/AP/Press Association Images.

Beirut[3] he could 'influence the purchase by Saudi Arabia of a large
order of Saladin [Armoured] cars [made by Alvis]' for the National
Guard. British officials were sceptical and rebuffed the fixer, because
Abdullah had previously said that he wanted to deal direct with the
British Government, and Feisal's banning of agents and commissions
one month before. But they could not easily ignore such dubious
unsolicited approaches. For, as Head of Defence Sales Raymond Brown
put it,[4] Saudi Arabia was 'one of the most important areas for British
business, and particularly in the Defence Sales field'.

As it happened, the British Government could discover whether the approach was genuine. For in Riyadh was a British Military Mission to the National Guard, commanded by Brigadier Adrian Donaldson.

The Mission was there because, almost six years earlier, in February 1963, Prince Feisal, soon to become King, had asked Britain for military training advisers to make the National Guard an effective force. Foreign Secretary Alec Douglas-Home told Prime Minister Harold Macmillan[5] 'it is in our interest that the present regime should survive and its principal prop be efficient'. Douglas-Home envisaged a Mission would provide intelligence, visibly and directly support the Saudi regime, and help Britain deal with any difficulties in relations with the Saudis.

The Mission arrived in August 1963. In 1964 Feisal forced King Saud to step down, and became King himself. During this power struggle the Mission helped Feisal and Abdullah by drawing up plans for Feisal's protection by the National Guard, and the occupation of key parts of Riyadh in the event of a revolt.[6] Not surprisingly, the Mission won Abdullah's trust.

In January 1969, diplomats agreed Donaldson should make enquiries about the Lebanese fixer.[7] Donaldson told them:[8]

[CENSORED] has made it clear to me that if we operate through him anything we need for the National Guard will be obtained. [CENSORED] wishes to operate only through Beirut at present and this I know presents great communications problems but I am sure that if the right machinery is established now a very considerable amount of business will follow.

British Ambassador Willie Morris pointed out[9] that because of Feisal's decree 'this puts us in very rocky waters'. He wanted Alvis to deal with the fixer directly. If this arrangement was exposed the diplomats could say:

we can hardly be expected to enforce on British companies Saudi regulations about the conduct of Saudi Government Departments. We made clear our willingness to do a Government to Government deal, but as Alvis were approached by an agent acting with the authority of the Department of the Saudi Government concerned, they could not be blamed for responding.

However, because of the censorship of this telegram, it is not possible to identify the person referred to by Morris as 'the authority of the Department of the Saudi Government concerned'.

Diplomats informed Harold Hubert of the Defence Sales Organisation (DSO)[10] of the plan for what Morris called 'a deniable fiddle'. Hubert said[11] 'he was completely flexible and would adopt whatever system we wished. At all events [CENSORED] could get his cut and no-one would have known about it at all'. Donaldson informed the Embassy[12] that 'the commission required is seven per cent'.

There is a clue to the identity of the Lebanese fixer and his Saudi client demanding a cut. A document from 1971,[13] sent to London by Morris, reads 'the history of Fustuq is set out in Annex B to the Ambassador's memorandum of 11 February 1970. The Embassy recommended against responding to his importunities until we got the clearest indication from Abdullah that he was Abdullah's man.'

Annex B of the Ambassador's memorandum of 11 February 1970[14] reads:

> In late 1968 [CENSORED] a Lebanese businessman [CENSORED] began a series of approaches to the [Defence Attaché] in Beirut, saying that he was in a position to secure sales to the National Guard. (He operates through a firm, [CENSORED] whose front man is a Chamounist politician)...

> In January, 1969, we instructed Donaldson to put to [CENSORED] our dilemma: [CENSORED] had told [Defence Secretary Denis] Healey he wanted government-to-government sales, and had instructed Donaldson to do nothing on Saladin sales without instructions from [CENSORED] others claimed to be speaking differently on his behalf. What were [CENSORED] wishes? [CENSORED] reply was to introduce Donaldson to [CENSORED].

> After consultation between the Embassy, [Foreign and Commonwealth Office and the DSO] it was agreed that [CENSORED] should be told to get in touch with Alvis.

Most of the documents relied on in this chapter were disclosed to me following an Information Tribunal case I fought against the Foreign and Commonwealth Office where the then Ambassador to Saudi Arabia, William Patey, gave evidence. The Tribunal found in my favour; though, as you can see, some of the documents are still partially censored.

However, even if Alvis did the dirty work, this deal was still very risky. Morris worried[15] that if Feisal found out that Donaldson had played the key role in bringing together company, fixer and buyer, Britain's relations with Saudi Arabia would be seriously damaged. Questions would be asked in London.

Further, Alvis already had an agent in the Middle East, Near East Resources.[16] Alvis did not want them to be involved in this deal nor pay them their normal commission,[17] as there would be less money for the other fixer. London told Morris[18] that '[Sulayman] Alamuddin [of Near East Resources] did help to prejudice the chances of a Saladin sale to the Saudi Army by being unwilling to share enough of his cut with [fixer Adnan] Kashoggi (and possibly Ghaith Pharaoun?), who then turned to Panhard'. Alvis therefore kept secret from Near East Resources that they were using another agent instead.[19]

Of course, as Morris realised, the simple answer was to pull out of the deal. He suggested:[20]

> the bold, simple, and pure course would be for me to go to [CENSORED] to quote his remarks on middlemen, and in effect denounce [CENSORED] for corruption. I do not think that [CENSORED] would thank us for it; Donaldson, not [CENSORED] would be disowned; the Mission would be wound up; the sales would go elsewhere.

In London diplomats dismissed his idea as 'out of the question'.

In March 1969, the Head of the Arabian Department at the Foreign and Commonwealth Office, Donal McCarthy, one of his colleagues, Hubert, the Defence Attaché in Beirut, and two Alvis salesmen met to discuss the next steps. The minutes[21] record the problem was that the fixer and his associates

> were demanding a letter from Alvis promising to pay them a commission of 7½ per cent on the main Saladin contract when it went through. For Alvis to do this, however, would be to put a dangerous document in the hands of [CENSORED] which could be used against them in many ways. It could be taken to the Panhard representative to persuade him to raise any commission offer he might have made; it could be kept to blackmail Alvis at a later stage over the main contract; or used

straightaway to discredit them with [CENSORED] in favour of a rival. [The Alvis salesmen] appreciated all these risks as fairly normal in a commercial deal of this kind...there was no question of course of Alvis paying a commission, or any major part of it in advance, though this would naturally obviate the need for a letter.

McCarthy said the letter

need not in itself harm [Her Majesty's Government] seriously if it were discovered. [Her Majesty's Government] would, of course, disown Alvis, though they would try to help to patch up any mess for Alvis later if possible...it was of paramount importance that [Her Majesty's Government] should be kept right out of any deal over the commission: if that deal became public and were associated with [Her Majesty's Government] then there would be wider and unacceptable damage to British official and commercial interests alike.

Hubert encouraged Alvis to get involved. He said

he hoped that Alvis would remember that this deal might provide an entrée for them to Saudi Arabia. The National Guard was being developed into a much more sophisticated force and much additional equipment might be required. The deal could also be useful for [the DSO] as it could lead to the introduction of Millbank Technical Services for the maintenance of the vehicles, and to other business following on from that. It was important generally for British equipment to be well represented. Equally, Alvis had no business in Saudi Arabia at present which they could lose if the matter of a commission were discovered. He pointed out that Vickers, with some £40 million at stake there, were quite prepared to make arrangements for commissions.

Alvis proposed to offer Near East Resources a sweetener to keep them quiet. Those present agreed that Alvis could write the letter the fixer wanted and that officials would stop meeting him.

Official Dilemmas about Involvement in Bribery

However, a junior member of the DSO's staff then introduced the fixer to Millbank Technical Services (MTS) in Beirut.[22] MTS explained

to McCarthy they might bid for a contract for back-up equipment if
the National Guard bought Saladins from Alvis. The fixer wrote to
MTS[23] 'asking to be appointed as consulting engineers for the project
([CENSORED] is supposedly a qualified engineer and the project does
contain a construction element)…The cut is 8 per cent.'

McCarthy pointed out:[24]

we cannot disown Crown Agents/MTS with their quasi-governmental aspect as easily as we can disown Alvis. [MTS] wanted, therefore,
to consult us in case we thought that there was too much danger of
embarrassment to [Her Majesty's Government]…I finally said that I did
not like the scheme at all, but that I saw no alternative way of getting
the business.

MTS hired the fixer about two weeks later.[25]

McCarthy moaned,[26] 'the Saudi circular banning commissions is all
very well. But as far as I can see its observance would frustrate orders,
whereas cooperating with [CENSORED] in contravention of it may
secure them.' He complained to the Saudi Ambassador in London,[27]
Abdurrahman Al-Helaissi, saying 'on a personal basis and not for the
record, that the ruling against agents was proving a farce; it prevented
legitimate business but [CENSORED] were in the van in evading it
and making their cut an effective condition of any business at all in the
military field at least. [Helaissi] wasn't surprised'.

The fixer was unable to secure a contract for Alvis or MTS and the
diplomats increasingly did not believe what he told them. One wrote:[28]

[CENSORED] may be a useful pawn, but I cannot believe that he has
the attributes or organisation of a real 'fixer'. The big deals in Saudi
Arabia are master minded by men of standing who have links with
the men at the top and an organisation both to take care of the lower
levels and assist the bidders in the preparation of their offers. The man
who signs the contract only does so when his signature has the firm
backing of a long line of recommendations starting from the bottom
of administration…without their 'Khashoggi' or their '[Kamal]Adham'
[Feisal's brother-in-law, head of the Saudi intelligence services, and
an extremely influential figure] the British companies would have
difficulty in finalising the contract. [CENSORED] hardly seems the
man to overcome this opposition.

At the Embassy in Jedda, diplomats were uneasy. James Craig, Morris's deputy, complained to London:[29]

the longer this affair goes on, the less I like it...Some governments are prepared to get involved in shady dealings; [Her Majesty's Government] are, I assume, quite rightly not...The Embassy can give a certain amount of help: we can advise on the choice of agent, we can sometimes check the agent's information, we can provide certain types of information ourselves (that X is married to Y's sister, for example). But we cannot and must not try to tell the company who is to be bribed and who is not. We cannot offer such advice without full, accurate and detailed information of backstage life in Saudi commerce and Government; and we cannot obtain such information without going down into the mire ourselves. I should have though it was self-evident that we ought not so to descend and it is highly doubtful, irrespective of the morality, whether we would be successful even if we did.
2. But that, after all, is what a local agent is for in this part of the world. That is precisely what Buqshan have done for the British Hovercraft Corporation (for your private ear B.H.C. paid Buqshan about 20% of the contract price and estimate that about three-quarters of this went to the Ministry of the Interior).

But, with a chance of a deal in the offing, London did want the Embassy to advise on the bribing and told Craig:[30]

while we understand your feelings, we do not think we can primly stand aside altogether. If we have a definite hint for example, that bribing a certain person will probably lead to the winning of a contract, we cannot very well sit tight and withhold the information, when doing so might mean that a foreign company would bribe into the contract. We do not have to tell a company in so many words 'who is to be bribed and who not' (though if we were sure about it we might neglect our duty to exports if we did not pass it on – unattributably). But we should surely be prepared to say to a company that they might find that X or Y could sway a deal if he was approached in the right manner.

In September 1969, Hubert learned that Alamuddin had discovered the arrangements with the fixer and advised:[31]

if [CENSORED] once had a value he no longer has I should have thought any Saudi operator with an ambition to get his cut out of this business would see to it that the project would not succeed while the present commercial arrangements exist.

Lester Suffield became Head of Defence Sales the same month. At the start of 1970, Morris wrote him a paper entitled 'Arms Sales to Saudi Arabia'.[32] He explained 'the question of corruption is obviously crucial,' and continued:

16. Though we know some sales have been made (e.g. Vigilants to the National Guard, the gift of arms to Jordan) without commissions, it has to be accepted that the normal choice for firms is between accepting the system or abandoning the idea of selling. We believe that in the course of considerable correspondence on this subject with the [Foreign and Commonwealth Office] and [Ministry of Defence] during the past year, the following general guidance has been accepted on our attitude to the system:

(a) Officials of [Her Majesty's Government], here and elsewhere, should acquire as much information as they can about the system and make it available to firms; but

(b) they should avoid getting themselves directly involved with this aspect of arms sales.

(c) Firms should be encouraged to take local advisers both to inform them and to act for them on these matters, rather than rely on officials.

(d) It must be made clear to firms that in this matter they are taking their own decisions, and the risks involved.

(e) Departments of [Her Majesty's Government] could not knowingly pay bribes without Ministerial clearance and that clearance would not be forthcoming. If commissions are to be paid on Government-to-Government sales (except for *bona fide* services) therefore the arrangements will have to be made by private firms manufacturing and supplying equipment.

(f) There should be the fullest exchange of information between [the DSO] and the Embassy; the extent to which *firms* will or should be expected to take officials into their confidence is more doubtful.

17. These rules are a matter of expediency, not ethics; the ethical course would be to advise firms to refuse regardless of consequences

to compromise with the system...The justification for the rules is that (a) [Her Majesty's Government] will be more vulnerable when (as we expect) these affairs become a matter of public scandal; (b) the system requires that firms work through agents (or 'advisers'); in the main they are only too inclined to let officials do what they should do for themselves; (c) our present troubles over National Guard arms purchases demonstrate the harm that can be done if officials get too involved (See Annex B); (d) the whole maze is so complex, the underworld involved so untrustworthy, that no advice can be given with certainty.

The fixer was still pestering British businessmen in Beirut. The Embassy in Jedda learned[33] that two had been approached about National Guard contracts and introduced to a firm called METICO. The Embassy knew METICO was the firm of Fustuq (Abdullah's man).[34] Diplomats described[35] how one businessman was 'taken to the METICO office where he had been given an assurance by [CENSORED] that he would arrange for the contract to be awarded'. The other was told 'he would not get the business if he did not appoint METICO as agents'.

At the beginning of 1970 Alvis let their agreement with the fixer expire. They had given Alamuddin, their official agent in Saudi Arabia, his notice three months earlier.[36]

As British chances of winning a National Guard deal appeared poor, at the Foreign and Commonwealth Office diplomats wondered what to do next. The desk officer for Saudi Arabia, Bill Fullerton, thought[37] Alvis might stand a better chance if they employed Khashoggi, 'one of the most powerful and wealthy of the Fixers on the Saudi scene'[38] for the 'real wheeling and dealing'. Fullerton mused,[39] 'though Kashoggi might be anathema [CENSORED] if the end result was that [CENSORED] got Saladdins [sic] and his required percentage, he might perhaps not mind Kashoggi's intervention so much?'. But, Fullerton's new boss, Antony Acland, who had replaced McCarthy, countered:[40] 'there is hardly room for [CENSORED] & Kashoggi all to get their cuts. If this is so, [CENSORED] will fear that the involvement of Kashoggi would reduce the amount available to them.'

Acland pointed out to Morris[41] that, as the fixer did not appear

to have the necessary leverage where it really counts, it seems that a bigger fixer will probably be required at some stage if the British deals are to be successful. Your theory that a company should go for the business first and that the fixers can then be expected to appear seems the right way to start undoubtedly, but in a case such as this, where no fixers of sufficient influence appear, what next? Agreed that [the Ministry of Defence] should not go looking for the right fixer, but does there not come a stage when the company should do so?

Acland suggested a new policy.[42]

Let us by all means try this direct approach and give it a chance to work. If nothing comes of it in due course, we might perhaps advise Alvis to put some pressure on [CENSORED] and say that if he cannot deliver the deal himself, why doesn't he get help from someone who can? If that in turn produces no results, it seems to us that there might be an argument for suggesting to Alvis that they pursue the matter further with Kashoggi, or any other fixer you may recommend.

Meanwhile Alvis had received[43] 'a letter from [CENSORED] the Lebanese firm handling [CENSORED] business pressing for renewed discussion of previous agreement'. As Alvis had no better alternative they renewed the agreement in April 1970.[44]

Millbank Technical Services and the Fixer

They did so because a new and bigger deal was now on the horizon. The National Guard was to be expanded, to comprise eleven battle groups with over 1,400 armoured vehicles, along with weapons, ammunition and technical support. The DSO reckoned[45] the deal would be worth £75–80 million (worth about £850–900 million today). They informed[46] Acland: '7½% commission should be paid across the board. This will be a total of about £6 million' (worth about £68 million today). Now the Saudis wanted a proposal by a consortium of the Ministry of Defence, Alvis and MTS.

The DSO wanted MTS to be the prime contractor, not Alvis. This was, said Suffield,[47]

because of the usual considerations that apply to any business in Saudi Arabia i.e. the need to pay 'commissions' and because also Prince Abdullah wished to give any purchase the appearance of a Government-to-Government deal, we proposed to Prince Abdullah that a middle course would be to make the UK package offer through [MTS].

As for commissions, the DSO told Acland:[48]

> Alvis have made their own arrangements. Previously the [Foreign and Commonwealth Office] have been reluctant to let MTS make similar arrangements because of their close connection with Government Departments. Since the time when this was discussed it has been made known in Saudi Arabia that 'Advisers' are permitted. It would greatly facilitate the setting up of suitable arrangements if MTS could be allowed to go ahead and negotiate such commission arrangements as they can. They would do this entirely on their own responsibility without any reference to the [Ministry of Defence].

Craig was sent to Beirut to give the fixer feedback on his previous efforts. Craig told his colleagues[49] that 'our meeting was arranged like something out of James Bond and I was taken up the mountain to [CENSORED] house for lunch'. There, he told the fixer that '[Her Majesty's Government] could not get mixed up in and did not want to know about any unorthodox payments'. He said bluntly, 'it seemed to us that everyone in the operation had played his part except [CENSORED] himself who had failed to obtain the decision to buy Saladins'.

The fixer and his associates

> later got on their high horse and said there were no repeat no unorthodox payments, only legitimate commission. When I tried to break through the hypocrisy they stalked round the room in high dudgeon.

Craig asked them why they had not secured a Saladin deal and the fixer's 'pride was hurt. He kept saying he could not accept the word 'fail' (*fashal*) so I withdrew it and substituted a circumlocution'. Craig concluded 'afterwards we went to the races and sat in the owners' box. I stayed only for the first race in which [CENSORED] horses came last and next to last. Absit omen [may the (evil) omen be absent].'

The draft agreement[50] between MTS and the fixer was to be valid for five years 'unless the implementation of this agreement is frustrated by instructions received from the Authority concerned in Saudi Arabia'.

MTS would pay 7.5 per cent of the total contract value to a Swiss bank account for any contracts won with the Saudi Army or National Guard.

The final agreement was signed on Friday 12 June. On Monday 15 June, MTS informed the Foreign and Commonwealth Office[51] that '[CENSORED] is due to visit the Ministry of Defence early this week, probably Tuesday'.

Acland told Morris[52] that 'the [Ministry of Defence] were optimistic that the deal had been or was about to be clinched and were of course anxious to receive [CENSORED] properly'. Lord Winterbottom, a Defence Minister, was asked to receive the visitor, Abdullah.[53]

At the meeting,[54] '[CENSORED], however, remained anxious that his dealings should be with the British Government so that questions of commission for agents in the Middle East did not arise'. A diplomat commented[55] that '[CENSORED] is merely establishing his position – he wants (as do [CENSORED], M.T.S. and Alvis) to involve [Her Majesty's Government] as proof of the honesty of the deal in order to enhance its presentational aspect to the [CENSORED] Council of Ministers'.

The Embassy in Jedda advised[56] that MTS and Alvis should

...put the onus on [CENSORED] to provide the service he has promised i.e. the contract...

3. As long as [Her Majesty's Government] remain the principal in Saudi eyes, the companies are subject to [Her Majesty's Government]'s guidance. Any departure from this understanding puts to hazard the whole exercise which is designed, as has been stressed previously, to afford [CENSORED] the protection of a deniable fix. The Companies' responsibilities outside any government-to-government contract are to pay [CENSORED] (or his firm [CENSORED]) an agreed commission, but this is no concern of [Her Majesty's Government].

However, because of the censorship of these documents, it is not possible to identify who is being afforded 'the protection of a deniable fix'.

Hubert, along with salesmen from MTS and Alvis, visited Saudi Arabia in October 1970, to discuss what equipment an expanded National Guard would need,[57] presenting their proposals to Abdullah in the spring of 1971.[58] The British package offered by MTS would cost about £112 million (worth about £1.2 billion today). Suffield reported:[59]

'Prince Abdullah expressed himself as satisfied with our proposals and said that he would put them to the Council of Ministers'.

A Memorandum of Understanding for the deal was drawn up. The Ministry of Defence planned that[60] 'MTS would handle the Fustuq aspects of any deal i.e. any commission arrangements'. But, again, no deal was forthcoming.

In July 1971, Hubert and Suffield visited the Embassy in Jedda to discuss what to do. They 'wondered if Fustuq was the right man'.[61] Morris pointed out 'the key is King Faisal's support for a substantial expansion programme for the National Guard, and Fustuq has absolutely no control over this'. They agreed[62] the Memorandum of Understanding would be 'presented to Prince Abdullah at the earliest opportunity'. However,[63] 'the timing of this should be...when there is a signal from Abdullah not Fustuq whose sense of timing has proved faulty on every occasion'.

The Americans Clinch the Deal

In November, the British learned that the Saudis had asked for bids from the Americans and the French.[64] Suffield said:[65] 'the temptation of business of this magnitude was causing various other members of the Royal family to come out in opposition to Abdullah's proposals and to suggest that their "clients" i.e. the US and France should be allowed in the bidding'. Prince Sultan, Abdullah's great rival, was able to manipulate Feisal's anger to frustrate Britain and Abdullah's plans.

Feisal was angry because he felt vulnerable. Since the mid nineteenth century, Britain had been responsible for the security of the sheikhdoms along the coast of the Persian Gulf, known as the Trucial States. Britain's planned military withdrawal from the Persian Gulf at the end of 1971 left Saudi Arabia and the other Gulf sheikhdoms to stand on their own feet.

Feisal had hoped that Gulf security after the withdrawal would be improved by the formation of a Union of Arab Emirates involving all nine Gulf sheikhdoms. The complex rivalries of the Gulf rulers made this impossible. By July 1971, the British realised that Bahrain and Qatar would not join any Union[66] and Feisal blamed Britain. Lastly, Feisal also blamed Britain for failing to persuade the Ruler of Abu Dhabi to settle a border dispute with Saudi Arabia.

In the summer of 1971, Abdullah was out of the country and Sultan persuaded Feisal to get back at the British. A copy of the confidential proposals Hubert and his colleagues had put to Abdullah was given to Khashoggi. He passed them to the American companies (for whom he was the agent) and asked them for a quote.[67] The Americans were then awarded the contract.

Abdullah did not tell Donaldson what had happened for another five months.[68] When he did, in January 1972, Hubert was in Jedda. At a discussion at the Embassy Morris agreed to ask Feisal to change his mind. Hubert reported:[69]

> much therefore depended on whether he was content to put his defence forces completely in US hands [the Americans were already the main suppliers of the Saudi Army]. If he did it seemed likely that we could expect only a few crumbs by grace of Mr. Khashoggi. If he hesitated something better might be possible.

Hubert and the diplomats had no qualms about sweetening Khashoggi if necessary:

> if a deal has to be done with Khashoggi it should be done. His own personal demands will probably be high, but that is the way business is done in Saudi Arabia, the King's edict about 25 percenters notwithstanding. Either Khashoggi is offered the cut he wants or we should pull out.

That would mean dumping Fustuq. So, Hubert continued,

> MTS will have to negotiate [CENSORED] out of as much of his commission as possible. As he claimed that [CENSORED] was taking 6½ out of the 7½% the 1% should be the basis of any negotiation though no doubt [CENSORED] greed will compel him to try to get something from both fixers.

Hubert thought this was feasible because '[CENSORED] whatever bravado he may display, will not step into a British court' to sue for breach of contract.

Hubert met Khashoggi within a fortnight of his return to London. Khashoggi told him:[70]

he wanted to operate for the British Government but at the same time wanted to ensure that any [Government-to-Government] business would leave his commissions protected. I told him naturally we should not interfere with commissions paid to him by firms, but did not comment on his first point.

Hubert reported,[71] 'K[hashoggi] knows about Fustuq since he mentioned the name first, but I doubt if he knows the detailed arrangements. I got an impression that he would not want to concern himself in any way with Fustuq and any existing commitments towards him.'

But, in early February 1972, the National Guard formally rejected the British plan. Fustuq later became a successful figure in the international bloodstock world. But in the race for the National Guard contract, his horse had come last.

MTS now cancelled their agreement with Fustuq.[72] The DSO told Morris[73] that MTS

dislike their present agreement with Fustuq...They visualise circumstances in which, if they subsequently got substantial business in Saudi Arabia through other channels they might make some small exgratia payment to Fustuq.

On 19 March 1973, the Americans and Saudis signed a Memorandum of Understanding for the modernisation of the National Guard.[74] Run by the Pentagon, the Office of the Program Manager, Saudi Arabian National Guard, still exists, with much of the work undertaken by the Vinnell Corporation, an American company owned by Northrop Grumman.

With a mega-deal at stake, the British Government had gone well beyond using agents to try and win a deal. Diplomats and DSO officials were heavily involved in devising the bribery scheme. Britain's relations with Feisal, a key figure in the Middle East, had been put at risk for the sake of a big arms deal.

However, in the 1970s, Britain developed a more lucrative 'special relationship', this time with the Shah of Iran.

4

The 'Special Relationship': Britain and the Shah of Iran (1970–78)

As with Saudi Arabia, Britain's arms deals with Iran were a significant part of a diplomatic relationship of great value to Britain. Iran's long-standing importance was a result of its location (on one side of the Persian Gulf opposite the Strait of Hormuz, which many of the world's oil tankers passed through, and bordering the Soviet Union) and resources. The Anglo-Persian Oil Company, founded in 1909, later became BP (British Petroleum).

After the Second World War the Anglo-Iranian Oil Company 'was Britain's largest single overseas investment and...with taxes to the home exchequer greatly exceeding royalties to the Iranian government'.[1] Unsurprisingly, many Iranians wanted to challenge British domination of the country's most important natural resource and so Iranian Prime Minister Muhammad Mossadegh nationalised the oil industry. In 1953, American President Dwight D. Eisenhower and British Prime Minister Winston Churchill authorised a joint operation by the American Central Intelligence Agency (CIA) and British Secret Intelligence Service (SIS) to organise a coup to remove him from power. The Shah promised the SIS's main agent he would dismiss Mossadegh by decree when the coup was underway.[2] The first coup attempt on 15 August 1953 failed and the Shah fled.[3] Less than a week later, after the second coup attempt succeeded, he was back, knowing he owed his throne to the British and Americans.

The Shah became one of Britain's key allies. Iran was a member of the Central Treaty Organisation, a military alliance against the Soviet Union. In 1970 Harold Wilson's Labour Government wanted close relations with Iran to ensure Britain's withdrawal of her armed forces from 'East of Suez' did not disturb Persian Gulf security. Britain was pleased the Shah was ready to assume responsibility for the Persian Gulf, be a bulwark against Soviet influence, and proposed co-operating

with the Shah on the security of the Indian Ocean.[4] The Shah agreed
to give up the Iranian claim to Bahrain.[5]

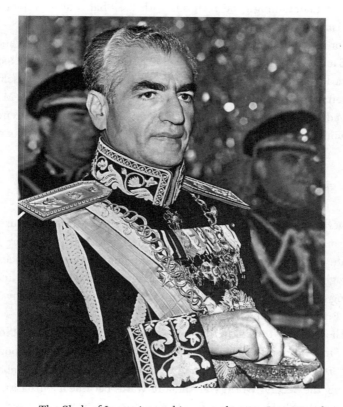

7.   The Shah of Iran, pictured in 1971, the year Iran signed
the first of several huge arms deals with Britain. British Head
of Defence Sales Lester Suffield authorised the payment of
commissions to the Shah's confidant Shapoor Reporter,
believing they were going to the 'Shah's fund'.

Picture by: AP/Press Association Images.

The Shah also exerted a powerful influence on world oil prices. In
1971 the Shah's leadership enabled the Organization of the Petroleum
Exporting Countries to increase the oil producers' revenues, and in
1973 he demanded more. An internal Foreign and Commonwealth
Office history[6] explained the Shah was 'attacking the vital British

interest of a secure and stably priced oil supply'. However, diplomats had concluded, 'Britain needed Iran more than Iran needed Britain', and so maintaining good relations with the Shah was an important British priority.

For most of the 1970s, Iran was Britain's main arms customer, ahead of Saudi Arabia, making up 24 per cent of all British arms exports from 1972 to 1978.[7] Britain's first mega-deal with Iran was the sale of Chieftain tanks in January 1971.[8] Millbank Technical Services (MTS) played a key role in the Iranian deals, as it had done in British attempts to win contracts in Lebanon and with Saudi Arabia's National Guard.

The Start of the Special Relationship

General Hassan Toufanian was the Chief of Military Industrial Organisation and Procurement in the Iranian Ministry of War. The Shah, described by diplomats[9] as 'moody and intensely suspicious', thought[10] 'Toufanian is not playing straight over [the tank] deal and is being got at by Germans'. The German Leopard tank was the rival to the British Chieftain.

The Embassy in Tehran told Head of Defence Sales Lester Suffield[11] the Shah was sending a 'personal envoy' to London, Shapoor Reporter. Reporter was born in Tehran in 1921,[12] worked for the British Embassy during the Second World War and afterwards became a journalist. He tutored the Shah's second wife – Queen Soraya – in English[13] and was close to the Shah, but combined journalism and tutoring with a career as an SIS agent.[14] In 1955 Reporter won British citizenship.[15]

Reporter, said the Embassy,[16] 'has to report direct to Shah who will then decide whether to go on with deal or not'. The Shah's choice was strange as 'Reporter is not an expert on tanks'. Secrecy was vital, said the diplomats, because 'Toufanian is not being told' about Reporter's mission.

Suffield replied[17] 'grateful for any advice before Friday on attitude we should take with [Reporter] and on closeness of relationship with Shah. Does this indicate need for payoff somewhere'. Ambassador Sir Denis Wright said[18] Reporter's relationship with the Shah is that of close and trusted confidant. The Shah has used him in the past to convey messages of particular delicacy and to negotiate various deals on behalf of the Iranian Government. He is well connected in the City, e.g. Lord Stokes [whose recommendation had led to the founding of the Defence Sales Organisation (DSO)].

The telegram continued:

> Reporter asked us with whom he should discuss his fee which on a deal of this size he would expect to be substantial. We told him to discuss this with you...I have known Reporter for past 17 years...his own opinions and advice can be coloured by self-interest, particularly pecuniary.

Reporter met MTS and DSO officials in London. Diplomats in London told the Embassy in Tehran[19] that Reporter would put the DSO's offer to the Shah immediately. Afterwards, the DSO expected Toufanian to complete the contract. The telegram said 'the cost of employing MTS has been absorbed in the [Ministry of Defence] equipment price as well as Reporter's fee in the event of a successful conclusion of the negotiations'. Further, 'for your own information, Reporter's fee has been described by him as a sum to be set aside for the "Shah's fund" and will amount to 1% of the value of the contract'.

Reporter took back to Tehran a letter from the Managing Director of MTS, R.G. Roe.[20] It described the

> provision by you of certain consultancy and advisory services in connection with a contract which it is hoped will be concluded between the Government of Iran and this Company for the supply of a quantity of Chieftain Tanks and associated equipment and ammunition. In the event of this contract being signed on the basis of the terms which we discussed with you and assuming that the value of the equipment supplied is of the order proposed i.e. approximately £56M, we would arrange to re-imburse you for your consultancy/advisory work in facilitating the conclusion of the contract.
>
> The terms which would apply as far as your fee is concerned would be that a figure representing 1% of the total basic [Free on Board] cost of the contract...would be arrived at and that the sum of money concerned would be paid to you in five equal instalments.

Reporter also carried a letter[21] from Defence Secretary Lord Carrington to the Shah. The letter conveyed Carrington's 'appreciation of your Majesty's action in authorising Mr. Shahpoor Reporter, O.B.E., to discuss with officials in my Ministry the proposed purchase...I trust that the proposals now being made will be entirely acceptable to your Imperial Majesty's Government'. I have seen no evidence that Lord Carrington was told of MTS's financial agreement with Reporter.

The Shah saw Reporter twice in the next week. After the second meeting, the Embassy told the DSO[22] the Shah accepted the proposals, and would 'give Toufanian fresh instructions without revealing part played by Reporter'.

Three days before Christmas Reporter told the Embassy the Shah would buy hundreds of Chieftains.[23] In January 1971 the Iranians signed a £52.3 million contract (worth about £600 million today) with MTS for 360 Chieftains. In June they bought another 437 Chieftains for £62.2 million (worth about £650 million today).[24]

In the mid 1960s, Britain could not win big arms deals in Iran. But, once Reporter was the agent for MTS, the DSO could sell through the back door. Now Britain was deluged with business from the Shah, who bought almost all his British arms from MTS. In December 1974, the Shah ordered 1,500 more tanks from MTS, most of which were more advanced versions of the Chieftain.[25]

Thanks to the Shah, MTS now expanded very rapidly. A report[26] by the chartered accountants Coopers & Lybrand in 1975 found MTS's turnover increased from £7 million (worth about £73 million today) in 1971 to approximately £60 million (worth about £453 million today) in 1974. At the end of 1974 MTS had 49 contracts; 37 were with Iran. Iranian arms deals made up 84 per cent of the value of all MTS contracts,[27] resulting in the company's 'dependence on the Iranian defence authorities'.

Reporter was knighted in the 1973 New Year Honours 'for Services to British interests in Iran'.[28] In 1974, the year the third massive tank deal was signed, he asked 'on instructions from [His Imperial Majesty]' for a rise to 1.5 per cent commission,[29] which he got. This did not stop him asking for more. In January 1975, Reporter wrote to Suffield[30] asking for a 'mark-up' of 2 per cent on a proposed Military Industrial Complex at Isfahan. He said 'my friend told [me] for the Saudis [the mark-up] is 25%!!'.

The Shah's Anti-Corruption Campaign

Meanwhile, the Shah had launched an anti-corruption campaign.[31] In the summer of 1974, he told American Ambassador Richard Helms that[32]

> he had been about to promote his trusted Genarmerie chief Farouknia to four-star General last month but threw him in jail instead when he learned he had been taking bribes from smugglers...now the crooked ones had better watch out because he was going to go after them.

In 1976, Iranian Prime Minister Amir Abbas Hoveyda formed a five-man High Council for the Eradication of Corruption.[33] British diplomats also noted:[34]

> there has been a recent purge within the Imperial Iranian Navy over bribery and corruption which has included the Commander-in-Chief, his Deputy, a number of admirals, and lower staff. We believe the prime area of corruption currently detected within [the Imperial Iranian Navy] concerns civil construction...there have been no suggestions that British firms were involved.

All contractors to the Iranian Ministry of War were required to sign an affidavit[35] swearing 'that the products and services contained in this agreement...do not include any commissions, rebates or fees payable to representatives, agents, advisers, consultants or third parties as remuneration for services of such representatives, agents, advisers, consultants or third parties'. Conveniently, MTS was exempt because it was a Government agency.[36]

In the mid 1970s British Ministers were told[37] that

> arms sales to Iran and the provision of technological assistance and support are usually negotiated on a Government-to-Government basis with the contracts being dealt with by Millbank Technical Services Ltd...this arrangement was reached at the express wish of the Shah in order to reduce the risk of bribery and corruption at all levels in the Services.

But actually the Shah wanted to limit all the pay-offs to himself and his inner circle.

Britain and Iranian Corruption Scandals

The first sign of trouble came when a scandal erupted over a British company which was trying to secure a contract to construct and equip hospitals in Iran. The editor of the diaries of Asadollah Alam, the Shah's Minister of Court, summarised what happened:[38]

> their principal agent was a well-known British peer whose political career had been blighted by involvement in a sex scandal. He was misled into believing that his local Iranian partner had passed on bribes to Alam. Alam was outraged when these allegations surfaced, professing ignorance of the entire affair. He duly received a letter of profound apology from Sir Anthony Parsons, acting as 'British Ambassador [and] guardian of the honour of England'.

The 'local Iranian partner' was Reporter. Parsons asked him what his fee was for. Reporter said[39] 'he operated a private fund on the Shah's behalf with Kleinwort Benson [a City of London bank] into which he paid his percentages on contracts. The income of the fund was used for purposes for which there was no budgetary provision eg the endowment of the chair of Persian Studies at St Antony's'. Parsons and Suffield wondered whether Reporter was bluffing companies into hiring him by invoking the Shah's name, and then pocketing the money himself. But, they thought,[40] Reporter would never have dared try such a 'stupendous con trick' in case the Shah found out.

MTS now decided to review its relationship with Reporter, asking a leading barrister, John Matthew QC, for an opinion. They were told[41] the relationship 'was perfectly legitimate'. Unfortunately Mr Matthew's opinion is not contained in any files I have seen, but officials did refer to it in other documents.

Matthew set out[42]

> three main criteria which commission payments needed to satisfy if any suggestion of corruption were to be avoided:
> (i)   the rate of commission must be reasonable, judged by contemporary standards;
> (ii) no payment should be made to a servant, employee or agent of the other party to a contract except insofar as both parties are aware of the position;

(iii) the payments should not be concealed in the principal's [here referring to the exporter's] books and he should be most circumspect if any suspicion (or, worse, knowledge) existed that the payments were being used for bribery.

However, where an agent is using commission 'for payments to employees of the other party to the contract', Matthew advised[43] that 'as a general rule the principal [exporter] is under no duty to "look behind" the payment to his agent, nor to enquire into the use which is made of it, by him'.

In the case of Iran, the ultimate recipient of the payments, the Shah, was the highest authority in the country. Hence the payments to him were not made 'corruptly' in the sense of the Prevention of Corruption Act 1906. Further, Reporter was acting for both sides. A Ministry of Defence official wrote 'the fact MTS used and still use Sir Sharpoor Reporter as an agent is as well known to the Iranians as to us'.[44] And, clearly, a 1 per cent or 1.5 per cent commission was a low amount by contemporary standards.

Meanwhile, another scandal was brewing with potential to cause serious damage to Britain's relations with the Shah. When the DSO negotiated the Chieftain deals in the early 1970s, officials asked the Iranians to choose between an American and British radio set for their tanks. Lieutenant Colonel David Randel was a DSO communications adviser. Two employees of the British company Racal gave him money believing he could influence the Iranian choice of radio set in Racal's favour. The Iranians chose Racal's radios.[45]

When officials learned of Racal's relationship with Randel, an investigation began. The Shah was informed in 1974.[46] Randel was arrested in April 1976[47] and accused, under Section 1 of the Prevention of Corruption Act 1906,[48] of 'soliciting and receiving corrupt payments from Racal in return for influencing contracts for defence equipment in Iran and Oman'. Two Racal employees were also charged. All three were tried at the Old Bailey at the end of 1977. They were found guilty in January 1978 of some of the charges relating to Iran, and jailed.

The British Government were obviously embarrassed a DSO official had been caught taking bribes. But, the real problem was Randel's involvement in the negotiations for the Chieftain deals at the time MTS's arrangement with Reporter had begun. In the run up to Randel's trial, his barrister had suggested[49] 'that if the case was proceeded with

Randel would claim in court that [Her Majesty's Government] were involved in the same kind of corrupt payments'. This would be a serious embarrassment for the Shah. By 1976, an internal Foreign and Commonwealth Office history[50] records, 'there was a general malaise in Iranian society'. The Shah 'had been unable to fulfil his promise of greatly increased wealth and improved social services for all Iranians, and Iran was very far from joining the ranks of the industrialised nations'. In October 1976 the Shah publicly admitted mistakes and in August 1977 he had, humiliatingly, been forced to sack his whole Government, including long-standing Prime Minister Hoveyda. By the time the Randel trial began, in November 1977, there were a series of student protests in Tehran.

British diplomats and officials were desperate to avoid the MTS/Reporter arrangement being mentioned at Randel's trial. For the the Shah's financial involvement in arms deals was not widely known. The American Secretary of State, Henry Kissinger, told the American Embassy in Tehran[51] that a check on the 'alleged involvement of [the] Shah in major defense contracts' had not turned up any 'derogatory information'.

For years, Ministry of Defence officials assured Ministers that the MTS/Reporter arrangement was 'not in any way improper'. But they did not feel it was legitimate enough to withstand scrutiny.[52] When diplomats discussed the Randel case with the Ministry of Defence a minute-taker wrote[53] 'MTS and [Ministry of Defence] *believe* (they have no proof) that Sir Shapoor pays this sum into the Pahlawi Foundation which is a well-known Iranian charity in which the Shah and Shahbanu [the Shah's third wife – Queen Farah] take a close interest'. They might have difficulty maintaining[54] 'this is a perfectly legitimate arrangement' when they did not know 'what Sir Sharpoor does with his commission' and could say only that they had 'no reason to suppose that he uses it for directly corrupt purposes'. As for the Pahlavi foundation, Parsons recalled[55] 'it was impossible to discover exactly how it functioned and impossible to judge its ethical standard'.

Suffield gave evidence at the trial. He confirmed[56] Reporter had been paid £1 million (worth about £4.7 million today) for the Chieftain contract. One week later in Parliament, the Minister of State for Defence said:[57] 'Sir Shapoor Reporter, who is a British subject, has been retained for some years by Millbank Technical Services Limited as its sole adviser regarding official defence sales to Iran…in that capacity he has received payments in return for those services'.

The Shah and his advisers were not pleased. Parsons recalled:[58]

our relations at the end of 1977 were in a peculiarly delicate state thanks to a corruption trial in London involving a serving British officer in which damaging allegations about the Shah were emerging in public. I was seeing Hoveyda, then Minister of Court, and the Shah frequently about the unfolding of this trial and was having a difficult time of it.

Toufanian demanded the British refund all the money MTS had paid to Reporter.[59] The truth about the payments was now important. If the money had not found its way to the Shah, then the DSO had been conned by Reporter (a hugely embarrassing admission to make) and could hardly refuse to refund the money. If the Shah had received the money, by refusing a refund the British would effectively be accusing him of hypocrisy, in front of his top officials. This would obviously enrage the Shah. Suffield's evidence related to one of the arms deals with Iran but overall Reporter had actually received a total of £7 million[60] from MTS (worth about £33 million today).

Again, Parsons had a[61]

heart-to-heart with Reporter in which he took the line that the fund had been started as a kind of emergency fund after the Shah's enforced flight to Rome in 1953 [when the first CIA coup attempt failed]. The income was used for state purposes and the fund was fed from a number of sources including the payments to Shahpour on the British defence contracts.

When Parsons met the Shah a few days later, the Shah thundered[62] 'he could not tolerate the insinuation that he had been receiving money paid by us to Reporter and that Reporter was a friend of his'. This further panicked British officials. A small group of Ministry of Defence officials, diplomats and SIS officers tried to establish the truth.

Foreign and Commonwealth Office Permanent Secretary Sir Michael Palliser sent Ministry of Defence Permanent Secretary Frank Cooper the conclusions Parsons had drawn, which were:[63]

the evidence strongly suggests that Reporter has over a long period been one of the many people who has handled the Shah's overseas investments: Reporter's specific responsibility being the account or accounts held by Kleinwort Benson. However, there is no independent evidence that the commissions which Reporter has been taking on defence sales have been going to the Shah.

One former DSO official recalled:[64]

I was told by [Suffield] that at some stage in the negotiations it had been made clear to him (by Reporter allegedly speaking on behalf of the Shah) that it would be necessary to include in the price a figure of 1% for the Pahlevi Foundation 'a charitable fund at the disposal of the Shah and used for various good works'...it was [Suffield]'s belief that he was carrying out the Shah's wishes.

The official believed that the Shah had asked for the increase in Reporter's commission because 'since [Suffield] was regularly seeing the Shah, Reporter would have been taking an awful chance if what he was putting in writing was not true'.

Bribery is payment in return for influencing a decision. It is astonishing that, believing the money was going to the Shah (who was the decision-maker), at his request, officials thought this arrangement was proper.

In the end, Palliser told Foreign Secretary David Owen,[65] 'it may well be impossible to establish the exact truth about the destination of the payments made to Reporter' which he still regarded as 'legitimate' because they were not 'clandestine'. The obvious thing for the Shah to do, with his regime coming under pressure, was to dump his old associate publicly.

Ending the Special Relationship

Further, at the time the Iranians had lost confidence in the Chieftain tank, and the engines used in it. There was a danger the Iranians would cancel the purchase of advanced versions of the Chieftain, then worth around £870 million (worth about £3.7 billion today).[66] The British had little choice but to play along with the Shah to preserve good relations with him.

The new Head of Defence Sales, Ron Ellis, agreed with Toufanian[67] to dump Reporter 'in a gentlemanly way', pay no further commissions on uncompleted contracts, keep the payments already made to Reporter secret, and negotiate a Memorandum of Understanding for arms deals between Britain and Iran.

Dealing with Reporter would be very tricky. Ministry of Defence officials regarded the Shah's denials about his relationship with Reporter as a 'bare-faced lie',[68] One quipped[69] the Shah was 're-writing history with a vengeance...I hope Reporter has returned the key to the Palace back door!'

The first problem was Reporter's letters promising him commission for each MTS contract. The DSO did not have copies of the letters (which were kept by MTS), but thought they were unlikely 'to include any duration clause or any arrangements for termination'[70] (the letter from MTS to Reporter[71] setting out his fee for the first Chieftain deal contained none). Reporter could sue for breach of contract, creating further extreme embarrassment. By the time Ellis was sent to talk to Reporter in early March 1978 the situation in Iran had deteriorated further. In January a number of protesters were killed in an anti-Shah riot in Qom.[72] In mid February there was another riot, in Tabriz, and Chieftains were used to suppress it.[73] Further public revelations about the 'Shah's fund' could lead to an explosive situation within Iran and a complete meltdown in Britain's relations with the Shah.

Ellis explained to Reporter[74]

> that since, as he has always claimed, the money was destined for the Shah if we don't stop payment on the instruction given the Shah would know automatically and this could damage our future relationships. He wriggled like mad but he could not refute the logic of the argument.

Reporter asked for compensation. Ellis felt Reporter would not sue for breach of contract but suggested a pay-off of £50,000 to £100,000 (worth about £230,000 to £470,000 today) 'if only to completely ease our mind'.

Fortunately for the DSO, the Inland Revenue started to investigate Reporter's income tax returns,[75] enabling Ellis to pressure him. Reporter agreed[76] to cancel his arrangement with MTS from 1 January

1978 'subject to him being able to settle to his satisfaction any UK tax liabilities'.

The second problem was Reporter's long career with the SIS. As Palliser explained to Owen:[77]

> Reporter's relationship with Britain goes back some 35 years. He was employed during the [Second World] war by the British Embassy in Tehran in a relatively junior capacity, but at some time after the war was taken on as an agent by our friends [a Whitehall euphemism for the SIS] because of the relationship of confidence he enjoyed with the Shah. The relationship stemmed from the fact that his father [Ardeshirji Reporter] had helped the Shah's father [Reza Pahlavi] to power. He played a role in the operation [in which the SIS's assets in Iran were placed under CIA control] to restore the Shah to his throne after the latter's flight to Rome during the Mossadeq regime in 1953.

Palliser continued:

> As regards Reporter's relationship with our friends, the latter are content to wind it up. It has not in fact been active for some years [Alam's diaries show the Shah's inner circle knew by 1969 that Reporter worked for the SIS[78]]. However, they are anxious to arrange an amicable separation, to minimise the risk that Reporter (who apparently feels that he has been victimised by the Iranians and abandoned by the British) should seek to 'clear his name' by telling his story to the press. I have just learned that this was done at a meeting with Reporter in Paris last week. He was told both that the relationship must be regarded as at an end, and that the Shah would be so informed. He took it well.

However, Reporter still worked for other British arms companies. Throughout the 1970s, the DSO[79]

> became aware from time to time that Reporter was seeking commissions from firms on defence deals ie asking for a percentage in addition to the one coming from MTS. Our advice to firms who consulted us was not to make any payments since the Shah had forbidden all agents fees [for companies but not government agencies] but we do not know to what extent the advice was heeded. Racal obviously knew better and, as the [Randel] trial has disclosed, paid him about 3%.

The British Aircraft Corporation (BAC) used Reporter to help them win a contract in Iran in 1976 for over 60 self-propelled Rapier missile units. In 1977 BAC was nationalised and became British Aerospace (BAe – now known as BAE Systems). After the Randel trial was over the DSO enquired about BAe's relationship with Reporter.[80] BAe 'had no intention of breaking their link with Reporter' because in their view, he was 'still in the Shah's confidence'. Because the new Memorandum of Understanding would ban commissions, they were coming to a 'new arrangement' with Reporter which they divulged to the DSO, but is not recorded in the available documents.

The Downfall of the Shah and Its Consequences

In January 1979 the Shah fled Iran. Needing to develop good relations with the new revolutionary Islamic regime, Britain refused to allow its old ally, the Shah, who was dying of cancer, asylum in Britain.[81] He died in Cairo in July 1980.

The revelations of the Randel trial now hit Reporter. He ranted to Ellis:[82]

you have no doubt seen some, if not all, of the kindnesses showered upon me by the 'honourable' members of the great British Press!! The net result was the ransacking of my house in Teheran and its virtual take-over by the Islamic Committees!!! This was my reward for years of service to U.K. You may also be interested to know that the tax people are still fighting what I hope to be a losing battle. This, despite, your solemn assurances.

The British Government now kept a wary eye on Reporter. When he applied to the Bank of England for exchange control consent to set up a company in Jersey with his wife, diplomats asked the intelligence services to investigate because[83]

the activities of Sir Shapoor Reporter are of concern to us. He owns property in Britain and we can assume, because of his past activities, that the present revolutionary government in Iran will be watching him very closely. In particular, they will be looking for signs that he is either directly plotting or aiding supporters of the Shah planning counter revolution.

Reporter was now the least of their problems. Officials told Prime Minister Jim Callaghan and his Ministers that[84]

> the changes in Iran have dealt a major blow to Western interests, a reliable military ally of the West has disappeared together with the military and intelligence facilities which it made available. The main guarantee of stability in the Gulf, after our withdrawal, has been removed.

Officials warned Britain's exports to Iran would be halved, with the loss of 35,000 jobs within one year. They also reckoned '*export sales* in the defence sector would be severely curtailed'.

Britain had around 50 arms deals with Iran.[85] On 6 February 1979 the Iranians repudiated six of the contracts worth £1.9 billion (worth about £8 billion today) and which supported 20,000 jobs. A Senior Commercial Officer at MTS later recalled:[86]

> when the revolution occurred something akin to panic broke out within the [Ministry of Defence]/[Royal Ordnance Factories – who manufactured Iran's tanks]...export approvals across the board for military contracts were withdrawn. The [Ministry of Defence] was faced with the nightmarish prospect of wholesale redundancies and disorganisation within the [Royal Ordnance Factories]...There were of course also the knock on effects into the sub-contractors...As a result, there was imminent danger of the partial collapse of a significant sector of the UK defence industry, with the attendant political and industrial consequences.

Fortunately, the Iranians had by and large paid for what they had already received. The largest potential losses therefore lay with contracts guaranteed by the Export Credits Guarantee Department (ECGD). Ministers reckoned the Government might lose around £114 million (worth about £420 million today) from cancelled contracts guaranteed by ECGD.[87] Further, they expected heavy redundancies at the factory in Leeds where Iran's advanced Chieftains were made (10,000 were employed on this one deal).

The Leeds factory needed to produce at least 50 tanks per year for five years to remain open before it started work on the next British Army order.[88] So Ministers agreed to try and sell some of the advanced Chieftains to Jordan,[89] and in November 1979 King Hussein bought 274 tanks worth £266 million[90] (worth about £950 million today).

After the Islamic Revolution in Iran, Owen commissioned a confidential report,[91] looking at why British diplomats (among many others) had failed to see it coming. The report, finished in 1981, said:

> the Embassy and [Foreign and Commonwealth Office] also saw no need to report on the private financial activities of leading Iranians, in particular the Pahlavi family, regarding corruption as a way of life in Iran. They believed that whatever the practice of the Pahlavi family might be the Iranians would assume that they were enriching themselves and regard it as normal behaviour for the ruling class. No particular interest was shown in the Pahlavi foundation, publicly described as a charitable institution but which is now known to have received a chunk of Iran's oil revenues for the Shah's private disposal. It now appears that the ability of some members of the Pahlavi family and their associates, including the head of SAVAK [the feared internal security service], to ignore the law and line their own pockets helped significantly to fuel resentment against the regime…a greater appreciation at the time of the extent of corruption and the popular reaction to it would have been a helpful contribution to the Embassy's political analysis.

Both in Iran and Saudi Arabia, the British Government had facilitated corruption. Officials and diplomats knew who was getting pay-offs, when, and how much they were receiving. They arranged deals through a subsidiary of the Crown Agents, MTS, to either circumvent local regulations (in Iran) or to give the deal an unwarranted respectability (in Saudi Arabia).

Arms deals can be an important part of any diplomatic relationship. But when pay-offs are being made to top people, exposure may destabilise a regime, or exacerbate its problems. However, as the British and Americans would soon find, corruption abroad could be politically explosive for them at home too.

5

Parting Ways: British and American Corruption Scandals (1975–76)

Today some people still think that bribery is accepted in many parts of the world as a way of life. However, even in the 1970s, a study[1] by the American State Department found that 'virtually all foreign governments have statutes forbidding official corruption'.

Only a minority of British and American exporters paid bribes in the mid 1970s. In Britain, Prime Minister Jim Callaghan learned[2] that 'about 10 per cent of our trade elsewhere in the world probably involved some type of practices which we would normally consider improper'. At around the same time, in America, 117 of the top 500 companies admitted making questionable or illegal payments to foreign government officials, politicians and political parties.[3]

Until 1975, those British and American companies that bribed overseas did so with impunity. Neither Britain nor America had effective laws to stop them. In Britain, as we have seen, officials condoned and sometimes facilitated dubious practices.

Even if the authorities in the exporter's or importer's country discover grand corruption, there are powerful incentives to take no action. In the exporting country, these are, among others, political embarrassment, the loss of contract(s) and jobs, and damaging impact(s) on foreign relations. In the importing countries, even if bribery is officially banned, action would have to be taken against the most powerful, their relatives and associates, a task requiring enormous courage.

Some scandals are, however, too big to ignore. In America the Watergate scandal of the 1970s resulted in the exposure of questionable or illegal payments by over 450 American companies both at home and abroad.[4] American public attention focused on Lockheed in particular. Legislation – the Foreign Corrupt Practices Act of 1977 – followed. In Britain, however, an arms trade corruption scandal of the 1970s was hushed up, and Britain's ineffective bribery laws remained unchanged until over 30 years later.

The Lockheed Scandal

The investigation into the burglary in 1972 of the Watergate offices of the Democratic National Convention, President Richard Nixon's political rivals, revealed Tom Jones, the chairman and chief executive of Northrop (one of America's largest arms companies), had authorised[5] illegal contributions of $150,000 to Nixon's re-election campaign.

Northrop's directors commissioned auditors Ernst and Ernst to investigate[6] 'the extent of the misconduct'. Although one American Government agency, the Securities and Exchange Commission (SEC), had access to the Ernst and Ernst report, it did not publish the section on Northrop's overseas payments.

Separately, a Senate Sub-Committee, chaired by Senator Church, was investigating American companies' influence on the country's foreign policy.[7] Unlike a British Parliamentary Committee, in America Congressional Committees can subpoena documents, and so Church obtained the Ernst and Ernst report.[8]

The Church Committee held hearings on Northrop, starting on 9 June 1975. Church himself opened by declaring[9] that the Northrop documents 'lay out in excruciating detail a sordid tale of bribery'. Tom Jones testified the next day and suggested[10] that, in at least one case, Northrop had exactly the same arrangements as another major American arms company, Lockheed.

The Church Committee and SEC subpoenaed all Lockheed documents relating to overseas commission payments from 1970 onwards.[11] In August 1975 Lockheed admitted in a press release[12] that it had paid $202 million in 'commissions and other payments to consultants' since 1970. Lockheed's Senior Vice President of Finance testified[13] that '$22 million was the total amount of payments that we know or think may have flowed to Government officials', a figure later revised[14] to between $30 million and $38 million (worth between $102 million and $129 million today). A series of Church Committee hearings between September 1975 and March 1976 publicised Lockheed's arrangements.

In February 1976, Carl Kotchian, the President of Lockheed, told the Church Committee[15] a high Dutch official, said to be Prince Bernhard,[16] Queen Juliana's husband, a war hero and highly influential figure in Dutch military and commercial circles, had received bribes from Lockheed. Bernhard denied the allegation. The Dutch Prime Minister, Joop den Uyl, established a Commission of Inquiry, the 'Commissie van Drie', to investigate.[17]

In his foreword to the Commission's report,[18] den Uyl said the Commission discovered 'attempts by aircraft manufacturers to exert improper influence on the procurement policy', but found no evidence they succeeded. But, he wrote,[19]

the Commission has come to the conclusion that [Bernhard], in the conviction that his position was unassailable and his judgement was not to be influenced, originally entered much too lightly into transactions which were bound to create the impression that he was susceptible to favours. Later he showed himself open to dishonourable requests and offers. Finally, he allowed himself to be tempted to take initiatives which were completely unacceptable and which were bound to place himself and the Netherlands' procurement policy in the eyes of Lockheed – and, it must now be added, also in the eyes of others – in a dubious light.

Britain's Ambassador in The Hague explained to London[20] that a prosecution might force Queen Juliana to abdicate, and cause a constitutional crisis weakening the Dutch monarchy. But the Dutch Parliament voted not to prosecute Bernhard. Instead he promptly resigned all his military posts and functions, which 'defused the affair as a political time-bomb'.[21]

The Church Committee also uncovered Lockheed pay-offs at the highest levels in Italy, made to secure the sale of C-130 aircraft to the Italian Air Force. A Lockheed document explained[22] that a 5 per cent price rise, advised by Lockheed's Italian consultant, was to 'provide for the probable contributions to Italian political parties'. The consultant told Lockheed[23] they 'must be prepared to go as high *as* $120,000 *per airplane* for the cumshaw pot'. Kotchian told the Church Committee[24] 'kumshaw is something you give to get something done'.

Lockheed won a contract for 14 C-130 aircraft in 1971. The pay-offs on the deal totalled $2,018,000 (worth about $9 million today).[25] In January 1972 Lockheed delivered the aircraft to the Italian Air Force.

The Church Committee published documents relating to this deal in February 1976, shocking Italy. The British Embassy in Rome warned London[26] the affair was having a greater political impact than revelations that the Central Intelligence Agency (CIA) had financed some Italian political parties. A diplomat, noting the CIA and Lockheed scandals were one of the two main reasons for the deteriorating political situation, hoped[27] that Italians would 'turn back from the Communist brink' (they did – the Communists came second in the June 1976 election). On 1 March 1979, former Defence Minister Mario Tanassi, former Head of the Italian Air Force Diulio Fanali and Lockheed's consultant, well-connected lawyer Ovidio Lefebvre, were found guilty.[28] Fanali's friend, Camillo Crociani, the former President of Finmeccanica, a major Italian arms company, who had also acted as a Lockheed agent, had fled to Mexico and was found guilty in his absence.[29]

Lockheed's shady dealings extended to Asia too. In Japan Lockheed made pay-offs to sell L-1011 TriStar airliners to All Nippon Airways (ANA). Their official agents in Japan were the Marubeni Corporation. Kotchian later recalled,[30] 'Mr [Toshiharu] Okubo [the Managing Director of Marubeni] advised me to make a pledge to pay money to prime minister [Kakuei] Tanaka'.

On 29 October 1972, the Japanese Government announced ANA would buy TriStar.[31] Lockheed paid money, intended for Tanaka, via Marubeni[32] in two instalments – $850,000 (worth about $3.7 million today) in June 1973, and $900,000 (worth about $3.6 million today) in January 1974. Lockheed also made pay-offs to others connected with the deal.[33]

Tanaka resigned as Prime Minister in 1974, before the Lockheed scandal broke, after a magazine revealed his questionable business deals involving friends and relatives.[34] In February 1976, Kotchian testified to the Church Committee. Investigations started in Japan and in August 1976 Tanaka was charged (with receiving a bribe) as well as Okubo (with offering a bribe).[35] Tanaka's arrest in 1976 shook the ruling Liberal Democratic Party, and Prime Minister Takeo Miki was forced to resign in October.[36] Tanaka and Okubo were later convicted.[37]

Lockheed had made questionable payments in the Netherlands, Italy, Japan, and other countries. In 1974 Lockheed's auditors asked lawyers for an opinion on Lockheed's payments in four countries, including Saudi Arabia and Japan. The lawyers said[38] the payments 'do not contravene any law of the State of California [where Lockheed's head office was located] or the United States', although their opinions were based on certain assumptions which later turned out to be factually inaccurate.[39]

The American Government's Response to the Lockheed Scandal

In America, like Britain, there was no law specifically outlawing bribery overseas. But some bribes could be illegal under other existing American laws.[40] It was illegal for American companies whose exports were financed by the Export-Import Bank or the US Agency for International Development (AID) to pay special commissions, or for American companies to claim tax relief on overseas payments which would be bribes if made in America. American companies paying bribes to win overseas business at the expense of other American exporters might be breaking antitrust laws.

The American Government could investigate the problem of bribery following the Church Committee revelations because of the securities laws. These laws, introduced in the wake of the Wall Street Crash of 1929, were designed to protect investors in shares and bonds from corporate misrepresentation, deceit and fraud. The laws forced companies to disclose, publicly, 'material' information, defined as 'those matters as to which an average prudent investor ought reasonably to be informed'. The SEC, which policed the securities laws, decided[41] questionable or illegal payments made by companies overseas were 'material' and should be disclosed, if they were a significant amount, related to a significant amount of business, or reflected on a company's 'quality of management'.

The SEC launched a voluntary disclosure programme in 1975. American companies which independently investigated questionable payments made in the previous five years, banned further payments, and disclosed to the SEC what they had done (although without naming the recipients of payments), would be unlikely to face legal action.[42] Eventually, over 450 companies confessed to making questionable or illegal payments worth over $300 million.[43]

The SEC Chairman, Roderick Hills, told Congress:[44]

the most commonly reported transactions were payments to foreign officials made in an effort to procure the enactment or favorable application of advantageous tax, customs, or other laws; to assist companies in obtaining or retaining government contracts; to persuade low-level government officials to perform their regular functions; or to meet extortionate demands by foreign government officials...the next most prevalent transaction, reported by 50 percent of the recent registrants [to the voluntary disclosure programme], involves foreign commercial payments made in a manner suggesting impropriety. Excessive sales commissions, over-compensated foreign business agents or consultants, or inflated invoicing to facilitate kickbacks to buyers' purchasing agents were recurrent techniques used to obtain business. These payments were channelled directly to the management or procurement officer of prospective private-sector buyers, or took the form of excess commissions or consultant's fees to be passed on as payoffs to government officials with intent to influence government contract decisions...most instances of reported abuse involved either the falsification of corporate records or the maintenance of incomplete records.

The American Inland Revenue Service began an investigation in 1976 into[45] 'intricate corporate schemes, outside normal internal audit controls, designed to generate large amounts of cash for illegal or improper use, and to reduce taxable income unlawfully'. By the end of 1976 it found[46] 'indications of slush funds or illegal activity' in over 270 of the 800 or so large companies investigated.

The American Government took firm action against Lockheed.[47] The Emergency Loan Guarantee Board, an American government body which provided loan guarantees to major companies whose failure could seriously affect America's economy, continued to support Lockheed on condition no further pay-offs were made. The SEC obtained an injunction permitting it full access to Lockheed's records. In April 1976 Lockheed agreed to establish a Special Review Committee to investigate and report its past practices.[48]

The Special Review Committee's report was sent to all shareholders in June 1977.[49] It said facts available to it[50] 'clearly showed that in the area of sales to foreign governments questionable practices existed including bribery'. Further,[51]

it was an established practice for Lockheed to make payments of large commissions to foreign consultants, in the belief that a significant part of some of the commissions would be used to obtain a favorable decision for Lockheed's products by such means as political contributions, bribes, payments to a customer's employees and payments to persons of influence seeking to extort money from the Company.

At around the time Lockheed's Special Review Committee was established, President Gerald Ford set up a Task Force on Questionable Corporate Payments Abroad. He said,[52] 'it is clear that a substantial number of U.S. corporations have been involved in questionable payments to foreign officials, political organizations or business agents'. He was taking action 'in the interest of ethical conduct in the international marketplace and the continued vitality of our free enterprise system'. In June 1976, he announced[53] he would ask Congress to pass a law requiring corporate disclosure of payments made with the purpose of influencing foreign government officials, and banning the falsification of corporate financial records.

New American Laws Banning Overseas Bribery

When Jimmy Carter became President in 1977, he decided to go further, and support[54] the 'passage of anti-bribery legislation which proscribes, with criminal sanctions, foreign bribery'. By the end of the year, Congress passed the Foreign Corrupt Practices Act.

Congress wanted to outlaw payments intended to 'influence the acts or decisions of foreign officials, foreign political parties or candidates for foreign political office'. A report by the House of Representatives on the draft legislation[55] argued bribery overseas was unethical, contrary to the expectations and values of the American public, eroded public confidence in the free market system, led to sub-optimal economic outcomes (as inferior companies could win contracts by bribery), and caused reputational damage to all American companies.

Importantly, the report claimed bribery was unnecessary because the SEC said that 'in every industry where bribes have been revealed... companies of equal size are proclaiming that they see no need to engage in such practices'. Representatives hoped American companies could resist extortion if bribery was illegal.

Representatives also spelt out clearly the foreign policy problem:

The revelation of improper payments invariably tends to embarrass friendly governments, lower the esteem for the United States among the citizens of foreign nations, and lend credence to the suspicions sown by foreign opponents of the United States that American enterprises exert a corrupting influence on the political processes of their nations. For example, in 1976, the Lockheed scandal shook the Government of Japan to its political foundation and gave opponents of close ties between the United States and Japan an effective weapon with which to drive a wedge between the two nations. In another instance, Prince Bernhardt of the Netherlands was forced to resign from his official position as a result of an inquiry into allegations that he received $1 million in pay-offs from Lockheed. In Italy, alleged payments by Lockheed, Exxon, Mobil Oil, and other corporations to officials of the Italian Government eroded public support for that Government and jeopardized U.S. foreign policy, not only with respect to Italy and the Mediterranean area, but with respect to the entire NATO [North Atlantic Treaty Organisation] alliance as well.

The Foreign Corrupt Practices Act banned all American companies from offering or paying a bribe to a foreign official (or their agent), foreign political party or candidate. It banned payments to intermediaries where there was 'reason to know' some of the payment might be used as a bribe. The SEC had found most bribery involved slush funds and inaccurate records.[56] The new law required all companies supervised by the SEC to maintain accurate and complete accounts and an adequate system of internal accounting controls.

Congress had already taken action on commissions in arms deals. In June 1976 the Arms Export Control Act became law.[57] American companies were now required to report to the State Department all commissions paid in arms deals. Commissions had to be 'reasonable' and 'not made to a person who has solicited, promoted, or otherwise secured such sale, or has held himself out as being able to do so, through improper influence'.

Geoffrey Edwards and the Foregone Commission

At the same time the Church Committee started its hearings on Northrop in 1975, the shady dealings of one of Britain's major arms companies were also in danger of being publicly exposed. But the outcome was very different. At issue were the commission arrangements made by Edwards in his successful campaign to sell the Saudis an air defence system in the mid 1960s.

To recap briefly, on 7 December 1965, the Saudi Defence Minister, Prince Sultan, had signed a 'Letter of Intent'. He promised to buy 40 Lightning fighter jets and 25 Jet Provost training aircraft from the British Aircraft Corporation (BAC), nine radar stations from Associated Electrical Industries (AEI), and training, logistics and other support services from Airwork. Each of the three companies had promised Geoffrey Edwards commission. BAC and AEI (and probably Airwork) understood that some of the commission would be paid to senior Saudi Princes by Edwards, so that the Princes would personally benefit from buying British.

The three companies could not draw up a final plan before the Letter of Intent was signed, because they did not have all the necessary technical information.[58] Therefore AEI and Airwork's prices were subject to technical surveys, to be carried out afterwards in Saudi Arabia.[59] This gave the Saudis plenty of room to haggle over the details of the contract later.

The Saudis could very easily secure more favourable terms as the three companies were not united. Although the companies formed a Saudi Arabian Air Defence (SAAD) Consortium, this was a façade and they negotiated their contracts separately.

BAC signed a contract first, in May 1966. They told the British Government[60] they included 'agency fees' of £48,500 (worth about £670,000 today) in the price of each Mark 53 Lightning (£775,000 worth about £10.7 million today – a commission of 6.3 per cent). Thirty-four of the 40 Lightnings sold were Mark 53s.

Now Sultan could be ruthless with AEI and Airwork. If the two companies could not satisfy him, the whole deal would collapse. As British Government officials realised,[61] 'the firms themselves would probably be involved in substantial losses because of commitments into which they have already entered in expectation of their negotiations succeeding, and might be in grave financial difficulties'. By October 1966, BAC had already started producing the Saudis' Lightning aircraft and had incurred £2.5 million (worth about £34 million today) in costs.[62]

Sultan had good reason to be tough. When the Saudi Council of Ministers agreed to buy the air defence system from Britain for just over £103 million, they had allocated a budget 10 per cent more than that figure, because of the uncertain outcome of the surveys.

However, AEI carried out surveys at the planned radar sites and found the range of temperatures there would prevent their radars working. More powerful (and expensive) radars[63] would cost £25.7 million compared with the £18.65 million quoted in the Letter of Intent (a 38 per cent increase). Airwork had also carried out surveys, but now the Saudis had specified substantial additional work.[64]

When AEI and Airwork increased their prices accordingly, Sultan threatened to cancel the deal. When negotiations resumed, he demanded large price cuts, which he eventually got. AEI told Edwards that they would now lose money on the deal. So, to prevent the whole deal collapsing (which would mean no more commission at all), Edwards agreed to forego all his commission from AEI,[65] and, 'so informed the various friends who considered themselves entitled to a share of his commission in compensation for their services'.[66]

The final contract, with Airwork, was not signed until September 1967. The final agreed cost for the air defence scheme was £118 million[67] (worth about £1.6 billion today).

Edwards had agreed to give up his £1.65 million commission (worth about £23 million today) from AEI on one condition – that no one else would receive any commission from AEI. However, AEI secretly promised a Lebanese middleman, Antoine Kamouh, £200,000 (worth about £2.75 million today) and £100,000 (worth about £1.35 million today) was paid to him in spring 1967.[68] Kamouh boasted about his coup in Beirut, where, as we have seen, the Saudis were well-connected. Ambassador Willie Morris in Jedda informed London[69] 'the news that [Kamouh] got this payment has got about, and Edwards' creditors have therefore concluded that they have been double-crossed'.

So when Lord Caldecote of BAC wrote to Edwards in November 1967,[70] after the Airwork contract was signed, to acknowledge the 'hard work, inconvenience and downright discomfort' that had been involved in winning the deal, he received a bitter reply.[71] Edwards was 'more than a little angry and very deeply concerned about the A.E.I. commission which you probably know about and which has caused me a great deal of embarrassment within Saudi Arabia'.

Edwards met Caldecote in January 1968. The day after Edwards followed up with a letter,[72] telling Caldecote that Kamouh 'had said that he was the only man who could secure the [AEI] contract...I know that none of this money that the Lebanese has received has gone to Saudi sources'.

Edwards ranted he had worked for AEI 'for seven years at my own expense to secure them a contract for £22m, only to find that some pseudo agent has received the commission that rightly belongs to me'. Because of the Kamouh payment Edwards considered his agreement forfeiting his commission was now null and void.

Edwards ended with a threat:

> I have taken legal advice and I am assured that I have every right to claim my commission in full and I think that I am being more than generous when I offer to accept £100,000 [worth about £1.35 million today] in settlement. You can be sure that I shall issue a writ against AEI in the immediate future unless settlement is forthcoming.

An internal BAC memo[73] confirmed:

> the Saudi Royal Family have now learned that [the Kamouh] commission was paid and Prince Abdul Rachman has made it very plain to both Geoffrey Edwards and Jack Baldwin [of the General Electric Company (GEC). AEI had merged with GEC but was known as AEI] that unless he receives some commission through Geoffrey no further orders in Saudi Arabia will be forthcoming for either G.E.C. or in fact for other British companies. This is particularly worrying to B.A.C. since there is a strong possibility of a substantial order for an additional number of aircraft which might well go to France if the present mood of disillusionment with British companies persists.

Geoffrey Edwards and Prince Abdul Rahman Sue AEI

AEI refused to back down. So Edwards sued AEI in May 1969 for 7.5 per cent commission – £1.65 million[74] (in 1974 he also demanded 2 per cent interest above the base interest rate).[75] British diplomats heard[76] 'a very strong rumour that Edwards had originally put in his claim because he was under pressure from Prince Abdul Rahman to pay the latter the amount due under the agreement between Edwards and the Prince'.

Within three weeks Caldecote told Morris about the case. He said[77] it '"must" be prevented from reaching the courts, and that he had tried, so far unsuccessfully, to persuade [GEC Managing Director Arnold] Weinstock to settle for £250,000 [worth about £3 million today]'.

At BAC, Company Secretary Brian Cookson worried[78] that 'the Writ and its attendant publicity will inevitably affect the Corporation'. AEI were affected already. Caldecote's handwritten notes of January 1969[79] record that Jack Baldwin of AEI had been 'asked to settle Abdul Rachman problem. Until settled Sultaan difficult with AEI'. Saudi administrative delays disrupted AEI's building schedule, costing AEI an additional £4 million (worth about £45 million today).[80]

Edwards had promised Prince Abdul Rahman 3 per cent of the installed cost of AEI's equipment (£660,000 – worth about £9 million today). Abdul Rahman believed he had earned his commission and so in October 1970 he sued AEI for his percentage too.[81]

In London diplomats worried that, if the case was not settled out of court, Britain's relations with Saudi Arabia would be seriously affected. After the 1973 oil shock had led to accelerating inflation in the West, Saudi Arabia was an important source of oil for Britain, as well as being the dominant power in the Arabian peninsula. How Saudi Arabia used its oil revenues was of fundamental importance for the stability of the international financial system,[82] and for the fortunes of Britain's new Labour Government.

Because the documents in the case contained[83] 'material which, if discussed in open court, could damage Anglo-Saudi relations', Edwards and AEI agreed 'to a system of editing and coding which would enable the documents to be used in court without their sensitive contents being made public'. The editing and coding was supervised by diplomats.[84]

Despite this precaution, in early 1974 diplomats[85] thought that 'given the damage to British commercial interests that disclosure to the Saudis of AEI's commercial practices could do, the point might come when [Her Majesty's Government] would have to consider "buying off" Edwards'. But they decided later[86] that their 'concern does not amount to £1.65 million'.

The British Government feared[87] that if Abdul Rahman forced AEI to disclose documents during his case, the Saudis would have access to information on AEI's commercial practices....it would no doubt have a serious effect on British firms' chances of doing business in Saudi Arabia and could sour Anglo/Saudi relations over a wide field. In particular, AEI's and GEC's commercial hopes both in Saudi Arabia and perhaps in other Arab countries would be severely prejudiced. The £10 million [worth about £75 million today] still owing to AEI from the contract [AEI had been forced, along with BAC and Airwork, to give the Saudis generous credit terms during the original negotiations in 1965] which gave rise to the Edwards case would be at risk.

Abdul Rahman knew what Edwards had promised him. He also knew about AEI's payment to Kamouh. But what he, and other Saudi Princes, may not have known was about all the other agreements Edwards had made. The discovery of these agreements could inflame jealousy.

After years of legal wrangling the trial date for the Edwards case was set for June 1975.[88] AEI were 'far from keen' on settling.[89] However, Abdul Rahman had lost interest in his case and AEI successfully applied to the court to have it dismissed for want of prosecution.[90]

BAC were still petrified that the Edwards case would go to court and publicly reveal embarrassing secrets. One month before the hearing, BAC asked a number of influential establishment figures to pressure Weinstock to settle.[91]

Diplomats strongly supported AEI's suggestion the case be heard 'in camera' (that is, not in public) or in arbitration (a means of resolving disputes by an impartial tribunal that the parties appoint themselves) because[92]

> inasmuch as [Her Majesty's Government] are concerned to promote good Anglo-Saudi relations and to promote British business they have an interest in avoiding a public hearing which might create ill feeling in Saudi Arabia (when details of commissions/bribes [?] are made public) and which might injure the chances for further British contracts in the future.

Edwards and AEI agreed to arbitration under Section 4 of the Administration of Justice Act 1970, and Mr Justice Eveleigh was appointed. The hearings began on 4 June 1975.[93]

Northrop and Saudi Arabia

Across the Atlantic, the first Church Committee hearings on Northrop would start five days later. Both the British and American Governments hoped their companies' dubious deals in Saudi Arabia would not become public.

The American Government already knew huge commissions had been paid for years on its Government-to-Government arms deals with Saudi Arabia, known as 'Foreign Military Sales'.

Back in 1969, Northrop had failed to sell Saudi Arabia its F-5 aircraft and sought a 'local representative' to help. After a 'survey of middle east sales representatives', Northrop selected two Liechtenstein companies, Triad Financial Establishment and Triad International Marketing, whose principal owner was fixer Adnan Khashoggi. Triad later sued Northrop over unpaid commissions. One of the judgments in the legal proceedings tells this story.[94]

On 4 October 1970 Northrop and Triad signed a one-year contract.[95] Northrop appointed Triad as its sole agent in Saudi Arabia, on a commission basis.[96] In July 1971, the first of seven phases of the Peace Hawk programme – the sale of F-5s and a comprehensive support programme – was agreed with Saudi Arabia.[97]

Peace Hawk (managed by the Pentagon as part of the Foreign Military Sales programme) was big business for Northrop. The seven phases of the programme eventually cost $4.2 billion. Northrop submitted its prices to the Pentagon which then sent a 'Letter of Offer' to the Saudi Government. When accepted and returned this 'Letter of Offer and Acceptance' was the agreement between the Pentagon and Saudi Arabia, which the Pentagon contracted Northrop to fulfil.[98]

For the first three phases of Peace Hawk, the Letters of Offer and Acceptance signed by the Saudi Government included as line items the commissions paid to Triad by Northrop.[99] The Pentagon 'recognized and allowed' these commissions, paid to American and Swiss bank accounts. In the legal proceedings, Northrop said[100] that, prior to 1978, 'Triad promised to bribe and bribed Saudi officials for the purpose of influencing their decisions concerning the Peace Hawk Program and to obtain business for Northrop'.

The commissions were substantial. The commission for Phase III was in excess of $5.5 million (worth about $25 million today).[101] In Phase IV, agreed in January 1975, Northrop sold 60 more F-5s and promised

Triad $23 million in commission (worth about $84 million today).[102] Although Northrop included the line item commission payments in its proposal to the Pentagon, these were now omitted from the Letter of Offer and Acceptance signed by the Saudi Government. For Phase V, Northrop promised approximately $45 million in commission (worth about $163 million today) to Triad.[103]

Two months before the first Church Committee hearings began (into Gulf Oil Corp) in May 1975, the Pentagon decided to ask the Saudis to approve the commissions in the two most recent phases of the Peace Hawk programme.[104] The Americans told Sultan about Triad's Phase V commissions in March 1975,[105] and Triad's Phase IV commissions in May.[106]

Tom Barger, a Northrop Director, went to alert Sultan that Triad's commissions might soon become public knowledge.[107] The American Embassy in Jedda warned Washington 'if members of the Royal Family are implicated, we will be in for painful time'. Ambassador James Akins pointed out[108] that '$45 million on a $300 million contract would be a first rate scandal. All excuses we would give, e.g. the British, French and Japanese are much worse, would be lame.' He correctly forecast:

> it is highly unlikely that the British, French or Japanese Governments would do anything to embarrass [the Saudi Arabian Government] or to expose the malfeasance of their companies. We, the U.S., must recognize that we will take the brunt of whatever reaction there is.

The day before the Edwards case began, Barger caught up with Sultan in Cairo.[109] Sultan was given the section of the Ernst and Ernst audit report dealing with Triad. He was indignant and demanded the Church Committee suspend its hearings to avoid it 'blackening' the Saudi Government. Sultan spoke of 'abandoning all procurement through US Dept of Defense despite investment Northrop planes'.

Sultan probably felt vulnerable. King Feisal had been assassinated three months before (by one of the other Princes), and this had led to changes in the Saudi Government. Sultan's half-brother and great rival, Prince Abdullah, Commander of the National Guard, was made Second Deputy Prime Minister, and was now ahead of him in the royal pecking order. And, as the Defence Minister, scandals affecting his Ministry could implicate him.

The American Government lobbied the Church Committee to prevent the names of top Saudis being mentioned.[110] Northrop's legal counsel did the same but the Church Committee refused to keep the Ernst and Ernst report confidential.[111]

On the day the Edwards hearings began in London (4 June), the State Department said:[112] 'the effect on Northrop's future and on Saudi-U.S. relations of the divulging of payments by Northrop to Khashoggi will depend on who else is named as getting money'.

It continued:

If the names of Prince Sultan, Prince Turki [the Deputy Minister of Defence and Aviation] or any other member of the Royal Family were to be connected with the receipt of payments from Northrop, we estimate that the results for Northrop would be serious and the effect on Saudi-U.S. relations potentially so. The allegations in such a case would almost certainly receive wide publicity in the U.S. and elsewhere...

5. Prince Sultan will in any case be sensitive to charges of corruption in his Ministry since he must bear the ultimate responsibility...

8. It is indeed ironic that U.S. companies which have been relatively the cleanest and the U.S. Government which has been scrupulously careful of Saudi funds seems likely to emerge from these hearings with a besmirched reputation to the benefit of others who have never been troubled by ethics in their arms dealings.

The Trial of Edwards v AEI

It was an accurate prediction. Over in London, Edwards's barristers were pleading his case.[113] In the run-up to the hearing, Edwards had read documents disclosed by AEI and now claimed AEI would still have made a net profit of £2.09 million on the Saudi contract, mostly made possible by Edwards giving up his £1.65 million commission. During an informal chat with a British diplomat,[114] an AEI accountant confirmed this was true.

On 5 June Northrop admitted that it had made payments to Adnan Khashoggi to ensure two Saudi generals did not block the sale of F-5s.[115] One week later the Church Committee hearings on Northrop had concluded. Although corruption had been publicly discussed, the State Department noted,[116] with relief, that 'there have been no allegations to date of involvement in commissions by Sultan or Royal Family (other than Prince Khalid [bin Abdullah])'. The only other three Saudis mentioned were the two generals and Khashoggi.

The considerable publicity in America about Northrop may well have affected AEI's tactics in the Edwards hearing. AEI's lead barrister said[117] he would ask Edwards about 'the disposal of very substantial additional sums which had been made available, particularly by BAC and Airwork (the 'slush fund')'. Edwards refused[118] to provide documents about money 'disbursed by [him] on behalf of the companies'.

Patrick Bannerman, the diplomat attending the hearing, was shown the documents Edwards had on Friday 13 June. He wrote:[119]

> they disclosed details of payments made to a number of influential Saudis. I was also told by Mr Edwards that he was not prepared under any circumstances to name names in oral evidence. To do so would be to break faith with his Saudi friends and could even jeopardise their positions and his own safety. I agreed that the documents and any oral evidence relating to them were extremely sensitive politically.

On Saturday 14 June, Sultan's Ministry of Defence and Aviation released a statement. It said[120] 'if some companies have been paying commissions to agents in return for real or imaginary services, the Government of Saudi Arabia is unaware of such payoffs, did not approve of them and will not tolerate them'. The Saudi Government asked the Americans for all relevant documents about 'payoffs and commissions and any other sums allegedly paid to two officers in the armed forces'. The statement threatened that 'just punishment will be meted against anybody who is proved to have deviated and betrayed the Government's trust'.

On Monday 16 June, in London, the Edwards hearing was adjourned for four days to allow for additional coding of particularly sensitive documents about Edwards's pay-offs.[121] Immediately Edwards told AEI he wanted to settle.

Bannerman wrote[122] that Edwards

> was very worried about possible leaks...[he] became increasingly worried both for his own safety and for the continued safety of some of those who had received money. The Northrop revelations and the effect

of King Faisal's assassination [by one of his nephews] on the position of some people in Saudi Arabia added to his anxiety.

As for AEI, 'when they saw how worried Mr Edwards was by their intention to proble [sic] the "slush fund" it was inevitable that they would push this issue as far as possible in hope of forcing Mr Edwards to withdraw'.[123] Edwards offered to withdraw the case, and in return AEI contributed £50,000 (worth about £300,000 today) towards his legal costs. This settlement was agreed on Thursday 19 June.[124]

The diplomats were 'all much relieved that this potentially embarrassing affair has been settled without publicity',[125] as were officials in the Defence Sales Organisation (DSO).[126] Now it could be business as usual.

Over in America, on Friday 20 June, six days after Sultan's public statement, the American Government told Northrop that commissions would not be allowed on Phase IV of Peace Hawk.[127] On 9 July, the Pentagon sent a circular to every company with a Foreign Military Sales contract with Saudi Arabia, Kuwait, Iran and Israel.[128] The circular required all companies to certify their contract price did not include any direct or indirect 'agent's fees' not approved in writing by the buyer country. On 28 July Northrop terminated their contract with Triad.[129] When, in August, the Saudi Government signed a Letter of Offer and Acceptance for an extension of Phase III of Peace Hawk, the letter imposed a total ban on commission payments. No commission was included in the Letters of Offer and Acceptance signed by Saudi Arabia for Phases V to VII of the Peace Hawk programme.[130]

Lockheed's turn was next. In September 1975, Chairman Daniel Haughton told the Church Committee[131] that Lockheed had paid Khashoggi $106 million in commission (worth about $385 million today). A Lockheed memo of August 1973, published by Church,[132] said that the company 'really have no way of knowing if the so-called under-the-table compensation is ever distributed to Saudi officials, or whether it stops at your own consultant's bank account'.

A few days after Haughton's testimony, the Saudi Council of Ministers issued Decree No. 1275 banning all commissions on Saudi arms purchases.[133] However, to the American Government's relief, back in Washington[134] 'no mention was made of identities of foreign government officials who may have received bribes...Senator Church announced that names had been deleted in order to avoid unnecessary embarrassment and difficulties in the countries involved'.

However, at this point, the SEC were still trying to obtain Lockheed's documents and a court case loomed. The American Secretary of State, Henry Kissinger, wrote to the Attorney General, Edward Levi,[135] asking for the 'names of officials of friendly foreign governments alleged to have received covert payments from Lockheed' to be withheld, as disclosure would 'have grave consequences for significant foreign relations interests of the United States abroad'. However, Kotchian's testimony to the Church Committee about the Netherlands, Italy, and Japan in February 1976 resulted in the names of Lockheed's consultants entering the public domain.

Northrop's troubles were not over. An investigation by its outside Directors found that the company had paid $30 million to foreign sales agents. The report said[136] that 'substantial amounts...were paid to individuals or organizations having principals who were then foreign government officials or who were or had been closely associated with foreign officials'. In 1979 Triad sued Northrop for commission payments that had not been made after Northrop cancelled its agreement with Triad in the summer of 1975. As these were due to be paid prior to the entry into force of the Foreign Corrupt Practices Act, they were treated as legitimate commissions during the subsequent litigation between Northrop and Triad. A Tribunal ruled that Northrop owed Triad $31.5 million (worth about $65 million today).[137] Long drawn out legal proceedings followed, but the decision was upheld by the American Supreme Court in 1987.[138]

Meanwhile, Kamouh, the man whom AEI had paid commission to instead of Edwards, was long dead, murdered in Paris in 1973.[139] According to author Anthony Sampson, his disappearance was 'in connection with his commission on British arms sales to Libya'.[140]

Edwards now divided his time between Jersey and Barbados. According to broadcaster Alan Whicker,[141] 'at his home he entertained an intriguing cast of characters from [Second World War fighter pilot] Douglas Bader and the President of Barbados to various shadowy figures from the Middle East'. However, one day 'he retreated to his house in Barbados, stopped eating, and simply drank himself to death...he left a pretty young wife and two small children and, drunk or sober, was seriously missed'. Nowadays, Jersey remembers him by an annual 'Geoffrey Edwards Memorial Handicap' race, held at Jersey Race Club.

As for Sultan, British diplomats said:[142]

> he has done well out of the granting of defence contracts: in 1975 his name was mentioned in the Western press in connection with the Northrop and Lockheed scandals but this does not seem to have damaged his position here.

Four years earlier, Morris had been more blunt, saying[143] 'Sultan has of course a corrupt interest in all contracts'.

Sultan's brother, Abdul Rahman, was by 1983, Sultan's deputy at the Ministry of Defence and Aviation,[144] remaining in post for over 25 years and throughout the Serious Fraud Office's investigation of BAE's Al Yamamah deal with the Saudis.

In the 1960s and 1970s both British and American arms companies made pay-offs overseas. BAC, AEI, Vickers, Alvis, Millbank Technical Services, Lockheed, and Northrop intended to pay bribes to win contracts. Both the British and American Governments knew commissions were planned or being paid, and tried to keep the details out of the public domain as best they could.

However, the SEC's investigation, followed up by the Church Committee, led directly to a new law banning bribery by American companies overseas, and a ban on dubious commissions in American arms deals.

In Britain, however, Edwards's dealings were kept secret. Indeed, they would still be so, but following my victory over the Foreign and Commonwealth Office at an Information Tribunal, the British Government had to put these remarkable documents about his secret legal fight with AEI into the public domain.

There was no scandal in Britain and no new laws. Only a year later, as we will see later, the DSO was approving huge commissions on two new Government-to-Government arms deals with Saudi Arabia. Britain now had a competitive advantage over the Americans (the Pentagon could not do the same), and fully intended to use it. However, doing so meant keeping her own scandals as secret as possible.

6

At Arm's Length: How the British Government Avoided Taking Action against Corruption (1976–78)

The Lockheed scandal in America had serious consequences. The Dutch Queen's husband was disgraced, and a former Japanese Prime Minister and senior Italian politicians and military figures were convicted. The American Government was forced to fetter the conduct of its companies abroad, but escaped untarnished itself.

In Britain, politicians and officials feared a similar scandal and its consequences. But they faced an additional problem. Unlike in America, in mid 1970s Britain many major companies were publicly owned, wholly or partly. So any dubious dealings which became public could lead to accusations that Ministers approved or tolerated bribery overseas. Prime Minister Jim Callaghan and his colleagues and officials needed to keep corruption at arm's length.

British companies were not immune to accusations of corruption in the 1970s. But unlike in America, the scandals were contained and no effective action was taken to address the problem of corruption.

British Petroleum and Commission Payments

British Petroleum (BP) was put under the spotlight. The British Government had a significant stake in the company in the mid 1970s (sold off in the 1980s) but the management still enjoyed day-to-day commercial independence.

In April 1976 the Chairman, David Steel, alerted the British Government to an investigation by the *Sunday Times* and Granada Television. Steel said[1] the journalists had discovered that between 1969 and 1974 BP had paid around £200,000 per year (a total worth about

£10.5 million today) to the Italian Oil Industry Association knowing that 'in all likelihood, the funds were being used for some non-commercial purpose'. Other major oil companies had behaved similarly.

Two days before the story was published, the Cabinet Secretary advised Callaghan[2] any public inquiry could upset the Italian Government and damage BP's reputation. It might lead to questions about whether similar enquiries were being made 'into the practice of British firms in e.g. Middle East countries where some form of "inflated commission" is the accepted practice if orders are to be obtained'.

The *Sunday Times* accused BP of 'buying Italian favours'. It claimed[3] BP had made 'secret Italian political contributions…in which political payments were calculated as a per centage of the money the companies could expect to make as a result of favourable legislation by the Italian Government'.

On 15 April Ministers decided to ask BP whether the accusations were true. Top civil servants interviewed Steel, the Company Secretary and Managing Director. The officials reported[4] that

> the account given in the Sunday Times is correct in substance. Payments were made by BP and other oil companies to all the Italian political parties that were members of the coalition Government, ie excluding parties at either extreme. These payments were related, in general, to the value of Government financial concessions to the industry… BP say that they were responding to pressures, rather than acting on their own initiative. They did not make a profit on these transactions but merely reduced their losses. And such payments were common practice in many other sectors of industry in Italy…the payments were made from London to a named Swiss Bank account. They were all regarded by BP as expenses wholly and reasonably incurred in the course of business.

BP also admitted 'payments were made to officials in Greece and Turkey and possibly other countries to facilitate business'. In Saudi Arabia 'an unusually high commission – £8m [worth about £48 million today] in relation to contracts worth £40m [worth about £240 million today] – is being paid under contract to three intermediaries in the Lebanon and Saudi Arabia'. These payments had not been revealed by the *Sunday Times*.

A new Ministerial Group on Special Commissions and Similar Payments agreed that an inquiry should be avoided.[5] The Chief Secretary to the Treasury, Joel Barnett, duly told Parliament[6] that while the Government was ready 'to root out bribery and corruption', Ministers believed effective international action was needed. But the Government faced little pressure for action.[7]

BP's activities threatened further embarrassment just one month later. A subsidiary company – Scicon – wanted to sell a police communications and computer network to the Saudi Ministry of the Interior. Scicon believed that Crown Prince Fahd had promised the contract to the French.[8] Callaghan saw a 'secret report'[9] (in other words, from the British Secret Intelligence Service (SIS) or Government Communications Headquarters) that Kamal Adham (the head of Saudi intelligence) wanted to pressure Fahd to open the competition to British companies.[10]

Adham's interest was not only in Saudi Arabia getting the best possible deal. In May 1974 Scicon had appointed a company called Arabian Electronic Projects of Jedda (AEP) as their agent for the next ten years.[11] Scicon agreed to pay 20 per cent commission to AEP's Managing Director via a Swiss bank account.[12] Subsequently Scicon won several contracts.

BP, one of the few British companies regulated by the Securities and Exchange Commission (SEC) in America, decided to join the SEC's voluntary disclosure programme and now needed to find out more about AEP. It discovered AEP belonged to Adham.[13] As this new contract was valued at up to £500 million[14] (worth about £2.6 billion today), it is not hard to understand why Adham wanted British companies to compete. His company, AEP, might earn the equivalent of what today would be £520 million if Scicon were successful, a very reasonable return for Adham and the company's valuable time.

BP did not know whether the Managing Director, Abdul Rauf Khalil, was a public official. So BP asked diplomats in London who checked with the SIS and the Embassy in Jedda.[15] The Embassy in Jedda told London:[16]

Abdul Rauf Khalil is a civil servant and in receipt of a regular salary from Saudi official funds. He is the chief assistant of Kamal Adham, the Head of the Foreign Liaison Bureau [that is, Head of the Saudi Intelligence Service] who has the rank of Minister. On behalf of Kamal Adham (and presumably on his own behalf as well) he does engage in private business. Since Kamal Adham, whose other function is special adviser to the King, is specifically authorised by the King to engage in private business, we assume Abdul Rauf is also authorised to do so. Abdul Rauf, on behalf of Kamal Adham, is currently engaged in advising Scicon Ltd and other member [sic] of the new consortium who hope to tender for the vast Ministry of Interior police communications and records project…the advice and support of Abdul Rauf and Kamal Adham is a vital factor in the coming negotiations.

Khalil told BP[17] that

he did not regard himself as being a Government employee; he was the personal assistant of Kamul Adum [sic], and employed by him. Second, Kamul Adum owns 23 companies, of which AEP is one. King Khalid had of course given his approval to these activities. Third, Kalil [sic] asserted that Government officials in Saudi Arabia have the right to involve themselves in business matters.

The Ambassador in Jedda, John Wilton, suggested Saudi Decree 1275 banning commissions should not be taken seriously.[18] It was only months after the Lockheed scandal but, Wilton told London,

Lockheed are still selling TriStars here, nor do Northrop and Khashoggi appear to have suffered. So far as the position in Saudi Arabia is concerned I am confident that BP's payments to Adham and Khalid [sic] will [do] us no harm so long as the present Saudi regime survives, even if they should become public. (It will not help if we are blamed for leaking them but it does not seem to have done the Americans much harm).

Satisfied by this explanation, officials at the Department of Trade recommended Callaghan write to Fahd in support of Scicon's bid. They told Callaghan[19] that the recipient of the commissions 'might be a Saudi Arabian Government official'. Further, they warned, BP's forthcoming statement to the SEC might publicly reveal Scicon's payments.

Not surprisingly Callaghan was suspicious and refused to write to Fahd.[20] Trade Secretary Edmund Dell then explained Fahd was expecting a letter and that Scicon would pull out unless one was sent.[21]

Very reluctantly Callaghan changed his mind, and berated Dell, telling him[22] to 'ensure that a similar situation, whereby my freedom of choice is limited by prior notification to a foreign Government, does not occur again'.

Later, the British Government received an advance copy of BP's statement to the SEC about Saudi Arabia. The statement[23] referred to Scicon as 'a subsidiary of BP' and Saudi Arabia as 'country P'. It read:

> This subsidiary has entered into seven contracts for the provision of services in that country. In the case of each such contract the subsidiary has agreed to pay a substantial commission to an agent or agents. In some instances persons in government service have an interest in these agencies, but this interest is maintained with the knowledge and consent of the government of country P. Compared with agents' commission in other countries, the commissions being paid in country P are high. BP believes, however, that the experience of its subsidiary in paying such high commissions in country P is not unique. Each such commission arrangement in country P has been provided for by a formal contract approved by the board of directors of the BP subsidiary or its immediate parent, the payments made have been booked as commissions or consultancy fees, and BP's independent auditors have been fully aware of these payments.

Luckily for Callaghan the full truth did not emerge. Scicon do not appear to have won the contract he endorsed. BP's final report to the SEC in May 1977[24] was drafted in elliptical terms, and virtually no individuals or countries where commissions were paid were named.

The Defence Sales Organisaton's 'Dirty Tricks' in Kuwait

Inside the Defence Sales Organisation (DSO) up until the mid 1970s, officials carried on their old ways. In Kuwait, the DSO used what one diplomat called 'dirty tricks'.[25]

In the summer of 1972 the Kuwaiti Government's chief arms procurement officer in London notified the British[26] that agents were to be 'formally excluded from arms contracts'. Then Ambassador to Kuwait John Wilton advised the DSO[27] that 'the system would not change in practice, and that whatever the man may be called, an agent/

fixer is indispensable to a company seeking to sell arms here: he alone knows exactly who to "fix" and how'.

One year later the DSO started negotiating the sale of 165 Chieftain tanks to Kuwait, against American and French competition. At a press conference, the Kuwaiti Defence Minister, Shaikh Sa'ad (who was Prime Minister from 1978 to 2003 and briefly Emir in 2006) said:[28] 'we absolutely refuse to let arms companies have agents and we refuse to deal through any middle man or broker'.

The DSO and Millbank Technical Services (MTS) used two 'channels' to negotiate the deal[29]. Bill Jones, a DSO official, gave one of the Treasury Solicitor's officials this account of what happened with the first 'channel':[30]

> Frank Nurdin of Racal – BCC was apparently a close friend of a Kuwait Colonel named Fahad Al Haggar who was the Chief Signals Officer in the Kuwait Army. Nurdin told [Head of Defence Sales] Sir Lester Suffield that Colonel Fahad could help the United Kingdom Government to get the Chieftain contract in Kuwait...Fahad told Jones that the United Kingdom Government would not get the contract unless a commission of 5% was paid to Fahad. Jones saw Fahad in his car and later went with him to his home. He asked Fahad why it was he wanted 5% and Fahad said that there were four other members of the Kuwait Armour Committee and he and the other four members would need to be paid 1% each...Apparently the matter was considered in London and Suffield took the decision to pay commission to Fahad...Jones was with Nurdin when the latter told Colonel Fahad that the commission would be paid.

The note continued:

> Colonel Fahad was told by Buckley of MTS that the contract for the sale of the tanks would be made with MTS and that the Commission has to be arranged with MTS and not direct with the United Kingdom Government.

Nurdin, who had been awarded the Order of the British Empire for services to exports in 1969,[31] was later accused of bribing DSO official Randel in relation to the Chieftain contract with Iran. As Nurdin and Randel's trial approached, diplomats worried about the existence of embarrassing documents held by the British Government concerning

Chieftain sales in Kuwait,[32] and feared Nurdin would claim the British Government condoned corruption. A letter Nurdin wrote to Suffield in January 1974[33] was unearthed, revealing that Nurdin had told Suffield the Kuwaitis wanted BCC Clansman radios for their Chieftains. In the letter Nurdin wrote: 'the Committees' spokesman discussed the Chieftain situation only on receiving further assurances from Bill [Jones] and myself of UK's 5% commitment to the Committee'.

When Defence Secretary Fred Mulley informed Callaghan about the trial of Randel and Nurdin, he warned:[34] 'we were considering in 1974/75 an arrangement which, if it had come to fruition, would have been corrupt; but it did not and no payments were made. Nevertheless mention of this in court will certainly cause great embarrassment'. When Suffield gave evidence he was asked about the Nurdin letter but warned not to disclose any names or countries. Suffield cryptically described the episode as 'an arrangement to do something which was not in the end done'.[35] The *Guardian* reported the next day[36] that Suffield 'said there had been agreement once to pay commission to someone in authority but in the end it was not carried out'.

The second 'channel' enabled the Ministry of Defence and Kuwaitis to agree a Memorandum of Understanding for the sale of 165 Chieftain tanks in 1975.[37] The agent, paid 3.5 per cent commission,[38] was Abdullah Ali Reza.[39] He was described by Ministry of Defence Permanent Secretary Frank Cooper as[40] 'a thoroughly respected citizen of Kuwait and his assistance in securing the contract has been crucial'.

In the 1960s the British Aircraft Corporation (BAC) had used Ali Reza as their agent[41] to sell 14 Lightning aircraft to Kuwait.[42] Not everyone in Whitehall shared Cooper's view of Ali Reza. Mulley told Callaghan[43] that MTS

hold a record of a meeting held in March 1974 which appears to indicate that some of the proposed commission to Ali Reza was for corrupt purposes. This record is disputed by MTS and [Ministry of Defence] participants in the meeting.

Though DSO officials thought the arrangement legitimate, the new Head of Defence Sales, Ron Ellis, wanted the commissions kept secret from Parliament. If Kuwaiti officials found out there could be[44] 'very awkward consequences', particularly as Shaikh Sa'ad had previously said agents were not permitted.

The British Government's New Guidelines on Arms Sales Commissions

Once Cooper learned of the Nurdin arrangements, approved by Suffield, he decided to rein in the DSO. The Lockheed scandal had shown the potential repercussions of public exposure. Cooper wanted the DSO to distance itself from commissions, no doubt to minimise the potential impact of any scandal later.

The 1967 policy[45] was still in force. The DSO could use agents who were 'persons or firms of repute' to 'promote exports where it is clear that the market could not be exploited without their help' and be 'remunerated on a basis which reflects the services rendered and can be defended as fair and reasonable'.

Cooper issued a new directive[46] to Suffield in June 1976, saying that public money was not to be used for illegal or improper purposes. Officials should not engage in or encourage illegal or improper acts, and the DSO should avoid employing agents. Where the DSO, MTS or another firm in a Government-to-Government deal used agents, they had to be reputable, and any commission above the going rate or above 10 per cent had to be approved by the Permanent Secretary of the Ministry of Defence. However, there was a get-out. In the last resort, said Cooper, what was illegal or improper would depend 'on the law *and* [emphasis added] practice of the country or countries concerned'.

Thus the DSO could not, as they had in the past, encourage 'illegal acts' (commissions being banned in countries such as Saudi Arabia, Kuwait and so on). But Cooper's guidelines allowed plenty of wriggle room. They would not stop commissions being paid by MTS and other private companies. And employing a 'reputable' agent provided no robust safeguard against bribery.

The British Leyland Scandal

Corruption was of course not just prevalent in military contracts. Civil contracts negotiated by nationalised British companies presented the same dangers for Ministers. And it was not only Middle Eastern countries that were problematic.

One year after Cooper's directive, a new corruption scandal erupted. On 19 May 1977 the *Daily Mail* exposed[47] 'the amazing truth about Britain's State-owned car makers'. The newspaper claimed that 'in a

8. Sir Frank Cooper, Permanent Secretary, Ministry of Defence, 1976–82. In June 1976 he approved huge commissions the British Aircraft Corporation and Cable and Wireless proposed to pay on Government-to-Government arms deals with Saudi Arabia.

© UPPA/Photoshot.

desperate effort to win overseas orders', British Leyland was paying millions of pounds in bribes. 'Not since the Lockheed Affair', claimed the *Daily Mail*, 'has there been such damning evidence of large-scale corporate corruption'. In particular, the *Daily Mail* alleged that Industry Secretary Eric Varley had 'nodded through' British Leyland's questionable methods.

In fact just weeks before British diplomats in Lagos had apparently been helping three British shipping companies – Swan Hunter, Sunderland and British Shipbuilders – smooth the negotiation of a bribe for Brigadier Shehu Musa Yar'adua, the effective deputy to the military ruler of Nigeria, General Olusegun Obasanjo.[48] The companies now cancelled the bribe intended for Yar'adua to avoid embarrassment. Officials told Britain's High Commissioner, Sir Sam Falle,[49] that Varley could not overrule them, as 'it would clearly be disastrous if it appeared that Ministers had in effect instructed nationalised industries to bribe members of foreign governments to obtain export contracts'.

The Daily Mail story about British Leyland was similar to those about Lockheed and Northrop. Unlike in America, the story had the added spice of the allegation that the British Government had 'nodded through' questionable payments by British Leyland.

Varley told Parliament:[50] 'I have not nodded anything through. I reject and repudiate such practices. I could never in any conceivable circumstances give them my approval or even discuss them or consider them except to repudiate them.' He told Keith Joseph MP[51] that the Government were 'totally opposed to any form of bribery or corruption. The Government will not tolerate any cover-up of these matters'.

The Daily Mail's source, Graham Barton, confessed one day later that the letter saying Varley had 'nodded through' questionable payments was a forgery.[52] The newspaper was humiliated and Varley successfully sued it for libel.[53] Barton and his wife were arrested and charged.

Ministers agreed that an inquiry into British Leyland's affairs should be avoided, otherwise, one diplomat wrote,[54] 'our exports seem bound to suffer. So, too, will our relations with influential foreigners who have been involved'. The Cabinet Secretary told Callaghan,[55] no doubt with the Lockheed scandal in mind, that 'once an inquiry were established it is difficult to know where it would stop'.

The weekend after the story was published Callaghan and a small number of Cabinet Ministers met at Chequers,[56] the Prime Minister's official country retreat. Chancellor Denis Healey said 'there was no doubt that bribery had been going on for years on a large scale in the Middle East and Africa'. Worryingly for Ministers, 'organisations responsible to Government (including [the DSO] and nationalised industries) had been involved'. Trade Secretary Edmund Dell 'asked whether we were ready to put people out of work?' Ministers agreed 'a Government enquiry at this stage would risk singling out British Leyland unfairly'. Instead the Chairman of the National Enterprise Board (which owned the Government's shares in British Leyland), Lord Ryder, would conduct a private inquiry.

Ryder's confidential report[57] found no evidence British Leyland had paid bribes overseas directly (this is not surprising, for, as we have seen, companies hardly ever paid commissions direct to decision-makers). As for indirect bribery, British Leyland's Chief Executive Alex Park told Ryder 'we have established that the company does not knowingly facilitate any bribery or any corruption at home or abroad. What we cannot establish beyond question is that any representative or agent never breaks the law of the country in which he operates.'

Ryder asked Park whether British Leyland queried what the agents did with their commissions. Park replied:

> we have neither the duty nor the right, in the absence of any concrete evidence of specific grounds for suspicion, to cross-examine these parties as to their observation of their own countries' laws. Were we to attempt to do so, this would rightly be seen as an affront and would destroy relationships of mutual confidence built up over the years. The effect on our export business would be disastrous.

The Ryder report highlighted one particular payment. In 1975 British Leyland won a contract to supply Land Rovers to the Saudi Arabian National Guard.[58] The *Daily Mail* published details of this transaction,[59] claiming it was approved by the Exchange Control Department of the Bank of England. Further, the *Daily Mail* said it knew the identity of the two beneficiaries who were 'both holders of high Government office'. It refused to publish their names 'in view of the almost certain capital repercussions which would be taken against the men in their homeland'.

Ryder reported[60] British Leyland's agent was Mr N. Fustok. According to Park, he 'held no official position in relation to the Saudi Arabian National Guard' but was the 'brother-in-law of the Commander' – Prince (now King) Abdullah. Fustok, said Ryder, was paid 15 per cent commission on the contract value of the sale of Land Rovers and Range Rovers to the National Guard, and 14 per cent commission on the net invoice value of spare parts. Park claimed[61] that

> the commission payment had not been associated in any way with the award of the contract. Mr Fustok's services were concerned with making sure that nothing happened within Saudi Arabia to prevent the contract

from being executed on time and thus ensuring that the penalty clauses in the contract did not operate.

Ryder asked Park if he thought 'Mr Fustok himself rendered bribes or improper benefits to public officials. Mr Park said that he had nothing to add.'

The Ryder report did not mention Saudi Decree No. 1275,[62] which stated unequivocally

it shall not be permissible for any company bound with the Saudi Government by any arms contract or the supply of the equipment necessary thereto to pay any amount as a pay-off to any middlemen, sales agent, representative or broker and this ban shall apply regardless of the nationality of the company or of the middlemen, sales agent, representative or broker, and whether the contract was between the Saudi Government and the company directly or through another country.

Conveniently British Leyland money was paid to Fustok's Chase Manhattan bank account in Geneva, Switzerland.[63] Knowledge of British Leyland's defiance of the decree was thus unlikely to come to light in Saudi Arabia.

Officials recognised Ryder's report begged as many questions as it answered.[64] They realised full publication would be 'very damaging' but that failure to publish might lead to accusations of a cover-up. They recommended a summary be published.[65]

Over in America, Lockheed had published the report of its Special Review Committee on 10 June 1977,[66] which clearly stated the company had paid bribes (as we saw earlier). Just under one month later, in Britain, Callaghan's Cabinet colleagues felt that partial publication of the Ryder report would lead to pressure for further information about British Leyland,[67] so they decided 'the best course therefore would be to rest on the argument that the report could not be published because of the prejudice to the Barton proceedings'.

Meanwhile, Varley was anxious. He had refused to permit the 'dash' payments by the three shipping companies in Nigeria, and told Parliament he had nothing to do with questionable payments. Varley's problem was that[68] a high proportion of all merchant shipbuilding orders in prospect apparently involve some form of questionable payment and there is a real risk that unless we are prepared to indulge in such practices, we will get very few contracts. The consequences for employment in the shipbuilding industry will be serious.

Now Varley had made his statement to Parliament 'officials will be consulting him about further cases where questionable payments appear to be necessary to secure shipbuilding contracts'.[69] Varley felt he could not permit such payments and threatened to resign if Cabinet colleagues overruled him to win business. Callaghan was asked by officials to 'calm him down'.

Varley told Callaghan[70] four suspicious cases had been put to him and that further cases were inevitable because aircraft and shipbuilding were nationalised industries. He complained that 'British shipbuilders would push every case back to Ministers if they could, so that they could escape all responsibility'. Callaghan said 'there were limits to what we could do to clean up the rest of the world' and the Government should satisfy itself that commissions were paid to 'credible Institutions' but not investigate further.

Callaghan and his colleagues discussed the issue two weeks later. In the meeting[71]

it was argued that no Minister should condone a corrupt practice if it came to his attention. However decisions about particular transactions about which there was some doubt should be taken by the Chairman and Boards of the companies for nationalised industries concerned, who should be willing to take the responsibility. Detailed cases should not be brought to Ministers for decision.

Other Ministers said they had statutory powers of direction over most of the nationalised companies, and could not duck the problem in this way. Callaghan told Varley, Dell and the Solicitor General to give further thought to guidelines.

Three months later Ministers reconvened. Dell had suggested:[72]

it was the responsibility of each board to manage the businesses entrusted to it in accordance with the statutes governing it and with declared Government policies where applicable, and it was for them, as for Boards of Directors of companies, to ensure that the conduct of their business overseas was acceptable in the countries concerned. The Chairmen of nationalised industry Boards should not therefore refer individual cases to Ministers but if they sought further guidance on the Government's general attitude, he proposed that the substance of the guidelines applicable in the Ministry of Defence in relation to defence sales might be disclosed in confidence to the Chairmen of the public sector bodies.

They later agreed[73] a statement about the new guidelines for nationalised industries should be made to Parliament only if pressure mounted.

In July 1978 the Bartons went on trial at the Old Bailey charged with forgery. Diplomats worried this might revive interest in the unpublished and confidential Ryder report.[74] The *Daily Mail* had published detail of British Leyland's dealings in Saudi Arabia but not the names of those involved. In the DSO, officials fretted[75] that 'much play could be made of the relationship between...Prince Abdullah and Fustuq with consequent souring of relations'. The Embassy in Jedda told London[76] that if Fustok's name came out, he would not

be pleased that commercial confidence had been broken, especially in such a sensational manner: and there will be others who will be worried lest the habit spread. Most serious of all would be for Fustok's connection with Prince Abdullah to be publicly revealed.

The Bartons' lawyers asked to see the Ryder report. Varley, and the Attorney General, Sam Silkin QC, considered halting the prosecution 'in the national interest'.[77] But instead they decided to release the Ryder report 'in the expectation that the Defence Counsel would make sensible and discreet use of it'.

In August 1978 Graham Barton was convicted. His wife was found not guilty. British Leyland claimed[78] that 'no evidence has been found of any contravention of English law, nor of a "world-wide bribery web"'. The Ryder report, which had found that British Leyland paid many commissions with no knowledge of what was done with the money, remained secret.

Britain's corruption scandals of the 1970s remained secret or were contained when made public. There was no broad ranging inquiry into the practices of Britain's exporters, like the SEC had carried out in America. Indeed, the main risk Britain's politicians and officials faced was getting caught with dirty hands. The solution was for Ministers and top officials to be kept at arm's length from any dubious practices. This now became the practice with the DSO's deals with Saudi Arabia.

Commissions and British Government Arms Deals with Saudi Arabia

Just after Cooper's new directive to the DSO about commissions in June 1976, a decision had to be made by officials about two new huge Government-to-Government arms deals with Saudi Arabia.

In 1973 Britain and the Saudis had signed a Memorandum of Understanding whereby BAC would undertake aircraft maintenance, training and building work for the Saudis up until 1978. This deal, known as the Saudi Arabian Air Defence Assistance Project (SADAP), ensured the equipment sold by BAC, Associated Electrical Industries (AEI) and Airwork with the help of Geoffrey Edwards could still be used by the Saudis. The 1973 deal was worth £253 million (worth about £2.3 billion today).[79] Now BAC told the DSO[80] they would pay 15 per cent commission if the 1973 deal were extended.

The other potential contract was a new project for Abdullah's National Guard known as the Saudi Arabian National Guard Communications (SANGCOM) project. The prime contractor would be Cable & Wireless, operating under Ministry of Defence supervision. Cable & Wireless told the DSO[81] they would pay 10 per cent commission to the Engineering and Trading Operations Company Beirut and 3 per cent commission to SIMEC International.

Suffield's submission to Cooper[82] about these deals claimed that the commissions were not 'exceptionally large in terms of the percentages commonly charged in Saudi Arabia for the sort of service being offered'. Cooper said[83] his responsibility was to ensure that the commission was 'no more than the going rate' and that they were 'a matter for the firms concerned and not for [Her Majesty's Government]'. He approved them. In September 1977 the SADAP project was extended to 1982.[84] In March 1978 the SANGCOM Memorandum of Understanding was signed.[85]

A draft of Suffield's submission to Cooper[86] was more blunt. It said that the service provided in return for the commissions 'although described as "technical consultancy", amounts in practice to the exertion of influence to sway decisions in favour of the client'. The following paragraph in the draft was also omitted from the final version:

> we would not wish to follow the recently introduced American practice in government-to-government agreements of informing the foreign government in the preamble to the letter of offer of the amount, and beneficiary if known, of any fees included in the price. The Americans appear to be powerful enough to get away with this 'take-it-or-leave it' approach but I do not believe we could afford to adopt this attitude. The French are certainly unlikely to adopt it...It would be unhelpful to consult the Saudi government on the subject in any way, since they would certainly not officially approve the payment of fees, although they undoubtedly expect appropriately discreet arrangements to be made. Statements to this effect are made by senior Saudis to visiting senior businessmen in somewhat elliptical language whenever a suitable opportunity occurs, for example by [His Royal Highness] Crown Prince Fahd ibn Abdul Aziz during a recent audience granted to Mr. [Allen] Greenwood, Chairman of BAC, in the presence of D.Sales 1 [a DSO official] and our Defence Attache [as we saw earlier, BAC had considered paying-off Prince Fahd in December 1963].

Cooper could authorise these commissions within his guidelines because:

1. He was not told the money might be used for illegal or improper purposes. In particular the submission omitted to mention Saudi Decree No. 1275. It also failed to mention the view of DSO officials that the payments were intended to 'sway decisions'.
2. The agents were being employed by BAC.
3. The submission gave no information to suggest the agents were not reputable.
4. The submission claimed the commissions were not excessive for the area.
5. Even if the commissions were for 'improper' purposes, Cooper could claim that, in the last resort, they were nonetheless the 'practice' of Saudi Arabia.

The submission did not say who was behind SIMEC International or the Engineering and Trading Operations Company Beirut. In fact, the manager of the latter was Mahmoud Mohamed Fustok.[87]

The company was founded on 4 March 1972,[88] just one month after MTS, having lost the large contract with the National Guard described in Chapter 3, had cancelled its commission arrangement with Fustuq.[89]

In January 1977, the Comptroller and Auditor General, Sir Douglas Henley, asked Cooper about the SADAP project.[90] In 1973 the Ministry of Defence agreed BAC could claim as a contract cost the 7.5 per cent (later increased to 8 per cent) of the contract price paid out in 'consultants' fees'.[91] The Ministry of Defence increased BAC's permitted profit to accommodate the rest of the commissions. BAC paid over £30 million (worth about £159 million today) in commission on the 1973 deal.[92] But the Ministry of Defence did not know who the recipients of BAC's commissions were, nor whether the Saudi Arabian Government had been officially informed of them. BAC had requested the commission payments be kept confidential.[93] So the Ministry of Defence excluded commissions from BAC's cost certificates, and hence kept them from the Ministry's own auditors.[94]

Cooper told Henley[95] he had

> sought from BAC assurances at the highest level that the agents to whom the payments are made are reputable companies or individuals; that they (BAC) regard their services as providing an adequate return for the payments which are made to them and, finally, that to the best of BAC's knowledge the appropriate authorities in the customer Government accept the position of the agents in relation to the contract. I have received assurances in writing accordingly.

Henley said[96] that BAC's auditors, Touche Ross & Co., had no means of identifying the recipients of the payments, and that, following the British Leyland allegations,[97] 'Parliament would now expect [the payments] to receive very special scrutiny and to be informed of the situation'.

Cooper asserted[98] officials had agreed to BAC's confidentiality request as 'a normal commercial precaution' and that 'we ourselves have not thought it necessary to know the identity of the recipients'. He said:[99] 'it is accepted Government practice to avoid over extensive enquiries. We must have regard for the risk of unnecessary interference in industry's business and for placing firms at a disadvantage with their competitors.'

Following Henley's questioning, Cooper amended his directive on commissions.[100] Where a firm sought Ministry of Defence approval for fees or commissions to be included in the price, written assurances were now required that the agent was reputable, and providing an 'adequate return'. In addition, 'to the best of the firm's knowledge' the customer Government should know about the agent.

Meanwhile, Mahmoud Fustok, who had graduated years before from the University of Oklahoma with a degree in petroleum engineering,[101] was now an extremely wealthy man and entered the international bloodstock world. Like Abdullah,[102] Fustok was passionate about horses. In 1978 he bought a substantial farm in Kentucky.[103] He also maintained stables outside Paris.

Through a mutual friend, he became close with Irish Taoiseach Charles Haughey, and Haughey spent holidays as Fustok's guest outside Paris.[104] In 1985 Fustok paid Haughey £50,000 via a mutual friend.[105]

The Irish Moriarty Tribunal, set up to investigate payments made to Haughey and Dáil member Michael Lowry while they held public office, stated[106] that 'Mr. Fustok's motive for making the payment was connected with Public Offices held by Mr. Haughey and both had the potential to and did influence the discharge of those offices in connection with the grant of Irish citizenship to relatives of Mr. Fustok'. Fustok, described by the Tribunal as 'related by marriage to the Royal Family of Saudi Arabia',[107] was killed in an accident in February 2006.[108]

Abdullah continued to benefit from his relationship with Britain. In 1981 he built a new palace for himself in Riyadh, with the construction work supervised by the British Royal Engineers.[109]

Ministers had devised rules designed to avoid them getting mixed up in bribery while allowing it to continue. Given they did not face the corruption scandals like those in America what would they decide to do about the wider problem of bribery in international trade?

7

Thwarted: How International Action against Corruption was Stopped in its Tracks (1975–80)

The revelations emerging from the Church Committee investigation attracted attention in America and around the world. In November 1975, the Senate called for an international code of conduct and set of rules to eliminate corruption.[1] In December, the UN General Assembly passed Resolution 3514 which called for exporting countries to prosecute those paying bribes overseas, and for co-operation between exporter and importer countries to prevent bribery, including the exchange of information. It asked the UN's Economic and Social Council (ECOSOC) to make recommendations on preventing corruption.

As we saw in Chapter 5, the American Government had taken a number of actions against corruption. There was action in other countries too. For example, in February 1976, high profile inquiries began in Japan and the Netherlands into Lockheed's activities.

British Ministers Discuss Corruption Overseas

So when, in April 1976, the *Sunday Times* accused British Petroleum (BP) of 'buying Italian favours', British Ministers realised they might come under pressure to take action too. Prime Minister Jim Callaghan set up a Ministerial Group on Special Commissions and Similar Payments.

Britain faced serious economic difficulties in the 1970s. Trade Secretary Edmund Dell told Cabinet colleagues,[2] 'we have to halt and reverse the long-term decline in our share of world markets...many of the growth markets are among those where these problems [corruption] arise most acutely'. And Britain was particularly dependent on exports compared with its main competitors. Department of Trade officials noted:[3] 'in 1976 and 77 UK exports represented 21–23% of GDP; this compares with 6–7% for USA, 12% for Japan, 16–17% for France and 23% for West Germany'.

As well as discussing the BP affair, Ministers considered a paper[4] on 'International Business Practice'. The paper drew a distinction between commissions 'ordinarily paid to overseas agents for their normal [in other words, legitimate] services' and 'special commissions', which were 'not supported by documentary evidence and are usually paid to an account in a third country, eg a numbered account in Switzerland'. The officials wrote: 'we have a strong impression, as distinct from hard evidence, that the payment of "special commissions" is common in business dealings in large areas of the world'.

The officials said their knowledge of corruption was 'incomplete and partial' because, one diplomat wrote later,[5] 'Ambassadors do not make a practice of reporting corruption unless they feel that British firms are being wronged by it or are behaving in a particularly scandalous way.' The parts of the British Government which knew most were the Treasury, Inland Revenue, and the Export Credits Guarantee Department.

Officials said[6] companies often reported 'special commissions' to the Inland Revenue, because payments made for trading purposes were tax-deductible. Companies also told the Bank of England (and the Treasury) about them because Exchange Control regulations required them to (in the 1970s, these aimed to protect Britain's balance of payments by restricting outflows of sterling). The Bank of England asked the Treasury to agree any commission over 10 per cent of the contract price. Officials tried to ensure only that British residents did not receive commissions, and that commissions were paid in step with payments received from the customer. The Export Credits Guarantee Department provided financial guarantees to exporters. If overseas buyers defaulted on their payments, British taxpayers would pick up the bill. In the 1970s around one third of all British exports were guaranteed in this way. Commissions paid by exporters had to be disclosed by companies on contracts worth more than £1 million (worth about £5.3 million today).

Officials reported commissions over 10 per cent were common, speculating this was because of the 'new rich oil markets in the Middle East and elsewhere where bribery has for centuries been endemic but which until recently has not emerged as such a striking factor in the international export scene'.

Ministers shied away from a public inquiry into BP (as they would do later during the British Leyland furore), but considered a more wide-ranging inquiry into corporate corruption, as the Securities and Exchange Commission was undertaking in America. Officials warned[7] that 'any enquiry which revealed the recipients [of bribes] could have major political repercussions' because 'in some "recipient" countries Heads of State, Ministers and Chiefs of Staff are directly implicated.' Further, 'any enquiry involving public disclosure of information about the affairs of companies and individuals which had been given in confidence would very seriously damage the effective working relationship between departments and the commercial world.'

A spirited discussion ensued.[8] One group of Ministers argued that 'acceptance of corruption as a fact of life in some other countries would only encourage its growth, and might also lead to British companies being discredited if a new regime with higher moral standards should take office'. They suggested a small committee, similar to President Gerald Ford's Task Force, should draft a code of practice for British companies and consider whether Exchange Control could do more than turn a 'blind eye'.

However, most Ministers wanted to avoid a general inquiry, because it 'would open the way to an examination of BP and other companies'. They acknowledged other countries had set up inquiries (by then America, Japan and the Netherlands had done so). But, they correctly observed, there was not the same political pressure in Britain for action (because there had been no similar public scandal).

Ministers considered the wider question of action against bribery in the light of President Ford's Task Force and the American proposal for an international agreement. Officials and Ministers felt Britain should take part in international discussions,[9] but that effective action could only 'be taken by Governments exercising their own jurisdiction in their countries'. They believed 'unilateral action...in the absence of an effective international agreement requiring parallel action by our main competitors would inflict very serious damage on our trading position in important areas of the world'.

One month later, the Chief Secretary to the Treasury, Joel Barnett, told Parliament[10] that it is not within Her Majesty's Government's power unilaterally to prevent corruption in other countries. What is needed is effective international action, and it is by our efforts to promote concerted action that we can best satisfy the wish of my hon. Friends – a wish which, as I have said, the Government fully share – to act against bribery and corruption wherever it is found. The Government will accordingly be pressing in appropriate international organisations for measures to be taken wherever possible to deal with this evil.

Big business was concerned about bribery too. At a meeting of the British Overseas Trade Board,[11] a group of business leaders and representatives from the Confederation of British Industry, the Trades Union Congress, and the Civil Service, members reported

demands for extra-contractual payments of up to 20% were rife and there was a clear danger of such practice spreading…within the UK and other developed countries. Among these countries there was still a bond of trust and morality, but this could be ruined by the very volume of improper practice in the rest of the world.

More enlightened business leaders such as Sir Frederick Catherwood, the Board's Chairman, cautioned those present against believing the lazy cliché that corruption was an accepted way of life in the developing world. He said:

there may always be corruption, but it will never be acceptable to the peoples of the third world. No one likes foreign companies to bribe their leaders and public officials, to divert into conspicuous consumption the funds which were meant to relieve poverty and build prosperity.

Catherwood had already taken the Swiss to task himself. At a meeting with Swiss bankers in Zurich he said[12]

he was seriously disturbed that [CENSORED] were now asking for bribes of up to fifty million dollars (sic) payable in Swiss francs before awarding contracts. The situation was also bad in several other developing countries and it could have seriously destabilising effects politically…One worrying factor was the role played by Swiss bank accounts in facilitating such payments: bribes were nearly always demanded in Swiss francs and recipients were protected by the strict Swiss legislation on non-disclosure of information.

The bankers replied that changing Swiss laws was futile as the bribes would simply be paid in Bermuda, the Cayman Islands or West Germany instead. Concerned though he was, Catherwood nonetheless told Dell[13] the British Overseas Trade Board saw unilateral action as 'ineffective and damaging to our exports'.

Guidance for British Business About Bribery Overseas

What should businessmen do? Barnett told Parliament[14] that 'all British companies should conduct their overseas business within the laws of their host countries' but that 'the high standards of business practice that we expect from British companies do not apply everywhere'. After the British Leyland allegations in May 1977, Callaghan asked Dell to review Government policy. Lord Ryder's confidential report on British Leyland had suggested this review should consider guidance for British companies overseas. That summer the British Government commended to Parliament an Organisation for Economic Co-operation and Development (OECD) recommendation made in June that businesses should not pay bribes, directly or indirectly, to public officials.

The Ryder report did not say how far a company should investigate its agents to ensure they did not use some of their commission to pay bribes. The Attorney General, Sam Silkin QC, had suggested[15] telling businesses that 'if you feel you have grounds for suspicion, you should investigate'. Officials disagreed[16] 'because in certain countries of the world [companies] will have grounds for suspicion'. They also worried that Silkin's suggestion would create pressure for the Inland Revenue, Bank of England, Treasury and Export Credits Guarantee Department to investigate the many commission payments they were aware of. The idea was dropped.

Dell argued to his Ministerial colleagues[17] that because of the range of practices prevailing overseas, guidelines for companies about discovering the ultimate beneficiaries of commissions would not be feasible. The existence of guidelines might encourage companies to ask the Government for advice in individual cases. Callaghan's Central

Policy Review Staff argued:[18] 'to try and impose on United Kingdom businessmen alone a greater conformity to western habits and practices could make them odd man out and our trade and employment would suffer accordingly'. Ministers agreed.[19]

British companies would have to rely instead on the advice of Britain's Embassies and High Commissions. Their advice varied depending on the local scene. In Cairo, the Embassy maintained 'a proper distance' but said[20] that

> British businessmen of long standing maintain that it is virtually impossible to get a contract…without making payments, and it is probably true that this is more the rule than the exception. According to our sources, bribes tend to be in cash, usually in hard currency abroad or sometimes through payments to Swiss banks etc…with big public sector contracts officials and Ministers…often also involved…the agents' commissions cover the payment of the appropriate monies and of course there can be very little check as to what money has gone where.

The Ambassador in Cairo, Willie Morris, who, during his time in Jedda, had not attempted to conceal from London his disgust at the corrupt behaviour of the Saudi Royal Family, reported that Sir Kenneth Keith, the Chairman of Rolls-Royce, had given Egyptian President Anwar Sadat two cars as part of an attempt to win contracts. Back in London one diplomat complained[21] that Keith was a 'menace' whose 'crude attempts at bribery cause embarrassment'.

From Jedda, Ambassador John Wilton advised London[22] that

> much is settled [in Saudi Arabia] by agreement between the senior princes. To secure a contract, a company must secure the support not merely of a senior prince, often through an established agent through whom very substantial commissions have to be paid, but also of many Ministers and officials down the line who, if seldom able to do much to help, are yet very able to hinder.

Rolls-Royce's three-year contract with Pennway Investment Corporation (principal shareholder, Head of Saudi Intelligence Kamal Adham), their 'regional consultant for the Islamic Middle East and agent in Saudi Arabia', was due to expire in early 1979.[23] Keith asked Foreign and Commonwealth Office Permanent Secretary Sir Michael

Palliser[24] 'how the embassy views Sheikh Kamal's current status in the Saudi power game and…whether we should renew or look elsewhere'. The Embassy in Jedda forecast[25] that Adham's retirement would lead to him losing influence. They advised Rolls-Royce to retain his services on a shorter contract and consider alternatives.

In the Far East, different rules applied. From Jakarta, Ambassador John Ford provided London with an 'anatomy of corruption' in Indonesia.[26] Indonesia's oil wealth had increased in the late 1960s and 'major contracts worth millions of dollars brought the commission agent into his own and it was possible for bribery to reach new levels of enormity'. He said agents would 'mark up prices by up to 50% to cover the costs of bribes necessary for sales to be made to, for example, the Indonesian Army'.

Corruption went right to the top of Indonesia's military regime. A lack of adequate oversight, said Ambassador Ford, meant it 'paid [for] people like Foreign Minister [Adam] Malik to establish shell companies to act as influence-broking "middle man" to set up contracts on a commission basis'. President Suharto, meanwhile, 'turned a blind eye on his wife's most energetic (almost obsessive) involvement in dubious money-making', and hence took no action against others. Mrs Tien Suharto was known 'locally as Mrs Tien Per Cent'. The Swiss Ambassador in Jakarta told Ambassador Ford about 'the numbers of leading Indonesians who find it necessary to visit Switzerland', but wryly observed that 'Indonesians are noticeably disinterested in winter sports and mountain scenery!'

Ambassador Ford recommended that smaller companies unfamiliar with the ways of the Orient should avoid Indonesia, as they would be 'in no position to resist the extortioner'. However,

> the experience of firms such as Shell, Unilever and ICI, who seem to have aschewed participation in any serious bribery or corruption indicates that a determination to be clean is ultimately recognised and pays off while those willing to bribe often find themselves subject to increasingly extortionate demands.

In Kuala Lumpur, High Commissioner Sir Eric Norris felt[27] that

> Malaysia has a long way to go along the corruption road before it catches up with Indonesia or Thailand. (One hard-headed British businessman has told me that he is surprised, not at being asked for bribes (which he

pays) but at the modest size of the sums demanded, by comparison with neighbouring countries.)

The Prime Minister, Datuk Hussein Onn, was 'probably incorruptible', and 'his wife is Persil white compared to Madame Soeharto [sic]'. Norris said corruption was worst in land deals, arms and aircraft sales, project tenders, customs and the police. Companies might lose contracts and delay projects by refusing to pay bribes, but 'British firms stand to lose more in the long term than they gain in the short by dishing out "slush money" or using any of the more shady ways of persuasion'. However, because Onn's example was not always followed, for low-level officials 'some modest lubricant will probably be the most effective means of persuasion. In short, my advice to British firms would be "Stay pure, but not fanatically so."'

The Americans Propose an International Agreement Against Corruption

The passage of UN General Assembly Resolution 3514 gave British Ministers and officials an opportunity to make the 'efforts to promote concerted action' promised to Parliament by Barnett. In March 1976, the Americans proposed an intergovernmental Working Group to draft an international agreement against corruption.[28] In June President Gerald Ford publicly said[29] improper behaviour by companies 'cannot be tolerated'. America had a duty to show leadership to advance the principles of 'free, honest and competitive economic behaviour'. He said: 'we must accelerate progress towards an international agreement'.

Following Barnett's statement in Parliament, British diplomats agreed to support the Americans.[30] ECOSOC passed a resolution[31] setting up a Working Group tasked with drafting, by mid 1977, an agreement to 'prevent and eliminate illicit payments' in international commercial transactions.

President Ford's Task Force were already working on a new law to require American companies to disclose commissions.[32] On 4 August 1976, his Foreign Payments Disclosure Act was sent to Congress.[33]

At the ECOSOC Working Group's first meeting, in November 1976,[34] the Americans were the only country to put forward a proposal (Britain had observer status, not full membership). They suggested countries should vigorously enforce their own laws against bribery, and exchange information. They also suggested that exporting countries force companies to disclose agents' commissions. This was intended to deter officials in importing countries from demanding bribes and make it easier for companies to refuse to pay them.

British officials were unimpressed, and found numerous practical difficulties with the American proposals.[35] But they had no constructive alternative to suggest. They agreed they could support an agreement condemning bribery, countries implementing their own bribery laws, and exchanging information in criminal proceedings. But they were reluctant to go further than these proposals, which would not alter the status quo, and tried[36] to convince the Americans to drop the idea of compulsory disclosure of commissions.

Other Western European countries and Japan were sceptical too. The developing countries were preoccupied with preventing 'the payment of royalties and taxes to illegal regimes in Southern Africa' rather than corruption.[37]

So when Callaghan flew to Washington in March 1977 to meet the recently elected President Jimmy Carter, officials told him[38] the Working Group had 'made virtually no progress'.

In America President Ford had clashed with Congress about the right approach to take. He had wanted companies to disclose agents' commissions, but not to criminalise corrupt payments made abroad.[39] Senator William Proxmire led those arguing for criminalisation. He proposed[40] an alternative law, saying: 'we cannot condone bribery abroad and expect the public to believe that the same kind of illegal payoffs do not occur at home. Corporate corruption knows no boundaries'. He argued that an international agreement, because it would take so long to introduce and be difficult to implement fairly, was 'really a prescription for doing nothing'. He denied American companies would be damaged by unilateral action. In 1976 senators did not hold hearings on President Ford's Foreign Payments Disclosure Act, but voted 86–0 in favour of the Proxmire bill instead.[41]

International Disagreement about How to Deal with Corruption Overseas

The new Carter administration proposed a new law criminalising overseas bribery[42] and at the next Working Group later that month argued other countries should do the same. British officials, along with their European partners, disliked this new idea.[43] They wanted a more 'modest' approach to the problem aiming at 'the creation of a strong world climate against bribery'. The approach might contain 'general principles and guidelines', involving 'codifying existing arrangements on the exchange of information' or developing 'model laws' or codes of practice. In other words, they did not want to change the status quo.

The American proposal struck at the heart of the problem. Should action be taken against the bribe payer, bribe recipient, or both? Although one could argue they have equal moral responsibility as both know the purpose of the payment (the payer, even if he does not know exactly what is done with his money, expects the award of a contract in exchange), many would say that the main responsibility lies with the party who makes the first approach. Sometimes it can come from the company or agent seeking a contract (for example, Geoffrey Edwards's attempts to cultivate contacts among the Saudi Royal Family). Sometimes it comes from a buyer who uses extortion in an attempt to obtain a bribe (for example, during Hawker Siddeley's attempt to sell two Hunter aircraft to the Lebanese Ministry of Defence in 1973).

In the discussions of the paper 'International Business Practice' Ministers had argued[44] that 'the main responsibility for stopping corrupt practices lay with the governments of the countries in which they occurred'. Thus British officials wanted[45] to stop the demand for bribes through 'action which will meet the prime requirement of ensuring that all importing countries enforce adequate legislation against bribery and extortion. Exporting countries should assist through recognised procedures with the enforcement of that legislation'. This approach differed fundamentally from that of the Americans, whose new proposal on criminalisation aimed to stop the supply of bribes.

The problem with the British approach is obvious. As we have seen (in, for example, Lebanon, Saudi Arabia and Iran), many demands for bribes came from extremely powerful people, or their friends, relatives or associates. Self-evidently it was unrealistic to expect those at the top of Government to take action in the worst cases of bribery in their countries, as they were themselves the guilty parties. Further, it was also unrealistic to expect others in these countries to put an end to corrupt practices, as this might require revolutionary change. In many countries those defying the regime could reasonably expect imprisonment, torture or death.

In addition, in many countries where corruption was most prevalent, Britain was actively helping maintain corrupt and undemocratic regimes in power. The British Government was one of the main backers of the Shah of Iran, while counselling him[46] to 'use minimum force in maintaining public order'. Although Ministers balked at selling him armoured cars and electric shock sticks to use against protesters, they agreed[47] British companies could sell tear gas and rubber bullets to help him suppress protests.

In Saudi Arabia, the British Military Mission was key to the effectiveness of the National Guard, the main counter-revolutionary force, and security ties deepened in the 1970s. By the time of the occupation of the Grand Mosque at Mecca, Saudi Arabia, by Islamic fundamentalists in 1979, Britain was providing training and assistance to the Saudi police and security services,[48] as well as SAS training for the Saudi Special Security Forces.[49]

Although the British officials who attended the UN Working Group discussions probably did not know the details of Britain's security and business dealings with the Shah of Iran and others, they must have realised that expecting importing countries to clean up corruption was hopelessly unrealistic. But adopting this stance was convenient, as it would be unlikely to result in any effective change or lead to an agreement targeting the supply of bribes that might be assiduously implemented by Britain but not by her competitors.

Britain is Isolated in International Discussions

By the summer of 1977, the Working Group had met four times, and produced an early draft of an agreement to 'prevent and eliminate illicit payments'.[50] The Americans lobbied for a Diplomatic Conference to finalise it. British officials worried that their passive approach was unsustainable as they would eventually have to decide whether or not to support the agreement.[51] One wrote 'the UK's position will be bearly credable [sic] if we can support only an agreement which goes no further than the provisions of existing domestic law'.

At the third G7 summit in early May 1977, the leaders of Britain, America, France, West Germany, Italy, Japan, and Canada agreed[52] that 'irregular practices and improper conduct should be eliminated from international trade, banking and commerce'. However, shortly afterwards senior Ministers met at Chequers to discuss the *Daily Mail* allegations about British Leyland. Callaghan said[53] that 'given the heavy reliance of the British economy on exports, it might be more difficult for us to accept as high standards in this matter as, for instance, the Americans'.

At the 1977 meeting of ECOSOC,[54] the Working Group was given until mid 1978 to finalise an agreement. British officials anticipated becoming full members of the Working Group. Now the British Leyland affair had raised the political temperature, Dell told officials[55] to 'play a more active part' and 'consider positive initiatives'. Ministers agreed[56] that 'strong efforts should be made to achieve effective international action'.

The Americans agreed to drop their proposal that companies should disclose agents' commissions (now absent from the bill going through Congress).[57] But Ministers still had to decide whether to propose to Parliament a change in Britain's corruption laws so they would apply to British nationals and companies when overseas. Generally, the law in England and Wales is 'territorial', following the long-accepted convention that each state regulates by law the conduct of those within its own territory and no other. It is much easier and quicker to obtain evidence and deal with cases if they are tried in the country where the crime was committed. In 1977, it was accepted that a British national or company paying a bribe while overseas could not be prosecuted in Britain, nor could someone in Britain who attempted, aided, abetted or procured an offence of bribery committed overseas be prosecuted in Britain.[58] But British citizens taking or paying a bribe in Britain (like David Randel and Frank Nurdin) could be prosecuted.

Dell told Callaghan[59] he did not want any extension of British jurisdiction overseas or change in Britain's corruption laws. Officials thought prosecuting British nationals or companies would be unfair if the bribe recipients were not prosecuted too. Dell also opposed the disclosure of commissions. So that Britain had something positive to say, he suggested advocating the negotiation of bilateral agreements with individual countries to deal with corruption.

When the Ministerial Group on Improper Trade Practices met in late October 1977, Silkin and Industry Secretary Eric Varley thought[60] that the American proposal might be politically necessary before long. However, Ministers' main objection[61] was that 'the United Kingdom would have to enforce rules which other countries only paid lip service to' and thus there could be 'seriously damaging effects on United Kingdom overseas trade'. They instructed officials to oppose the American proposal.

In Washington, the Americans were disappointed with the negative response from Britain and other developed countries. Dell told his colleagues that the prospect of an international agreement was remote, saying[62] 'I do not think there can be any question of our unilaterally imposing new obligations on ourselves, in spite of the willingness of the United States to go some way in this direction'. On 19 December 1977, the Foreign Corrupt Practices Act became law in America, making it illegal for Americans to pay bribes overseas.

Bilateral agreements, British officials decided,[63] would need foreign partners whom Britain could be confident would prosecute their own nationals where appropriate. As one official had pointed out,[64] bilateral agreements would be unlikely with countries where corruption was rampant:

> the Governments of most Middle East countries voice concern from time to time about corruption, and they occasionally indulge in purges of varying intensity. However this is often window dressing because corruption is endemic and the purges are not infrequently prompted for reasons concerned with internal political manoeuvres...There is not in our view any country in the area with a standard of government and business ethics sufficiently close to our own...To the extent that rulers and their relations are beneficiaries of corruption, the UK could find itself in an impossible position if a bilateral agreement laid upon us an obligation to report all cases of corruption coming to our attention to those in authority in the countries concerned. We would need to be highly selective in what was reported otherwise we could be drawn into the internal politics of these countries with the risk of an unfortunate backlash on our trade and economic links.

With the Foreign Corrupt Practices Act now American law, in 1978 the Americans pressed again for a Diplomatic Conference to conclude an international agreement. To the dismay of the British,[65] the French, like the Americans, now said exporting countries should prosecute their own nationals for bribery committed overseas. By June 1978 Britain was the only country in the Working Group refusing to extend her jurisdiction overseas to tackle bribery.[66]

British officials believed[67] the French about-turn was cosmetic and that the French would not prosecute their nationals, leaving Britain at a competitive disadvantage in international trade. Big business agreed.[68] Officials thought[69] the American/French proposals would be 'likely to inhibit UK exporters' and hence be effective in Britain. As Ministers had promised Parliament in 1976 that Britain favoured effective action, they would now be embarrassed if Britain was the only developed country unable to sign an international agreement.

Officials were thus keen to delay or disrupt progress. In the Working Group they raised Southern Africa, hoping[70] the developing countries would block progress by insisting the agreement should ban payments to Southern Africa. However, this ruse failed as the developing countries were 'more reasonable on this occasion' and agreed to discuss Southern Africa at a later stage.[71]

British officials now tried to block agreement at the 1978 ECOSOC meeting to a firm date for a Diplomatic Conference[72] because, unless there was time for further discussion of the draft agreement, 'the UK could eventually face the choice of being the one major developed country refusing to ratify or of accepting jurisdiction over nationals for the offence of bribery abroad'. Dell told Callaghan[73] that Britain should ask for a 'preparatory committee at which further discussion of the main issues can take place. This will afford us more time to secure an acceptable outcome.' At ECOSOC a Diplomatic Conference was agreed in principle, but a decision on the date deferred until mid 1979.

The new Trade Secretary, John Smith, told Callaghan[74] that Britain should not back down yet, as there was still time for further discussion. Silkin objected,[75] pointing out that if the American/French proposals were not accepted, any agreement would be ineffective because 'persons committing acts of corruption abroad will continue to do so with impunity, where the State in which the corruption takes place is unable or unwilling to proceed against the bribing or the bribed'. He argued that maintaining

> a negative posture would be quite inconsistent with our repeated claim that the problem of international corruption should be solved at the international level and that we are striving with other States to achieve an effective international instrument to this end.

He suggested Britain could argue that a certain proportion of developed countries should sign the agreement before it came into force, and that there should be regular monitoring. This would deal with concerns that Britain would be at a competitive disadvantage.

But Smith, supported by Chancellor Denis Healey, argued[76] that it would be 'an unacceptable result if we were to end up prosecuting British businessmen for alleged bribes given overseas when those demanding the bribes, and exporters from other countries willing to pay them, went scot-free'. The Home Secretary, Merlyn Rees, doubted[77] whether some exporting countries would use their powers to prosecute their own businessmen who bribed abroad, and thought it would be difficult to prosecute in Britain. He thought, along with Smith and Healey, that all countries should enforce their own laws against corruption instead. Varley and diplomats also backed Smith.

Isolated, Silkin made one last attempt to change his colleagues' minds. He pointed out that their view about what would work ignored reality. He wrote to Smith:[78]

> The problem will not, in my view, be solved by the philosophy that each country must stamp out corruption within its own borders. As we both know only too well from past experience, in a number of countries where expensive investment is taking place there are certain individuals who appear in effect to be above the local law and who make fortunes out of corruptly selling contracts to the highest bidder. The names of some are well known to our departments. Others are more shadowy. We know that this practice holds to ransom commercial enterprises operating from developed countries and compels them, I am sure against their wishes, to accept dubious practices to the point at which these become almost the norm. Only too regularly the existence of a 'slush fund' is embarrassingly uncovered.

Callaghan agreed with Smith,[79] and Britain continued to resist the American/French proposals.

The next Working Group meeting in February 1979 made good progress towards an agreement. Diplomats thought Britain should now make concessions to avoid isolation.[80] Foreign and Commonwealth Office Minister of State Frank Judd met privately with Silkin.[81] Judd said 'he was very concerned that corruption in international trade should not escalate: decent businessmen were coming under increasing pressure to offer bribes'. They agreed that resisting the American/French proposals was now 'foolish'. Silkin said that because under the Prevention of Corruption Act 1906 the Attorney General had to give permission for a prosecution, he could take into account whether or not the agreement's objectives were being achieved before deciding to prosecute in any particular case.

The Ministerial Group on Improper Trade Practices reconvened in March 1979. Officials identified a major loophole in the draft agreement.[82] Only individuals of exporting countries who bribed abroad would be prosecuted, not companies. So, 'a company will be able to evade the agreement entirely, merely by employing non-nationals to carry out corruption for it abroad'.

Ministers felt[83] that 'any agreement was likely to hurt United Kingdom exporting companies' because, officials pointed out,[84] they 'will be inhibited compared with some of their competitors' in 'respect of actions which secure valuable export contracts'. Thus Ministers said[85] that monitoring other countries' activities should be a precondition of any British concession on prosecuting nationals who paid bribes abroad. In addition, they wanted companies covered as well as individuals, to make the agreement acceptable.

In May 1979 the Conservative Party won the General Election, and Margaret Thatcher became Prime Minister. She appointed John Nott as the new Trade Secretary.

The Failure to Reach International Agreement

At around the same time, the final Working Group meeting took place. There the Americans and other developed countries agreed in principle that companies as well as individuals should be prosecuted for overseas corruption. The draft agreement[86] also contained monitoring provisions. However, the developing countries decided to use the draft agreement as a bargaining chip.[87] They refused to attend a Diplomatic Conference unless a separate Code of Conduct for Transnational Corporations (which the developed countries disliked) was also agreed.

Now developing countries appeared uninterested in the draft agreement and were threatening to block it, an alternative was for the exporting countries to ignore them and make their own agreement. If the demand for bribes could not be stopped, the supply still could. The Americans discussed this with British officials in January 1978,[88] and raised it in informal discussions with European countries in June.[89]

At a meeting, British officials argued[90] that an agreement (in the OECD) would 'imply that Western countries were the sole cause of corrupt practices in international trade', and that it might not be implemented by all. The Americans said 'it "took two to tango" and that if one partner was constrained the dance would cease. [They] thought that a "cartel" of Western countries in this field could make a substantial impact.'

Nott had made his feelings clear years before when responding to Barnett's statement in Parliament about the BP allegations.[91] He declined to support the international action against bribery Barnett proposed. Nott argued that importing countries must take ultimate responsibility for the problem, and that 'our major companies are operating in the real world and that we would deplore any humbug in the British Press, or from Labour Members [of Parliament], that damage their interests'.

Officials were now pushing at an open door. They told Nott[92] that the draft agreement

is likely to affect UK interests adversely without, in all probability, making a significant impact on the problem of corruption in international trade. We do not believe that it can be improved sufficiently to make it a more effective instrument. Our paramount aim should be, therefore, to render it harmless.

This would also solve an obvious political problem:

Our [G7] summit commitment to international work in this field would make it very difficult internationally to adopt an openly destructive approach. This would also be very controversial, in domestic political terms. There is, moreover, some political merit in continued participation in the international work, since it provides a useful line of defence when individual cases involving payments overseas by nationalised industries occur...a collapse in the negotiations (if generated principally by others) or a long stale-mate would be to our advantage.

Sticking to the line that effective action in importing countries was essential to eliminating corruption, officials recommended rejecting the American suggestion of an agreement between exporting countries only. Nott agreed,[93] saying 'he did not wish the UK to make any move which would seriously impede British exporters to the Middle East'.

At the ECOSOC meeting in July 1979, no agreement was reached. The Minister of State for Trade, Cecil Parkinson, suggested[94] that Britain should continue to oppose the American/French proposals and take no initiative to accelerate or collapse the discussions. His colleagues agreed. Lord Strathcona at the Ministry of Defence said[95] that he attached 'particular importance in this context to avoiding any developments which might make our export firms in the defence sector less competitive in world markets'. In the autumn of 1979, the UN General Assembly agreed to leave a decision about a date for a Diplomatic Conference to the 1980 ECOSOC meeting.[96]

At the 1980 ECOSOC meeting,[97] the Americans again pressed for a date for a Diplomatic Conference. Again the developing countries insisted this should be linked to agreement on a Code of Conduct for Transnational Corporations, and so again no agreement could be reached.

Knowing that any progress was now very unlikely, British officials became less inhibited at showing their true feelings. Diplomats in New York suggested that developing countries should be blamed for the stalling of progress on the anti-corruption agreement. If the UN General Assembly could not agree a way forward, one wrote,[98] 'how much better it would then be if the USA simply repealed their domestic legislation. Amen to that'. Another told Parkinson[99] that the Americans had 'created their own problems by domestic legislation outlawing bribery by US companies…the White House is under unavoidable pressure to subject everyone else to the same misery'.

And there the American push for an international agreement against corruption ended. It would be another 17 years before one was concluded.

In America, the Foreign Corrupt Practices Act was criticised. In 1978 President Carter set up a Task Force to identify disincentives for American exporters. Its report[100] argued that the Act was a major concern because its ambiguity and lack of enforcement history created uncertainty for American companies. The report said the losses from foregone business were significant but unquantifiable. It also concluded that the Act was reducing corruption in international business by American companies.

An evaluation of the impact of the Act by the American General Accounting Office in 1981[101] drew similar conclusions. It found 30 per cent of exporters had lost business because of the Act's anti-bribery provisions. However, 60 per cent of American companies reported changing their company code of conduct because of the Act, and 70 per cent felt that questionable payments had been reduced.

In the meantime, British companies were continuing their old ways with impunity.

8

'Business as Usual' (1980–2001)

At the start of the 1980s, corruption was, of course, still a significant factor in international trade and the internal politics of many countries. British diplomats fretted over the security of the 'traditional regimes of Arabia', in the light of the Islamic revolution in Iran, and the occupation of the Grand Mosque at Mecca, Saudi Arabia, by Islamic fundamentalists, in 1979. They thought[1] a major weakness of these regimes was 'corruption, whose full extent is scarcely guessed at by their subjects, and which is the skeleton in the cupboard of all the ruling families'.

In Oman, the current Sultan, Qaboos, overthrew his father in a British-backed coup in July 1970. British diplomats thought Qaboos, then only 30 years old, was young and callow. By the mid 1970s they were worried that[2]

> a small group of largely expatriate Arabs has come to control a large part of Government, particularly in awarding contracts. These people have achieved representation in the formal areas of Government which allow them to control both policy and access to the Sultan.

One of the 'Omani Mafia' was Qais Al-Zawawi, who became Minister of State for Foreign Affairs in 1973 and Vice-Chairman of the National Development Council in 1974. In early 1981, Ministry of Defence officials reckoned[3]

> he now enjoys more power than any other Minister but can scarcely be said to have used it wisely. The spending spree which followed his appointment enriched Qais and a few others but impoverished Oman and led directly to the financial crisis of early 1975...he has continued to profit (sometimes excessively) from his position and influence.

However, they observed wryly, 'there is evidence that he became genuinely concerned about the country's finances'.

Turning to Saudi Arabia, diplomats wrote:[4]

the line between public office and private purse is as blurred in Saudi Arabia as elsewhere in the region. Commission payments are an established element of business practice. But the scale of transactions in development projects and oil have magnified the temptations – and the resulting fortunes. The Saudi Government revealed its acute sensitivity on this issue in December [1979] when revelations in Rome of [Ente Nazionale Idrocarburi – an Italian oil company]'s commission payments to Saudi officials forced [Saudi company] Petromin to cut all supplies to Italy. It is suspected that most senior princes and Petromin officials have oil allocations at their personal disposal, and in a tight market will expect to be suitably rewarded...the prospects for an effective anti-corruption drive look dim unless senior figures, including Prince Fahd the Crown Prince, back it. But allegations against Fahd himself, and especially his sons, are if anything multiplying.

A British Aerospace (BAe) salesman confirmed to the Foreign and Commonwealth Office in 1981[5] that in arms deals with the Arab world 'once the political framework had been set (and this was essential), it was still necessary for the fixers to get to work'.

Prime Minister Margaret Thatcher was keen to mount an arms sales drive during her time in Downing Street. At the end of 1980, she and her Ministers told the Defence Secretary,[6] Francis Pym, 'to exploit all possible opportunities to extend overseas markets for defence sales'.

In March 1981, the new Defence Secretary, John Nott, visited Saudi Arabia, Oman, Qatar, the United Arab Emirates and Bahrain. He told Thatcher that Arabs were 'well disposed towards' British military equipment. He warned:[7]

we must, however, recognise that without recourse to the 'Arab methods' employed by the French and by our major competitors, we will, of necessity, always be at some disadvantage. To be really sure of gaining contracts in this region one has not only to demonstrate the quality of equipment and to offer competitive prices and delivery dates, but also to give cause for the right individual to see personal advantage in their negotiation. The French indulge their Middle Eastern customers to a range of physical, financial, and proprietorial pleasures which would be outside our Parliamentary sanctions – and these practices pay. Indeed two years in my previous appointment [as Trade Secretary] led me to the sorry conclusion that in the project business, orders are increasingly won by those who give them away, or bribe them away.

Origins of the Al Yamamah Deal

It was during the 1980s that BAe, which during the 1970s had become Britain's main arms exporter,[8] decided to provide the Saudi Prince overseeing their largest contract with a programme of benefits which would, 20 years later, result in Britain's own version of the Lockheed scandal.

The big prize was another jet fighter sale to Saudi Arabia under a Government-to-Government Memorandum of Understanding. In the 1970s, the British Government had decided to permit commissions in its arms deals with the Saudi Government. With the failure of international action against corruption in the UN, and the Thatcher Government anxious there should be no impediments to arms exports to the Middle East, dubious practices would be firmly institutionalised in British arms deals with Saudi Arabia in the 1980s and beyond.

In the 1960s the British Aircraft Corporation (BAC – BAe's predecessor) had sold 40 Lightnings and 25 Jet Provost training aircraft as part of the Saudi Arabian Air Defence (SAAD) scheme. In 1972 BAC sold ten Strikemasters (as the Jet Provost was later known).[9] In 1973, BAC became the lead contractor for the Saudi Arabian Air Defence Assistance Project (SADAP), agreeing to maintain the Lightning and Jet Provost/Strikemaster aircraft, train pilots and undertake related construction work. The Saudis bought eleven more Strikemasters in 1976,[10] and in September 1977 the SADAP project was renewed[11] under a second Memorandum of Understanding, earning BAC a further £635 million (worth about £3 billion today). In 1982 the project was renewed under a third and final Memorandum of Understanding, for some £350 million[12] (worth about £910 million today).

This was big business for BAe. However, early on Whitehall officials and BAe Chairman Sir Frederick Page recognised that to continue BAe's work in Saudi Arabia in the long-term another aircraft deal was necessary,[13] as by the 1980s the Lightnings were rapidly becoming obsolete.[14] The obvious replacement was the Tornado, the aircraft that became the backbone of the British, West German and Italian air forces in the 1980s.

Well before then, in 1975, the British Government approved the release to the Saudis of North Atlantic Treaty Organisation information about Tornado.[15] One year later Prince Sultan, still the Saudi Defence Minister, visited Britain but a planned demonstration of the Tornado prototype was ruined by bad weather.[16]

To win another major deal, BAe needed close relations with all the key players on the Saudi side such as Sultan. But BAe needed to court other influential figures. The rising star in Saudi Arabia was Prince Bandar bin Sultan, one of Sultan's 33 children.[17]

Bandar had married one of King Feisal's daughters. In 1978 Bandar helped his brother-in-law, Prince Turki bin Faisal, the new Head of Saudi Intelligence, overcome the opposition of the Israeli lobby to the sale of ultra-modern American F-15 fighter jets to Saudi Arabia.[18] At this time Bandar became good friends with American President Jimmy Carter,[19] and the link-man between Carter and Crown Prince Fahd, the real power behind the scenes in Saudi Arabia. When, a few months after the Islamic Revolution in Iran, the Saudis increased oil production and kept their price below that of other oil producers in the Organization of the Petroleum Exporting Countries to compensate for the fall in Iranian production, Carter thanked Bandar[20]. Later Bandar developed a 'personal friendship' with President Ronald Reagan and his wife Nancy.[21]

The British had spotted Bandar's potential early. In 1972, Ambassador Willie Morris in Jedda had told Head of Defence Sales Lester Suffield[22] that Bandar 'is not only the son of the Minister of Defence but also a popular young officer and the leading advocate amongst them of the virtues of the Lightning and the British connection' (having learned to fly at RAF Cranwell). Morris prophesied he 'may be a valuable asset to our position here in defence sales'.

With his connections and recent experience in arms sales, and as the son of the Defence Minister, by 1980 Bandar was a key figure for BAe, with whom he was developing a relationship. In July, Bandar told Sir Frederick Rosier,[23] BAe's chief in Saudi Arabia, he wanted BAe to get an extension to the SADAP project in 1982. In December Bandar asked to see Foreign Secretary Lord Carrington. Diplomats told Carrington[24] that Bandar 'was likely to talk about the possibility of very large contracts for the British in the defence field, having himself (with Wafiq Said) been directly involved in negotiating some recent very large contracts with the Americans on behalf of his father'.

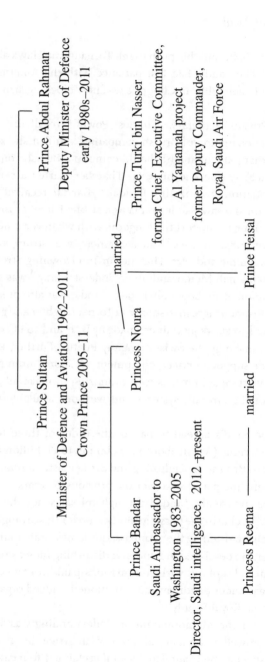

Figure 8.1 Some Saudi royals connected to the Al Yamamah arms deal

The Al Yamamah Deal

In early 1984 Britain began a big push to sell Tornado and Hawk aircraft to the Saudis.[25] The Saudis had lost patience with the Americans,[26] because the pro-Israeli lobby in Congress was now blocking arms sales to Saudi Arabia.

Thatcher's Private Secretary, Charles Powell, recalled:[27] 'Mrs. Thatcher, a great champion of British companies and British exports, was very keen that [Al Yamamah] should come to a British company, British Aerospace'. At the end of 1984, Thatcher started a series of important negotiations by meeting Bandar.[28] Bandar recalled[29] that Thatcher told him she saw Saudi Arabia as a strong friend of Britain's and would be willing to support the kingdom with whatever it needed. In the spring of 1985, he says,[30] an agreement was struck with 'a handshake between me and Mrs. Thatcher in Ten Downing Street'.

The first Al Yamamah Memorandum of Understanding[31] was signed by Sultan in London on 26 September 1985. Bandar was also present.[32] The British Government agreed to supply 72 Tornado fighter and ground attack aircraft and 30 Hawk jet trainers made by BAe, and 30 PC-9 basic training aircraft made by the Swiss company Pilatus. Further, Britain agreed to provide support services, equipment, weapons, ammunition and electronic warfare systems, as well promising to make all future developments of the aircraft, systems and weapons available to the Saudis.

In return, the Saudis agreed to pay 'of the order of three to four billion pounds sterling' (worth about £6.75 billion to £9 billion today) and to sell back to Britain the Lightning and Strikemaster aircraft (and related equipment and parts) sold over the previous 20 years.

The deal was, unusually, funded through oil sales not the Saudi defence budget.[33] A clue to the possible motivation for this arrangement lies in a despatch[34] written by then Ambassador James Craig four and a half years earlier. He described to London 'a disturbing increase during [1980] in private sales of oil, with commissions paid into Swiss bank accounts – illegal under Saudi law, but sanctioned, indeed organised, by members of the Royal Family'.

Two weeks after the Memorandum of Understanding was signed, diplomats sent Powell a summary account of an article in an Arabic language news sheet named *Sourakia*.[35] *Sourakia* claimed 'four cavaliers' benefited from Al Yamamah, taking £600 million in 'commission' in

9.   A British Aerospace Tornado Air Defence Variant fighter. Twenty-four were sold in the first Al Yamamah deal (1985). The Saudis are now replacing them with Eurofighter Typhoon aircraft.

© Nicholas Gilby. Picture courtesy of the Royal Air Force Museum.

10.   A British Aerospace Tornado Interdictor/Strike fighter-bomber. Forty-eight were sold to the Saudis in the first Al Yamamah deal (1985) and 48 more in 1993.

© Nicholas Gilby. Picture courtesy of the Royal Air Force Museum.

total. Diplomats said Powell should 'simply refuse all comment'. Eleven days later, the *Guardian* published a story[36] headlined 'Bribes of £600m in jets deal'. However, these allegations were never investigated and the truth never established.

11.   Saudi Minister of Defence and Aviation Prince Sultan (seated, left) and British Defence Secretary Michael Heseltine (seated, right) signing the first Al Yamamah Memorandum of Understanding in London, September 1985. Standing behind Sultan is his son, Prince Bandar.

Picture by PA/PA Archive/Press Association Images.

On 17 February 1986, a second Memorandum of Understanding was signed, which set out in detail how the Al Yamamah programme would be managed.[37] On 3 July 1988, a third Memorandum of Understanding was signed, in which Britain agreed to supply additional aircraft, weapons and ships.[38]

BAe and Prince Turki Bin Nasser

Behind the scenes BAe paid for physical, financial, and proprietorial pleasures. The key beneficiary was one of Sultan's nephews, Prince Turki bin Nasser, who was married to one of Sultan's daughters, Princess Noura. Turki bin Nasser was a Royal Saudi Air Force (RSAF) officer and by the end of the 1980s was in charge of the Al Yamamah programme, now BAe's most important contract. From 1989 to 2002 Turki bin Nasser and his entourage received over £60 million in benefits and cash from BAe.

Not surprisingly BAe wanted to confer these benefits via a third party. It needed someone both it and Turki bin Nasser could trust. So they turned to someone who had been connected with the RSAF for 20 years, Tony Winship.

Back in 1969 Winship, aged 37, had retired from his duties as an RAF Wing Commander. He joined Airwork in Saudi Arabia, commanding the RSAF's Lightning Conversion Unit (where Saudi pilots learned to fly the Lightning aircraft).[39] Soon after arrival, Winship got the opportunity to provide service to the Saudis above and beyond the call of duty, courtesy of Geoffrey Edwards.

The situation in Yemen was an irritant to the Saudis. Aden had been a British colony until 1967 when the British withdrew in the face of a radical insurgency and the People's Republic of South Yemen (PRSY) was founded. The PRSY was hostile to the traditional Gulf monarchies and provided a safe haven to the Popular Front for the Liberation of the Occupied Arabian Gulf, which was dedicated to overthrowing the Sultan of Oman and the other Gulf monarchies.[40]

The Saudis sponsored attempts by Yemeni rebel groups to overthrow the new PRSY Government,[41] and, unsurprisingly, tensions on the Saudi/PRSY border ran high. The problem was, the SAAD Consortium Manager explained,[42] 'the Saudi Air Force cannot operate without the services provided by these British firms'. Airwork refused[43] to let its pilots 'undertake combat duty for the Saudis while in the company's employment'. Edwards was, however, able to avoid any souring of relations between Airwork and the Saudis by striking a secret deal.[44] Airwork pilots could give the company one hour's notice and resign to join his mercenary organisation. Airwork agreed to give pilots wanting to rejoin the company following combat 'sympathetic consideration'.

In November 1969 PRSY forces captured Wadi'a, on the Saudi side of the border, and the Saudis asked Airwork for three pilots to fight back.[45] Winship, Morris reported to London,[46] flew one sortie against the PRSY. After a few days the PRSY forces retreated.[47]

Having demonstrated his loyalty to the Saudis by flying against their arch-enemy, Winship was no doubt trusted by them. Hence he was the ideal man to manage BAe's Al Yamamah benefits programme. By the late 1980s, Winship worked for BAe, and hired a company called Travellers World to deliver BAe's benefits for Turki bin Nasser.

At that time, Travellers World was a subsidiary of The Travel Company, which described itself[48] as one of the top dozen business travel agents in the UK. It was turning over £35 million per year (worth about £64 million today), and its clients included former Beatles Paul McCartney and George Harrison, composer and impresario Andrew Lloyd-Webber, and the Saudi Royal Family.

The Managing Director of Travellers World was Peter Gardiner, who had been organising holidays for Turki bin Nasser, his family and, occasionally, associates, since 1977.[49]

In 1989 Gardiner learned from Turki bin Nasser's driver[50] that 'there was a man called Winship who worked for BAe, who was now involved with [Turki bin Nasser] and that he was responsible for making travel arrangements for him'. He wrote to Winship introducing the company and offering its services.

Between 1990 and 1992, shortly after Gardiner started doing business with Winship and BAe, Gardiner bought all the shares in Travellers World from The Travel Company.[51] Business from Winship from 1989 made up 70 per cent of Travellers World's revenue, and, according to Gardiner 'the company could not survive without it'.[52] The company's vulnerability made it easy for Winship to control.

The services provided by Travellers World for Turki bin Nasser, all paid for by BAe and managed by its representative Winship, were diverse including travel (the most important part) and also[53] 'summer schooling for Saudi children; medical facilities for [Turki bin Nasser's] entourage; aircraft flight training; property management and refurbishment; general purchases for Saudi guests; [a] wide range of security services' and other payments requested. About 60 per cent of the services provided by Travellers World on Winship's behalf were for Turki bin Nasser and his family and entourage, with the remainder for other top Saudis.[54] Gardiner said:[55]

> all the services were under [Turki bin Nasser's] control and I believe that Winship was doing what [Turki bin Nasser] was guiding him to do. If [Travellers World] provided a poor service or made mistakes then this would have greatly upset [Turki bin Nasser] and with the influence I believe he had, could have affected BAe's involvement with the Al Yamamah programme.

Winship, according to Gardiner,[56] 'wanted to keep everything as confidential as he possibly could...because the whole programme was sensitive, in particular the lifestyle of the Saudi Royal Family. Also the fact that BAe were funding it'. So an elaborate coded invoicing system was developed[57] to disguise the services BAe paid for.

BAe paid Travellers World monthly. Every month Gardiner or one of his senior staff would take a set of invoices to Winship, along with the supplier invoices for all the month's expenses. A master statement summarised the month's spending, containing a description of each item, and the net cost. To each net cost was added Travellers World's 10 per cent management fee, increased to 12.5 per cent in the early 1990s.[58]

Travellers World grouped items on the master statement by beneficiary, each with their own code.[59] 'PB' was Principal Beneficiary (Turki bin Nasser). 'PN' was his wife, Princess Noura. 'PF' was his son, Prince Faisal bin Turki. 'PH' was his daughter, Princess Haifa bin Turki. 'GBH' was General Beherey, an RSAF General. 'SO's were Serving Officers in the Saudi Armed Forces. 'B' (Base) was Winship's operation in Britain and his personal expenses. Travellers World staff used subheadings to categorise each beneficiary's expenses, such as 'London visit', 'Milan visit' or 'medical'. The total for each beneficiary was calculated, and these amounts were then added together to provide the final Travellers World fee for the month.

Travellers World staff turned the master statement into a series of separate invoices for each beneficiary's expenses. Each invoice sent to BAe typically contained a brief mundane description such as 'accommodation services and support for overseas visitors reference PB'. Winship then sent a summary invoice to BAe's accounts department at Warton Aerodrome, Lancashire.[60]

Winship carefully checked all the invoices and underlying documentation provided by Gardiner. He told Gardiner that he should have the only copies of the invoices (sent to BAe) and the master statement, ensuring the confidentiality of the programme,[61] as the only person working for BAe who had a record of the full truth would be Winship. But for years Gardiner kept copies of the documents documenting every single transaction.[62]

The Travellers World documents for July 2001 are an example of how the programme worked. Turki bin Nasser's chargeable expenses (excluding air fares) amounted to £312,991.95, categorised as

'Preswick visit', 'London visit', 'Paris visit', 'tuition', 'LA visit', 'security' and 'medical'.

For his Preswick visit, Travellers World paid his two American Express credit card bills, totalling £100,432.40. For his London visit, Travellers World gave him £3,000 in cash. His stay at the Hyatt Carlton Tower in London's exclusive Knightsbridge district cost £30,433.07 (including £2,000 in tips), and his visit to Maxims-de-Paris, just by Place de la Concorde, cost £55,490.34. Travellers World provided 75,000 French francs as spending money. That month Travellers World also charged BAE (the company had been known as BAE Systems since November 1999) £54,360.80 for his air fares.

The chargeable expenses of Princess Noura ran to £353,987.20 in July 2001. This covered, among other things, security arrangements for a Los Angeles trip, limousine hire in Cannes and Athens, stays in top hotels in Athens and Italy, telephone calls, an American Express credit card bill and yacht hire.

Prince Faisal bin Turki cost BAE £63,272.81 in July 2001, which paid for stays in leading hotels in London, Milan, and Cannes, as well as limousine hire in Cannes. Travellers World also gave Princess Haifa bin Turki £5,000 cash for a London visit (£5,625 was charged by Travellers World to BAE).

The 'serving officers' cost BAE £148,658.53, including air fares, London hotel stays, fees for English private schools, and car hire for a visit to Houston. General Beherey's stay at the Dorchester Hotel on London's Park Lane cost BAE an additional £7,550.59. The Saudi Defence Attaché lived in a house in London's exclusive Mayfair district. Travellers World paid the rent,[63] which was £130,000 a year by 2002, as well as the electricity and water bills.

Winship's 'base' costs for July 2001 were £49,480.39, including spending £218.88 on office stationery, £84.59 on electricity and £32.50 on 'designer plants'.

Once the subtotals for each beneficiary were added up, the master statement for July 2001 came to £995,927.27. A summary Travellers World invoice dated 31 July 2001 and addressed to BAE at Warton stated the subtotals for each beneficiary (coded as 'reference PN', 'reference SO', and so on) with the final demand of £995,927.27. Travellers World's bank statement for 17–23 August 2001 records a direct credit transfer from BAE Systems 'ref: – Travellers World' for £995.927.27.

In the July 2001 master statement Turki bin Nasser's tuition expenses included £1,200 for 'Bolton Lee'. Winship had introduced Turki bin Nasser to theatre student Anouska Bolton-Lee, whose previous boyfriends included Hollywood actor Leonardo di Caprio. Bolton-Lee said[64] she was Turki bin Nasser's mistress in London from 2001 to 2003. Although she did not know it at the time, BAE (through Travellers World), not the Prince, paid the rent for her flat[65] in the posh West London district of Holland Park, as well as for cash she was given.[66]

In America, Turki bin Nasser owned a substantial property in Beverly Hills, California, comprising three housing complexes, an indoor and outdoor swimming pool, wine cellars, cinema, discotheque, cigar humidor, staff quarters and an arsenal. Travellers World paid significant amounts for security, limousines and transportation for the Prince's entourage,[67] while his family were resident.

Over the years, Travellers World also paid for:

1. The hire of a large freighter jet (in September 1995) to transport Princess Noura's Rolls-Royce and crates of furniture from America to Saudi Arabia.[68]
2. Charter helicopters, private jets, and hotel accommodation[69] for the six week honeymoon of Turki bin Nasser's son, Faisal and his new wife, Princess Reema bin Bandar, Bandar's daughter.
3. Major holidays for members of the Saudi royal family[70] including Crown Prince (now King) Abdullah's son, Prince Abdul Aziz bin Abdullah and his wife Princess Abeer bin Turki[71] (Turki bin Nasser's daughter).
4. A complete professional video unit and studio to record the wedding of Abdul Aziz and Abeer in Saudi Arabia.[72]

Gardiner kept management summaries of the amounts being charged by Travellers World for the programme. After September 1991, the amounts rarely dipped below £100,000 a month. The total for 1991 was just under £1 million. Over the following three years, the programme charges averaged around £3.1 million per year. For most years from 1995 to 2001, between £6.5 million and £7 million was charged every year by Travellers World for the programme. Three times the monthly bill exceeded £1 million (in September 1996, August 1997, and August 1998). From 1995, money was also used to build up a reserve fund for

Turki bin Nasser on Winship's instructions.[73] This was done by adding a further 2.5 per cent on to the 12.5 per cent commission charged on some items to BAe.[74]

From January 1991 to February 2002 Travellers World charged £59,340,696 for the programme and BAe reimbursed the company for every penny.

In Gardiner's view,[75] 'Winship's operation including [Travellers World], was a highly efficient and sophisticated means to give [Turki bin Nasser] what he wanted. He received a double benefit of the money; he had the value of it and the additional benefit of the management of the money.'

As for Gardiner, he said:[76]

I did not consider at any time, until 2002, that what [Travellers World] were doing was either illegal or immoral. Services paid for by BAe through [Travellers World] were treated with secrecy and sensitivity not because they were regarded as illegal but because of fear of divulging the Saudi royals' lifestyle and security issues. These people were targets because of there [sic] enormous wealth, position and power. The payments were never ever regarded as immoral, I believed what we were doing was right and was normal business practise [sic] for this type of business.

Gardiner's belief he was not acting illegally[77] derived from advice from his lawyers and auditors who had full knowledge of the benefits programme. What did the British Government know about the Travellers World programme and other dubious practices of the Al Yamamah deal?

Before Al Yamamah was signed the Ministry of Defence knew substantial commissions had been paid by BAe on the SADAP project.[78] Defence Sales Organisation (DSO) officials privately believed the purpose of the commissions was to purchase 'influence'.[79] Publicly the British Government has said that the Ministry of Defence paid no commissions.[80]

Ministers told Parliament[81] that 'any use of agents by companies associated with Al-Yamamah is a matter for those companies [concerned], but the prime contractor, British Aerospace, has assured us that it operates in accordance with the laws and regulations of Saudi Arabia'. Saudi laws, noted Ministry of Defence officials in 1991,[82] 'do not permit the employment of agencies and the payment of agency fees in the procurement of weapons and related services'.

In the early 1990s the Parliamentary watchdog, the National Audit Office, investigated the way Al Yamamah was reported in the Ministry of Defence's accounts. A draft letter from the Comptroller and Auditor-General Sir John Bourn to the Ministry of Defence Permanent Secretary, Sir Christopher France, in March 1992,[83] said:

> there has been a great deal of speculation in the Press about the payment of commissions. Our examination confirmed to our satisfaction that the Department have not paid commissions. My report does not, however, refer to the question of whether commissions have been paid by British Aerospace.

Those and the following words were omitted from the final version of the letter:[84]

> A thorough investigation into the profitability of the sale would reveal whether substantial commissions have been paid. There are, of course, guidelines [the 1977 Cooper guidelines] to cover such circumstances. We would need to see evidence that these have been followed, if appropriate.

Auditors showed the draft report to BAe, whose points on commission were 'taken on board'.[85] However, apart from Chairman Robert Sheldon MP and his Deputy, Sir Michael Shaw MP, no members of Parliament's Public Accounts Committee were allowed to see it. The report remains the only National Audit Office report never to have been made public.

British arms companies continued to pay commission to agents throughout the 1980s and 1990s. Alvis was doing so at around the time BAe was paying the bills for the programme for Turki bin Nasser.

Alvis's Business Practices in Indonesia

In the early 1980s Alvis, one of Britain's leading arms companies, appointed a Singaporean businessman, Chan U Seek, as its agent. He was asked to win Alvis contracts from the Indonesian Army for Scorpion armoured fighting vehicles, but failed to secure a deal. In January

1995, by using different agents, Alvis won a £78 million contract for 50 Scorpion and Stormer vehicles, and another £81 million contract for a further 50 vehicles in August 1996. In 2001 Mr Chan sued Alvis claiming he was owed £6.2 million commission (worth about £8.2 million today) from the 1995 and 1996 deals.

Alvis Chairman and Chief Executive, Nicholas Prest, a former DSO employee, described to the court in the litigation *Chan U Seek* v *Alvis Vehicles Limited*, the 'typical' way Alvis managed its agency agreements:[86]

> The terms of appointment would normally be limited to a particular transaction or type of business, and/or would be for a particular period of time. If, during that time, Alvis believed that progress towards a contract had been made, the agency agreement would typically be extended for a further period in the expectation that a contract would be finalised during that period. Once it becomes clear that the initiatives of a particular agent have not borne fruit, the retainer either expires or is terminated by Alvis.

As for commission payments:[87]

> Alvis's practice over the years has been to pay agent's commission due on contracts secured during the term of their Agreements pro-rata on receipt of the funds. Our standard term Agency Agreement provides that commission will be paid within 30 days of receipt of the funds…I believe that such a provision is very standard in companies within the UK defence industry.

Peter Levene was Chief Executive of Alvis in 1982 and asked Mr Chan, whom he knew well, to identify an agent for Alvis in Indonesia.[88] In May 1982 Mr Chan introduced Alvis to Yoesie Salim,[89] and in March 1983 Alvis appointed him as a marketing consultant.[90] In November 1983, Alvis wrote to Mr Chan promising him 4 per cent commission if the Indonesian Army bought Scorpion vehicles.[91] According to Prest:[92]

> Knowing that high level political support would be necessary for a major Scorpion project, Yoesie Salim had introduced Alvis to a colleague of his, a Mr Soekarno (married to President Suharto's sister or half sister) in the hope that he would use his personal contacts within the higher

echelons of government to exercise influence over resourcing decisions. On the recommendation of Mr Chan, and decided by Peter Levene, both Yoesie Salim and Soekarno were appointed as [United Scientific Holdings]/Alvis representatives for Scorpion in 1983.

Later, once Alvis had concluded Yoesie Salim and Soekarno could not win a deal, the agreements with them were terminated, but the letter from Levene to Mr Chan was overlooked.[93]

In 1989 Rini Soewondho, an Indonesian woman who ran a company called P.T. Surya Kepanjen (PTSK), approached Alvis at an arms fair in Kuala Lumpur, Malaysia. Rini secured Alvis a $5 million contract in 1991 for spares for some of Indonesia's armoured vehicles, and PTSK was then appointed as a consultant for Alvis in Indonesia.[94] Rini undoubtedly provided a wide range of legitimate services for Alvis,[95] and introduced Alvis to the eldest daughter of President Suharto, Madam Tutut.[96] Rini recalled[97] that

at that time, arrangements for the presidential budget [needed for the purchase] could only be made if it was supported by President Suharto. This usually meant seeking support from a member of 'his inner circle'. I managed to arrange a meeting with a member of 'his inner circle' and as a result I was able to confirm with Alvis that the presidential budget could be obtained.

Lionel Steele, Alvis's International Sales Manager, said[98] that Rini 'had explained to me that on-top budgets would be approved by the President only if he were approached via one of a number of companies which he knew and trusted'. He testified that the Chief of the Indonesian Army had told him 'the President's family...would automatically want to be involved in any large contract'.[99]

According to Prest,[100] Steele and another colleague

recommended the appointment of another consultant to assist in this process [obtaining additional funds for the Indonesian Army for the purchase] because, whilst Rini clearly had excellent contacts and influence with the Army, her influence in the budget allocation function of central government was less strong. The person identified by her to assist us was someone we came to refer to as Madam Tutut. Her real name was Mrs Siti Rakhmana, who is the eldest daughter of the then President Suharto...[Madam Tutut] encouraged us to make arrangements with her associates to put a Consultancy Agreement in place. She provided her services through a company called Global Select.

Global Select and Alvis signed a contract in May 1994.

After the 1995 deal was agreed, the Indonesians expressed interest in a further contract for Scorpion and Stormer vehicles. Prest recalled:[101]

we encountered competition from the [South] Koreans who were offering a competitive vehicle on generous credit terms. We were able to see off this competition by obtaining support from Indonesian Ministry of Defence staff. Madame Tutut was instrumental in achieving this,

this time through another company she owned called Basque.[102]

Prest testified:[103]

There were two crucial factors which enabled us to secure the 1995 and 1996 contracts. The first was Rini's contacts with and influence with the Army which Alvis was able to make use of by prioritising within the Armed Forces an immediate demand for the Scorpion vehicle. The second was, on Rini's recommendation, our being able to appoint consultants, Global Select and Basque for each respective contract, which consultants, through Madame Tutut, were instrumental in enabling the Armed Forces to secure the necessary funding, over and above their existing budget.

Overall Alvis paid £16.5 million in commission to the various agents involved in the two contracts via offshore accounts.[104] These payments were described in court by Prest as a 'tax'.[105]

To pay for their armoured vehicles the Indonesian Ministry of Finance borrowed $105 million (for the January 1995 deal) and £65 million (for the August 1996 deal).[106] Britain's Export Credits Guarantee Department (ECGD) provided guarantees to the bank making the loans to the Indonesians. Alvis told ECGD the amount of commission paid[107] but, under the procedures used at the time, did not have to disclose the identities of the agents. In 1998 a financial crisis hit the Far East, affecting Indonesia severely. In September of that year, the British and other Governments agreed Indonesia could reschedule the debts it could not afford to pay at that time.[108] ECGD paid the bank

$46.6 million in guarantees for the first loan, and £67.5 million for the second loan. Under the rescheduling agreement the British taxpayer will not get this money back until June 2021[109].

BAe and its Agents in the 1990s

Internal BAe documents, uncovered during the Serious Fraud Office (SFO) investigation into BAe and published on the internet by South African investigative journalists or used by British prosecutors, give an insight into BAe's extensive use of agents in the mid 1990s.[110]

In 1995, BAe had 299 advisers. The SFO found[111] that 'the Company referred to these advisers as either "overt", that is advisers who conducted their work openly as BAe's in-country representatives, or "covert", that is those whose relationship was regarded as highly confidential'.

An internal BAe note from April 1995[112] explains the need for confidentiality:

1. Rules or regulations in the relevant country (including clauses in Government sales contracts) forbidding the appointment of intermediaries, agents etc
2. Tax implications when the adviser wishes to pass on money to a third party but cannot declare this to his authorities
3. General embarrassment or possible press interest due to a large fee or a sensitive subject.

In 1995, BAe had 225 overt or 'brass plate' advisers, and 74 'confidential advisers', paying its confidential advisers just over £21 million.[113]

A BAe document around that time[114] suggested that 'in order to increase security and confidentiality of Marketing Adviser Payments consideration should be given to the possibility of making these payments through a company set up for the purpose and given a name which has no connection with BAe'. Three methods were suggested. Under the first method, the BAe business unit would pay the amount due to the front company, which would then pay the adviser. One disadvantage was that 'the system would deter casual observers but would still be obvious to anyone investigating'. The second method was the same, except BAe's Head Office in Farnborough, Hampshire, would pay the front company, so the business unit would not know the adviser's name. But the disadvantage was 'the system is still transparent if investigated'. The third method was to form a front company 'as offshore marketing subsidiary of BAe with sufficient expert Directors (and staff?) to be credible'. The front company would receive regular income from BAe via a levy from each business unit which used advisers. The front company would then pay advisers in the normal way. The advantages were 'this is the most covert version...the arrangements can be justified if investigated, and would be difficult to penetrate anyway. Covert paperwork can be removed offshore'. The disadvantages were inconvenience, and 'advisers would have to be persuaded to accept that the new company gave them sufficient comfort'. As we will see, something similar became BAe's chosen method.

Another BAe document[115] from that time, titled 'Covert Agreement Preparation and Storage', gives further detail, revealing that BAe had 'about 350 covert agreements in existence', with the original signed copies 'held by the custodian in Switzerland'. BAe had a referrals committee which approved each covert agreement; the advisers were then controlled by a Marketing Manager. At BAe's Head Office a computer list was held of 'all requests for percentages to include in bids and the answers'.

A BAe document from 1996[116] summarises work into the feasibility of 'setting up of an Offshore Company to make the payments to confidential Advisers' and 'Maintenance of all confidential records offshore'. The document concluded that 'offshore company locations in Europe have been checked' and 'the best appears to be Liechtenstein'. As for storage, this 'would be most convenient in Switzerland'.

The American investigation into BAe found[117] that

in February 1998, [BAe] engaged Uniglobe Aktiengesellshaft (Uniglobe), a trust company in Vaduz, Liechtenstein, to create Red Diamond Trading Ltd., (Red Diamond), an offshore company, located in the British Virgin Islands, in order to, [among other things], conceal [BAe's] brokering relationships. Although not a subsidiary of [BAe], Uniglobe structured Red Diamond in a manner in which Red Diamond could not act without [BAe]'s written agreement. [BAe] was the ultimate beneficial owner of Red Diamond.

The purpose of Red Diamond was to facilitate payments to third party brokers hired by [BAe]. Prior to Red Diamond's creation, [BAe]

was responsible for all agreements with and payments to its brokers...
Red Diamond operated with intent to circumvent the normal payments
reviews and at the specific direction of the senior management of [BAe].

The SFO found that Red Diamond was[118] 'so structured that it would
be extremely difficult for an enquiring outsider to pierce its veil. Its
existence was known only to a small group of [BAe] executives.' As we
will see, BAe used Red Diamond to make pay-offs around the world.

In America, arms companies could not operate with such impunity.
In the 1980s, for example, Lockheed paid $1 million (worth about $1.6
million today) for 'influence'[119] to win a $79 million contract (worth
about $134 million today) from the Egyptian Government for three
C-130 aircraft, and was fined $24.8 million (worth about $36 million
today) in 1995 for breaking the Foreign Corrupt Practices Act[120] (at
the time, the largest ever fine recorded for a breach of the Act[121]). In
Israel, the General Electric Company (GEC) participated in a bribery
scheme in the 1980s to win two military contracts. One was a $100
million contract (worth about $198 million today) to supply tools,
equipment, testing facilities and training to support F-110 engines
GEC had previously sold to Israel, and the other was to supply 75 F-110
jet engines, worth over $200 million (worth about $353 million today).
The company was fined $9.5 million (worth about $14.6 million
today) in 1992 for breaking the Foreign Corrupt Practices Act and
other laws.[122]

The Origins of the OECD Anti-Bribery Convention

However, the international climate started changing when in 1988
the Foreign Corrupt Practices Act was amended. Congress left the
Act's basic structure unchanged, but made the accounting provisions
less draconian, and introduced new defences against the accusation
of bribery.[123] But Congress now required the President to pursue
negotiations with Organisation for Economic Co-operation and
Development (OECD) countries to ensure their nationals could be
prosecuted in their home country for overseas bribery.[124] Thus the
American effort to negotiate an international agreement against
bribery, halted at the end of the 1970s, began anew.

An OECD 'Ad Hoc Group on Illicit Payments' started work in 1989,[125] issuing a Recommendation to OECD countries in 1994.[126] This recommended that 'member countries take effective measures to deter, prevent and combat the bribery of foreign public officials in connection with international business transactions'.

The Recommendation was not legally binding,[127] but led to follow-up work. In 1996 the OECD agreed it was 'necessary to criminalise the bribery of foreign public officials'.[128] Shortly afterwards, the OECD Anti-Bribery Convention was drawn up, and signed by OECD Ministers in Paris in December 1997.[129] Britain and America both ratified the Convention one year later, with the Convention entering into force in February 1999.[130]

At long last the Americans had got the agreement among exporting countries they had been pushing for when Thatcher's Government came to power. In the Convention each participating country promised to make it a criminal offence for its nationals to bribe, attempt or conspire to bribe, directly or via intermediaries, a foreign public official overseas. Under Article 5, the investigation and prosecution of bribery 'shall not be influenced by considerations of national economic interest, the potential effect upon relations with another State or the identity of the natural or legal persons involved'. The Convention provided for systematic monitoring of how OECD countries were implementing it.

In 1999 BAe and GEC agreed to merge British Aerospace with Marconi to create a global arms company. The new company was known as BAE Systems plc. America was hugely important to BAE because of the unrivalled size of its military budget (which made up 37 per cent of global military spending in 2000[131]). In 2000, BAE earned more revenue from America and Canada than from Britain, the rest of Europe or the Middle East.[132]

Over an 18-month period, BAE took two actions which would lead to the public exposure of its dubious dealings for the first time. Firstly, in November 2000, BAE's Chief Executive, John Weston, wrote to American Defense Secretary William Cohen. Weston told Cohen[133] that because of

> the size of the Company's presence in the US following the [Marconi Electronic Systems] US merger, the importance of the US to the Company's long term strategic objectives and the prospective

convergence of the English law of corruption with the [Foreign Corrupt Practices Act], it was agreed that the Company should develop [a Foreign Corrupt Practices Act] compliance program for its non-US businesses to operate as if these businesses were, in fact, subject to the [Foreign Corrupt Practices Act].

Weston also promised that within twelve months, BAE's subsidiary companies would adopt compliance programs to ensure that BAE met the OECD's anti-bribery standards.

Secondly, BAE decided to end their long-standing arrangement with Gardiner's company, Travellers World. Following the 11 September 2001 terrorist attacks in America, the British Government decided to bring in a new Anti-terrorism, Crime and Security Act. This law contained two sections extending the reach of Britain's old corruption laws overseas. Under Section 109, a British national or company bribing overseas would be liable for prosecution in Britain, if the bribery would have been an offence if committed in Britain.

The Act came into force on 14 February 2002. On 23 January Gardiner met Winship. According to Gardiner, Winship[134]

said that BAe was very concerned about the military contracts they had in the United States and that the US government had strict regulations on certain types of commission payments. BAe was on the point of becoming a prime contractor for a major military jet programme in the United States, the joint strike fighter F35, which was worth billions of dollars. Winship also said that the BAe directors had been required to sign a declaration confirming that BAe were not involved in any behind the scenes commission payments and this related not only to current contracts but also to how BAe had conducted itself in this area in the past. Winship then said that BAe were going to be pulling out of the arrangement with [Travellers World].

Winship indicated the business would be continued, but 'in future [Travellers World] would be paid from sources other than BAe'.[135] Gardiner did not believe he, BAe or Turki bin Nasser had broken the law up to the end of 2001, but was now worried.

On 19 February Travellers World's solicitors wrote to Gardiner, advising him[136] that if you continue to make payments and transact business in the manner you have done up until Christmas 2001 the Company and its directors are at risk of being prosecuted for a criminal offence under the 1889 [Public Bodies Corrupt Practices Act] and 1906 [Act].

Gardiner also took advice from a leading criminal barrister, Orlando Pownall QC. Pownall advised:[137]

I am confident that the activities of [Travellers World] and BAe did not amount to an offence at common law or by statute prior to the Anti-terrorism, Crime and Security Act 2001…as there was no jurisdiction in this country to prosecute the offer of services to those who performed a public duty abroad.

But, now the 2001 Act was in force, Travellers World

would in my judgment, be at risk of prosecution if they continued to provide travel and other services to [Turki bin Nasser] in the knowledge that these services were intended to influence and encourage continued participation in the [Al Yamamah] project. It is furthermore my view that BAe are at risk of prosecution if they continue to provide funds to [Travellers World] in respect of the payment for such services. Likewise, [Turki bin Nasser] is also at risk of prosecution for accepting those services.

Travellers World continued to make arrangements for Turki bin Nasser and his entourage, but only when the company's solicitors advised Travellers World would not be in breach of the 2001 Act.[138] At the end of February 2002, Travellers World arranged and paid for a trip to Italy for the Prince, Princess Noura and around 20 others.[139]

However, as BAE was now unwilling to pay the bills, Travellers World invoiced Turki bin Nasser for the services direct, on Winship's instructions.[140] For the first four months of 2002, Travellers World billed Turki bin Nasser £699,374.49 for its services. These payments almost exhausted Turki bin Nasser's reserve fund. So, on 18 April 2002, Gardiner wrote to Winship[141] telling him that because Winship was 'unable to confirm that any new payments would be made to Travellers World for past and current services,' Travellers World had no 'option other than to cease operating the BAe programme'.

On 30 May 2002, Gardiner wrote to Peter Wilson, the Managing Director of BAE's International Programmes, describing the 13-year programme[142]. On 19 June Gardiner met with BAE executive Damian Turner[143] and they agreed the programme would cease.

The SFO Investigates BAE

The programme now over, Gardiner tried to keep Travellers World alive, but failed and the company closed.[144] Concerned by regular media stories alleging questionable practices in the Al Yamamah contract, Gardiner decided to approach the SFO in March 2004.[145]

The SFO had first received allegations about Al Yamamah in 2001.[146] The OECD reported:[147]

> According to contemporaneous SFO and [Ministry of Defence] documents, the case was initially not taken beyond a discreet internal inquiry of the allegations' implications, despite the availability of substantial documentary evidence and witnesses who allegedly had first hand knowledge of suspicious transactions. According to SFO documents, the case was not initially investigated because of insufficient evidence but this conclusion was drawn quickly and apparently before the available evidence had been properly explored.

Later, said the OECD,[148] 'the UK authorities recognised that an insufficient investigation had occurred'.

Gardiner's impeccable documentary record provided the 'additional evidence' the SFO needed.[149] On 29 July 2004 the Director of the SFO, Robert Wardle, decided to investigate BAE.[150] The SFO was looking at[151] 'certain payments made by BAe to Saudi Arabian officials, families, friends and associates' and 'the investigation is principally concerned with BAe and allegations that the said payments represented inducements to obtain and/or facilitate the continuation of the Al Yamamah defence contract'.

The British Government, faced with an investigation into the country's biggest arms company, as the Americans had been in the 1970s, would now find their ostensible commitment to fighting corruption overseas seriously tested.

9

An Investigation Interrupted: The SFO and BAE Systems (2004–10)

The Serious Fraud Office (SFO) investigation of BAE Systems's dealings in the Czech Republic, Romania, Saudi Arabia, South Africa and Tanzania began in July 2004.[1]

It was a high profile test of the ability of the SFO to bring a prosecution under the Anti-terrorism, Crime and Security Act 2001, which had come into force over two years earlier. In July 2004 (over five years after Britain had ratified the Organisation for Economic Co-operation and Development (OECD) Anti-Bribery Convention) no one had ever been convicted for bribery overseas under that Act, or the Prevention of Corruption Act 1906. In America, between the ratification of the OECD Anti-Bribery Convention and July 2004, there had been 19 Enforcement Actions (that is, successful prosecutions) under the Foreign Corrupt Practices Act.[2]

Further, the British appeared to lack the appetite to enforce the 2001 Act. The Home Office had estimated when the 2001 Act was passed that there would be 10 to 20 corruption investigations and one to two prosecutions per year.[3] In March 2005, there were just two full investigations underway,[4] and there had been no prosecutions in the three years since the 2001 Act came into force.[5]

As with the previous criminal investigation into bribery in Britain's arms deals in 1978 (when two Racal employees and Lieutenant Colonel David Randel of the Defence Sales Organisation (DSO) were convicted), the SFO's investigation into Al Yamamah was potentially extremely embarrassing for the exporter, customer and the British Government.

There were similarities with the Randel case. The Iranians then were Britain's biggest arms customer, as Saudi Arabia was in 2004. And, like with Iran, the investigation might reveal the dirty secrets of very powerful people, long used to benefiting personally from arms deals.

The key difference, however, was that in the 1970s a British company bribed a British officer (who threatened to reveal what he knew about the Shah). If the SFO charged BAE, the conduct of the Saudi Royal Family would have been the focus of an Old Bailey trial. For BAE the stakes were very high. The Eurofighter Typhoon was BAE's newest fighter aircraft, but the company had not managed to sell it overseas. BAE reckoned[6] a sale of Typhoon to Saudi Arabia would be Britain's largest export contract in a decade, and worth £40 billion.[7]

The SFO Investigation of Al Yamamah

In November 2004 the SFO told BAE[8] it was suspected of false accounting, and in February 2005 that it was also suspected of corruption. Section 2 of the Criminal Justice Act 1987 allows the SFO to gather evidence by compelling individuals to be interviewed, requiring them to produce relevant documents and permitting the police to search premises. The SFO issued a number of Section 2 notices to BAE, interviewed senior BAE executives, and compelled the disclosure of a large amount of documentation.[9]

Meanwhile, BAE and the British Government were working hard to sell Typhoon to the Saudis. In July 2005 Prime Minister Tony Blair and Defence Secretary John Reid both visited Riyadh, and according to the Saudis,[10] 'openly expressed a desire to supply Saudi Arabia with these planes'.

On 14 October 2005 the SFO issued Section 2 notices to BAE, asking it to reveal the identities of the consultants BAE used in Al Yamamah and other contracts around the world. BAE complained to Attorney General Peter Goldsmith, saying:[11]

> it seems clear from the section 2 notice relating to the Al Yamamah programme that the SFO has received information from [Her Majesty's] Revenue and Customs with the names of consultants engaged by the Company and the amounts paid to them, notwithstanding written assurances of confidentiality given by the then Inland Revenue to the Company and a conversation between the Permanent Secretary at the Ministry of Defence (Sir Kevin Tebbit) and the then head of the Inland Revenue (Sir Nicholas Montagu) at which the highly confidential

nature of the information to be provided by the Company to the Inland
Revenue was explained.

BAE claimed:[12]

> disclosure to the SFO of the information relating to Al Yamamah
> requested in the section 2 notice would be regarded by the Saudi Arabia
> government as a serious breach of confidentiality by the Company and
> the UK government. The Company believes that if this information
> is provided there is little prospect of it remaining confidential
> with consequent jeopardy to the next tranche of the Al Yamamah
> programme relating to the sustainment of Tornado aircraft [a £2.5
> billion deal to upgrade 80 Tornados was signed in September 2006[13]]
> and the sale of Typhoon aircraft being agreed between the UK and Saudi
> Arabia governments.

BAE also argued[14] that the SFO should stop its investigation because
Britain's relations with Saudi Arabia would be damaged, claiming
the Saudis had already complained to the British Government about
the investigation. BAE told the SFO[15] that the 'allegations [were]
unfounded for the principal reason that the support services provided
to Saudi officials were provided for and paid for under the contractual
arrangements that underlie the Al Yamamah programme'.

Tebbit lobbied Robert Wardle, the Director of the SFO, and the
office of his boss, Goldsmith,[16] in November 2005. Goldsmith and
Wardle[17] agreed to ask Ministers whether they thought the public
interest favoured continuing the investigation. By doing so, they hoped
to make it impossible for BAE to refuse to hand over the names of its
consultants in Saudi Arabia.

The Cabinet Secretary sent Goldsmith's office a note in December
2005,[18] approved by Blair, Reid and Foreign Secretary Jack Straw. It
claimed Al Yamamah sustained 10,000 to 15,000 jobs in Britain and
2,000 more in Saudi Arabia, saying BAE's main interest was the
upgrade programme for the Tornado jets bought in the 1980s and
1990s. The first phase was already agreed, with the second coming up.
However, the note conceded, there was not a high risk of the Saudis
halting this programme.

The note explained that the Tornado upgrade programme and
potential Typhoon sale were

a central element in the viability and competitiveness of BAe Systems, the UK's main global defence contractor. Indeed were the contract to be called off and future business to be placed elsewhere, it could have a material impact on BAe earnings, and potentially on UK defence industrial capabilities.

The note suggested that if the SFO investigation continued, there was a 'high risk' the Saudis would not buy Typhoon. Further, a 'central consideration' was the importance of Britain's relationship with Saudi Arabia in respect of counter-terrorism and the search for Middle East stability.

Five days after the Cabinet Secretary's note was sent, the British and Saudi Governments signed a new Memorandum of Understanding to replace the Tornado Air Defence Variant aircraft sold in the Al Yamamah deal with Typhoon aircraft.[19] In January 2006, Goldsmith and Wardle decided the investigation should continue.[20]

The SFO followed the 'money trail' from BAE to its consultants. They asked the Swiss authorities to inspect certain bank accounts[21] (it is almost certain they obtained details of which bank accounts to look at from BAE's disclosures made under the Section 2 notices). This request, Wardle later told Parliament,[22] aimed to find out whether 'the person or individual who finally got the payment was either acting as an agent or a public official'.

Typically, when investigators ask to look at bank accounts, the account holders are alerted and told the reason.[23] The High Court heard[24] that

the reaction of those described discreetly as 'Saudi representatives' was to make a specific threat to the Prime Minister's Chief of Staff, Jonathan Powell: if the investigation was not stopped, there would be no contract for the export of Typhoon aircraft and the previous close intelligence and diplomatic relationship would cease.

The damage, Wardle said later,[25] would have been caused by the 'probing into the bank accounts. We were told that that would offend the authorities in Saudi Arabia because they regarded that there were obligations of confidentiality'. By the autumn of 2006, he said,[26] SFO investigators were 'on the point of planning to travel to Switzerland to look at the material and liaise with the authorities there'.

The Termination of the SFO Investigation

The Saudi threats prompted a new attempt by the British Government to stop the SFO investigation. The Cabinet Secretary wrote to Goldsmith's office[27] in September 2006 warning that 'there are very strong indications that the severe damage to the public interest…we feared was likely in December 2005 is now imminent'. A few days later Goldsmith's office replied[28] that the Attorney General was 'of the firm view that, if the case is in fact soundly-based, it would not be right to discontinue it on the basis that the consequences threatened by the Saudi representatives may result'.

Helen Garlick, the Assistant Director of the SFO, challenged the Cabinet Secretary's view. On 27 October 2006 she wrote to Goldsmith's office,[29] noting 'the continued assertion by the Saudis that the SFO investigation breaches confidentiality provisions in the [Al Yamamah] contract'. She queried the lack of

> any risk analysis as to why the Saudi government would allow the personal interests of [senior figures in Saudi Arabia] to result in damage that extends far beyond the [Al Yamamah] contract and other UK commercial interests, to wider bilateral and geo political interests.

And she pointed out, 'the purpose and intent of our investigation was transparent to the Saudi side without apparent prejudice to the viability of the new phase of the Al Yamamah contract signed in December [2005]'.

At the time Garlick was drafting her letter, the author, unaware the British and Saudi Governments were putting strong pressure on the SFO to halt its investigation, was starting a sabbatical to carry out much of the research on which this book is based. To my great surprise, I discovered that, in May 2006, the Department of Trade and Industry had released two files on the negotiation of Al Yamamah to The National Archives at Kew, in South-west London. The files mostly concerned the debate within the British Government in the mid 1980s about whether BAe should be given a substantial loan guarantee for the atypical oil-for-arms Al Yamamah deal.

In these two files was the first Al Yamamah Memorandum of Understanding,[30] signed in September 1985, which had never been made public. It was classified '[Royal Saudi Air Force] Secret'. It described the overall structure of the Al Yamamah deal, stating that the arrangements would be 'elaborated' by the end of March 1986 in a further Memorandum of Understanding and Letters of Offer and Acceptance.

One file also contained a confidential telegram from Riyadh written by the leader of the British Al Yamamah negotiating team, Colin Chandler. Chandler was a former Group Marketing Director of BAe and became Head of the Defence Export Services Organisation, the new name for the DSO, in May 1985.[31]

On 5 January 1986, Chandler, British Ambassador Sir Patrick Wright, the Director General of the Ministry of Defence's Saudi Armed Forces Project, and Dr Maurice Dixson, the Commercial Director of BAe's Military Aircraft division, met Saudi Defence Minister Prince Sultan and two Royal Saudi Air Force generals to conclude the Al Yamamah negotiations.[32]

Chandler's telegram to London[33] revealed the price of the first 20 (of 48) Interdictor/Strike variant Tornados had risen from £16.3 million in May 1984 (worth about £38.7 million today) to £21.5 million (worth about £48.4 million today), and the price of each Hawk trainer from £4 million (worth about £9.5 million today) to £5.3 million (worth about £11.9 million today). This was a price rise on both types of aircraft of 32 per cent over that short period.

I gave these documents to Rob Evans, whom I had known for some time. Evans was one of the two journalists (David Leigh being the other) working on the *Guardian*'s award-winning investigation into BAE. The *Guardian* published the documents on 28 October 2006, the day after Garlick's letter to Goldsmith's office, alongside an article entitled 'The secret Whitehall telegram that reveals truth behind controversial Saudi arms deal'. In the article,[34] the *Guardian* claimed that the price increases detailed in the Chandler telegram equalled £600 million (worth about £1.35 billion today), the same as the amount 'alleged at the time in Arab publications was exacted in secret commissions paid to Saudi royals and their circle of intermediaries in London and Riyadh, as the price of the deal'. The *Guardian* also printed excerpts of briefing papers for Prime Minister Margaret Thatcher contained in the files. One document described Sultan as 'not highly intelligent...He has prejudices, is inflexible and imperious, and drives a hard bargain.'

The Saudis, said a Ministry of Defence official later,[35] were 'shocked' by the article. On 3 November 2006, according to the official,[36] a meeting was held between [the Director of the Saudi Armed Forces Project] and a senior Saudi Arabian General closely associated with the Al Yamamah programme. At this meeting, the General conveyed the [Saudi Arabian Government's] displeasure that these documents, and other material, had been released in public...he said that the [Saudi Arabian Government] was greatly concerned by the comprehensive breach by the [British Government] of security understandings between the two Governments, which greatly undermined the trust between the Governments.

In Whitehall, panicked officials, alarmed that I might uncover more secrets about Britain's arms deals with Saudi Arabia at The National Archives, ordered a group of civil servants to see if 'any other sensitive records had been released in error'.[37] Ninety-eight files were reviewed, and documents from 13 removed from public view.[38] An Information Tribunal, having reviewed this evidence and other secret material, concluded[39] that

the revelation of the disclosure of the [first Al Yamamah Memorandum of Understanding] did cause real and actual prejudice to [Britain's] relations with [the Kingdom of Saudi Arabia], albeit contributing to the prejudice caused by the SFO investigation and the revelation of other sensitive documents at the same time.

In November 2006, some in the media and Parliament began a campaign to try and put pressure on the SFO. The *Daily Mail* called[40] for an end to 'this silly fraud probe' and argued 'the Attorney General must act now'. Conservative MP Michael Jack accused the SFO of 'gumming up the works'.[41] The *Daily Telegraph* quoted a Conservative Party frontbencher as saying[42] 'the SFO have had long enough. These people can't bumble around for ever.' Wild claims were made by the *Daily Mail* and *Daily Telegraph* (and others) that the SFO investigation would cost 50,000 jobs. But, the Eurofighter consortium's own report showed the Saudi Typhoon deal would involve fewer than 5,000 jobs in the UK.[43]

Meanwhile, the SFO was trying to obtain evidence[44]

to address the question of who (under the Saudi constitutional arrangements) was the principal contracting party in relation to the Al

Yamamah contract, and whether the financial arrangements which lay at the centre of the investigation had been approved or authorised by the principal.

Goldsmith had been pressing Wardle to address this legal problem since April 2006. So, on 30 November 2006, Wardle met Sir Sherard Cowper-Coles, Britain's Ambassador to Riyadh. Cowper-Coles told Wardle[45] that if the investigation continued the Saudis might cease counter-terrorism co-operation with Britain, and that 'British lives on British streets were at risk'. Cowper-Coles had been told[46] nine days before 'that all intelligence cooperation was under threat'.

Wardle and his team considered asking BAE to plead guilty to corruption on a limited basis. Blair's office asked Goldsmith to speak to Blair before BAE was approached. Before they spoke, Cowper-Coles met Wardle again and told him[47] that if the investigation continued Saudi Arabia would cease intelligence and security co-operation with Britain.

Blair wrote to Goldsmith.[48] He said that there was now a 'real and immediate risk of a collapse in UK/Saudi security, intelligence and diplomatic cooperation' which would have 'seriously negative consequences'. Blair complained of the 'critical difficulty' the investigation 'presented to the negotiations over the Typhoon contract'. He said his view was endorsed by Straw, Reid, and formed after advice from 'the Government's most senior national security official advisors'.

Blair and Goldsmith met three days later. Goldsmith said[49] 'he was concerned that halting the investigation would send a bad message about the credibility of the law in this area, and look like giving in to threats'. Blair said that 'a supervening national interest' was at stake, and that 'the British people would regard these as higher interests'.

In discussion it was said that

> any proposal that the investigation be resolved by parties pleading guilty to certain charges would be unlikely to reduce the offence caused to the Saudi Royal Family, even if the deal were accepted, and the process would still drag out for a considerable period.

Further,

> it was important that the Government did not give people reason to believe that threatening the British system resulted in parties getting

their way. But the Government also needed to consider the damage done to the credibility of the law in this area by a long and failed trial, and its good reputation on bribery and corruption issues compared with many of its international partners.

Over the next three days Goldsmith read through 20 files which contained the SFO's case.[50] On 12 December, Wardle met Cowper-Coles for a third time. One day later, Wardle decided to halt the investigation because he 'was satisfied that pursuing the investigation into the Swiss accounts, or indeed attempting to bring any prosecution which involved naming the Saudi Princes, would result in a withdrawal of cooperation including cooperation in respect of security'.[51] Wardle later confirmed[52] that, even if he had believed halting the investigation would be incompatible with Article 5 of the OECD Anti-Bribery Convention, which states prosecution decisions 'shall not be influenced by considerations of national economic interest, the potential effect upon relations with another State or the identity of the natural or legal persons involved', he would have done the same.

On 14 December, Goldsmith announced in the House of Lords[53] that the Al Yamamah investigation was over. He said the SFO could not guarantee bringing a prosecution and needed another 18 months to investigate. Goldsmith himself felt it unlikely there would have been a prosecution, had the investigation been allowed to run its course. Immediately two non-governmental organisations, Campaign Against Arms Trade (in which I was heavily involved) and The Corner House, launched a Judicial Review (see www.controlbae.org.uk).

British Compliance with the OECD Anti-Bribery Convention

The OECD had already called on Britain to pass a new modern bribery law which unequivocally outlawed bribery of foreign public officials. It had also complained that no company or individual had been indicted or tried for bribing a foreign public official since Britain's ratification of the OECD Anti-Bribery Convention in 1998.[54] In January[55] and March 2007,[56] the OECD said publicly it had 'serious concerns' about whether the discontinuance of the Al Yamamah investigation was consistent with the Convention.

While the Americans had amended the Foreign Corrupt Practices Act almost immediately after they ratified the Convention in 1998, in Britain progress towards a new bribery law had stalled. A draft Corruption Bill, published in 2003, had been widely criticised.[57] After further public complaints by the OECD in June 2007 about Britain's progress,[58] another consultation on a new corruption law was published in late 2007.[59]

In December 2007, because of the Judicial Review, the SFO was forced to publish the documents which told the story, described in this chapter, of how its investigation was halted. As a result, the OECD was able, in 2008, to publish a detailed analysis of the British Government's decision-making process,[60] saying what it had seen 'reinforced and intensified the serious concerns' it had 'about whether the Al Yamamah discontinuance was consistent with the Convention'. With access to detailed evidence, the OECD could conclude[61] that it was 'disappointed and seriously concerned with the unsatisfactory implementation of the Convention by the UK'. Now under significant international pressure, six months later the British Government published a new draft Bribery Bill.[62]

Inside the SFO's Al Yamamah Investigation

The detail of the Al Yamamah investigation was revealed by the Wikileaks website in March 2011. A cable from the American mission to the OECD[63] gave details of a meeting of the OECD Working Group on Bribery, held in Paris one month after the SFO investigation was halted, in January 2007.

Garlick told the meeting the Al Yamamah investigation had four parts. The first part investigated the relationship between Prince Turki bin Nasser and BAE. The SFO found that two subcontractors (one being Travellers World) had paid Turki bin Nasser up to £70 million prior to the entry into force of the Anti-terrorism, Crime and Security Act 2001, which made bribery overseas illegal in Britain. The SFO decided[64] to concentrate on BAE's activities after this change of the law, reflecting an 'operational judgement rather than any acknowledgement that acts before that date could not be prosecuted'. After the change in the law, Garlick said[65] that the 'SFO had evidence indicating that BAE had conspired to circumvent the 2001 Act and another 3 million pounds were paid to Turki [bin Nasser]'.

Garlick told the OECD that the second part of the investigation was into BAE's 'overseas agents'. BAE made payments 'to marketing consultants employed at the behest of the Saudi Government after implementation of the 2001 act, but no documents were produced to substantiate the provision of any genuine services by the consultants'. The third part of the investigation looked at payments made by BAE to 'an unnamed senior Saudi official'. Garlick said 'the SFO sought Swiss banking records regarding agents of BAE. The SFO found reasonable grounds that another very senior Saudi official was the recipient of BAE payments', but the SFO was never able to examine the Swiss bank accounts.[66]

The fourth part of the investigation was into BAE's applications for loan guarantees from Britain's Export Credits Guarantee Department (ECGD). Al Yamamah was a Government-to-Government deal underpinned by Memoranda of Understanding. To meet its obligations to the Saudis, the Ministry of Defence placed a contract with BAE. In this contract, the Ministry of Defence guaranteed to use best endeavours to ensure the Saudis paid for the arms.[67] BAE agreed to hold the Ministry of Defence harmless if no payment from the Saudis were forthcoming (in other words, BAE agreed to take the loss, even though they had no contract directly with the Saudis).

As the revenues from Saudi Arabia were so substantial, not surprisingly BAE sought insurance for the possibility the Saudis did not pay. Since 1989 ECGD had provided this insurance[68] by giving BAE consecutive insurances and indemnities for Al Yamamah. The last indemnity was issued in 2006 for five years (but cancelled in 2008).

Garlick told the OECD[69] that 'the SFO investigated potential fraud against the ECGD and discovered false representations by BAE to conceal the corrupt dealings, which would constitute conspiracy to defraud under [British] law'.

Would an SFO prosecution have failed? The key problem was that of 'principal's consent', as the Prevention of Corruption Act 1906 is based on the agent/principal concept. Generally, 'the informed consent of the principal to the agent's actions is a defence to the agent's liability for breach of trust'.[70] In the 1970s, leading barristers, such as John Matthew QC, hired by Millbank Technical Services, believed that questionable payments would not be illegal if made with the principal's consent (see Chapter 4). As we have seen, BAE's main defence to the allegations against it was that the Saudi Government had consented to the payments it made, and Goldsmith considered this the main obstacle to any prosecution.[71]

However, in March 2005 the British Government had given a categorical assurance to the OECD that principal's consent could not be a defence to an accusation of corruption under the 1906 Act.[72] Further, the SFO did not itself think BAE's defence was viable because 'the company would be unable to show that any possibly relevant official had provided consent on an informed basis'. In fact, the SFO agreed to consult Cowper-Coles only because of Goldsmith's concerns.[73]

Because the SFO investigation was terminated, we will never know who was right. However, the combination of an inadequate law (the 1906 Act) and no enforcement of it (resulting in a lack of clear case law), undoubtedly put a serious obstacle in the SFO's path.

The Saudis, by threatening to end counter-terrorism co-operation with the British Government, indicated they were willing to breach their obligations to other countries under UN Security Council Resolution 1373, adopted in the aftermath of the 11 September 2001 terrorist attacks in America. The resolution required states to 'take the necessary steps to prevent the commission of terrorist acts, including by provision of early warning to other States by exchange of information' and 'afford one another the greatest measure of assistance in connection with criminal investigations or criminal proceedings relating to the financing or support of terrorist acts, including assistance in obtaining evidence in their possession'.

The British Government knew much of the Saudi intelligence was likely to be obtained by torture. Sandy Mitchell, a British citizen and anaesthetic technician at the Saudi Security Forces Hospital in Riyadh, was falsely accused by Saudi intelligence of bombings in Riyadh in 2000. As detailed in Mark Hollingsworth's book *Saudi Babylon*,[74] Mitchell was tortured and has subsequently suffered from Post Traumatic Stress Disorder and other serious long-term health problems. When the Saudis threatened to torture his wife, he confessed to carrying out bombings in league with the British Embassy. Three other Britons – Ronald Jones, William Sampson and Leslie Walker – were also tortured and made to confess to a terrorist bombing. By 2003 all were released.

The British Parliament's Joint Committee on Human Rights says[75] that 'complicity in torture is a direct breach of the UK's international human rights obligations...complicity in torture exists where a state... systematically receives information known or thought likely to have been obtained from detainees subjected to torture'.

Richard Alderman, who succeeded Wardle as SFO Director, said[76] that 'the damage that was done by [the halting of the Al Yamamah investigation] was great and will last for a very long time...It was very regrettable and very unfortunate'. In 2007 the Americans formally protested to the British Government about it.[77]

BAE soon got its prized new deal. Early in January 2007, less than one month after the SFO investigation had been halted, Sultan said publicly that the Saudis would take delivery of Typhoon aircraft very soon.[78] In September 2007 the British and Saudi Governments agreed a new deal[79] whereby the Saudis would buy 72 Typhoon aircraft, manufactured by BAE, to replace the Air Defence Variant Tornados sold under Al Yamamah. This deal, called Al Salam, was worth £4.43 billion initially, with weapons and long-term maintenance expected to increase its long-term value to £20 billion.[80] BAE told ECGD[81] that 'no agents had any part in obtaining or negotiating this contract and that no commissions or fees were paid'.

12.   A prototype Eurofighter Typhoon fighter. The Saudis agreed to buy 72 in September 2007, just nine months after the termination of the Serious Fraud Office corruption investigation into the Al Yamamah deal.

© Nicholas Gilby. Picture courtesy of the Royal Air Force Museum.

One month later, the red carpet was rolled out for King Abdullah, Prince Bandar and other senior Princes as they paid a State visit to Britain, culminating in a banquet at Buckingham Palace. In April 2008, the High Court ruled that Wardle's decision to terminate the Al Yamamah investigation was unlawful.[82] However, in July 2008, the decision was overturned in the House of Lords.[83] The investigation never reopened. In February 2011, Cowper-Coles, who had a profound impact in convincing Wardle that the SFO investigation should be stopped because of Saudi threats, became BAE's international business development director,[84] focusing on the Middle East and south-east Asia.

The American Investigation of BAE

But meanwhile, the Americans had decided to open a corruption investigation into BAE, including its dealings in Saudi Arabia. BAE admitted[85] that it did not subject the Travellers World programme to the standards of the Foreign Corrupt Practices Act, thereby breaching the assurances given by Chief Executive John Weston to American Defense Secretary William Cohen in November 2000.

American investigators also found that BAE[86]

used intermediaries and shell entities to conceal payments to certain advisors who were assisting in the solicitation, promotion and otherwise endeavouring to secure the conclusion or maintenance of the [Al Yamamah deal]. After May and November 2001, and until early 2002, in connection with [Al Yamamah], BAES agreed to transfer sums totaling more than £10,000,000 [worth about £13.2 million today] and more than $9,000,000 [worth about $12 million today] to a bank account in Switzerland controlled by an intermediary. BAES was aware that there was a high probability that the intermediary would transfer part of these payments to the [Saudi] official. BAES undertook no or no adequate review or verification of the purpose of these payments, and therefore BAES failed to comply with the foregoing representations made to the Department of Defense.

The SFO investigation and media allegations that BAE had paid bribes on arms deals prompted BAE into action. It asked the former Lord

Chief Justice Lord Woolf to form a committee and undertake a review of 'ethical conduct in BAE Systems plc'.

BAE told the Committee[87] that 'it does not believe that it has done anything that would constitute a criminal offence'. However, 'the Chairman [Dick Olver] and Chief Executive [Mike Turner], in discussions with us, acknowledged that the Company did not in the past pay sufficient attention to ethical standards and avoid activities that had the potential to give rise to reputational damage'. But BAE were determined that there would be no raking over the past. The Committee's task 'was not to conduct an inquiry into the truth or otherwise of the criticisms made of past conduct'.[88]

An inquiry into the truth would not have been unprecedented. Thirty years earlier, Lockheed's Special Review Committee, composed of Lockheed directors, had argued[89] that 'if the Committee were to make meaningful and effective recommendations to put an end to questionable practices...the Committee had to obtain knowledge of precisely how those practices had arisen and been perpetuated'. They had then proceeded to do exactly that.

BAE pledged to develop and implement a 'global code of ethical business conduct and reviews of key areas of ethical risk'. The Committee said:[90]

> one such risk area is the use of 'Advisers' to help obtain defence contracts. Most of the criticisms made against the Company (and indeed the defence companies more generally) have concerned allegations that such Advisers have engaged in corrupt practices. The Company, because of the ethical and reputational risks involved has taken radical action in terminating or reviewing all existing contracts it held with such Advisers.

As for the new Al Salam deal with Saudi Arabia,

> the Chairman and the Secretary to the Committee were provided by the Company with commercial information about the contract. On the basis of this information, it appeared to the Chairman that the contract should not in itself create any risks of unethical conduct by the Company.

The Americans and SFO also investigated BAE's deals in Eastern Europe. In 1999, the Czech Republic, Hungary and Poland joined the North Atlantic Treaty Organisation (NATO). NATO expected these countries to spend an extra $10 billion so their equipment was up to NATO standards.[91] This created a big opportunity for arms companies, which had suffered through a downturn in military spending since the end of the Cold War.

In 2000 the Czech Republic wanted to buy 24 to 36 new fighter aircraft to replace its Soviet-era MiG-21 aircraft.[92] In May 2001 the American and French companies withdrew from the competition[93] because[94] of 'concerns about the integrity of the process', leaving BAE and Saab only. In December the Czechs awarded a £900 million contract (worth about £1.2 billion today) for 24 Gripen fighters to BAE and Saab.[95] However, the Czech Government was unable to pass a Finance Bill in the Czech legislature which was necessary to fund the purchase.[96] So, in 2004, the Czech Government paid £400 million (worth about £488 million today) to lease 14 Gripen jets for ten years instead.[97]

In 1999 Hungary announced its intention to buy used fighter aircraft, and in June 2001 awarded Lockheed Martin the contract. A few days later, this decision was reversed[98] and the Hungarian Government decided to lease 14 Gripen jets from BAE and Saab for twelve years instead.[99] On 3 February 2003 Hungary signed an amended lease for more modern versions of the Gripen.[100]

To win these deals, BAE paid more than $19 million to companies associated with their agent. BAE accepted[101] that 'there was a high probability that part of the payments would be used in the tender process to favor BAES'.

BAE is Charged and Fined

On 29 January 2010 the SFO decided to charge BAE agent Count Alfons Mensdorff-Pouilly with corruption. The Count, from Luising in Austria, was charged[102] with conspiring

> to give or agree to give corrupt payments (contrary to section 1 of the Prevention of Corruption Act 1906) to unknown officials and other agents of certain Eastern and Central European governments, including the Czech Republic, Hungary and Austria as inducements to secure, or

as rewards for having secured, contracts from those governments for the supply of goods to them, namely SAAB/Gripen fighter jets, by BAe Systems plc.

The SFO's barrister told the Court[103] that 'from 2002 onwards, BAE adopted and deployed corrupt practices to obtain lucrative contracts for jet fighters in central Europe'. It was, he claimed, a 'sophisticated and meticulously planned operation involving very senior BAE executives'. The SFO alleged Mensdorff-Pouilly paid 'public officials to favour BAE's bids to supply Gripen jets', and that the purpose of three offshore entities created in Switzerland was to 'channel money to public officials'. The SFO alleged 'significant cash withdrawals' were often made within days or weeks of important procurement decisions, and that Mensdorff-Pouilly was paid $17 million in return for 'marketing reports' which were, the SFO's barrister alleged,[104] copied and pasted from the internet.

However, these claims were never tested in a trial. Mensdorff-Pouilly denied the allegations 'wholesale'.[105] The SFO dropped the charges when both they and the American Department of Justice announced in February 2010 they had settled with BAE.

In return for BAE pleading guilty for an accounting offence with regards to a deal in Tanzania, the SFO agreed to halt its investigation into BAE, and not prosecute the company for any conduct before February 2010.[106]

Negotiations for a deal in Tanzania had begun in 1992 when Siemens Plessey Electronic Systems attempted to sell a radar system to the Tanzanian Government for use at Dar-es-Salaam International Airport. In late 1997, BAe bought the British arm of Siemens Plessey Electronic Systems.

A Tanzanian businessman, Shailesh Vithlani, acted as an adviser to Siemens Plessey Electronic Systems from 1993.[107] A BAe committee decided to extend his contract in 1998.[108] Vithlani was promised 31 per cent of the price if the radar contract were secured. Because the percentage was so high, BAe Chairman Dick Evans approved Vithlani's reappointment.

British Aerospace Defence Systems Limited, as Siemens Plessey Electronic Systems was now called, signed a radar contract on 10 September 1999 for $39.97 million (worth about £54 million today). About one week before, BAe had changed its relationship with Vithlani.

On 2 September, Red Diamond Trading Limited signed a contract with a Panamanian company called Envers Trading Corporation, which was controlled by Vithlani.[109] In return for 'the provision of certain advice and various services as required', Envers would receive 30.025 per cent of the radar contract price. The next day BAe concluded an agreement with a Tanzanian company called Merlin International Limited, also controlled by Vithlani.[110] The same services were to be provided, in return for 1 per cent of the contract price.

The SFO found[111] that 'acting through Merlin, Vithlani was referred to by the Company as an "overt" adviser while acting through Envers, he was referred to by the Company as a "covert" adviser'.

BAe and Red Diamond were required to make payments to Merlin and Envers respectively, on receipt of payments from the Tanzanian Government due under the radar contract.[112] From January 2000 to December 2005, about £7.7 million was paid to Envers (mainly) and Merlin.[113] The money due to Vithlani as a 'covert' adviser went from BAE to Red Diamond, and then to Envers.[114] The money due to Vithlani in his 'overt' role went direct from BAE to Merlin.

BAE accepted that[115]

there was a high probability that part of the $12.4 million would be used in the negotiation process to favour British Aerospace Defence Systems Ltd…it was not possible for any person considering the accounts to investigate and determine whether the payments were properly accounted for and were lawful.

Indeed, prosecutors could not establish what Vithlani did with his money.

Reviewing this evidence, Mr Justice Bean concluded that BAE had tried to conceal[116]

the fact that they were making payments to Mr Vithlani, 97% of them via two offshore companies, with the intention that he should have free rein to make such payments to such people as he thought fit to secure the Radar Contract for [BAe], but that [BAe] did not want to know the details.

BAE agreed to plead guilty under Section 221 of the Companies Act 1985[117] for failing[118] to keep 'accounting records which were sufficient to show and explain payments made pursuant to (a) a contract between Red Diamond Trading Limited and Envers Trading Corporation, (b) a further contract between British Aerospace (Operations) Limited and Merlin International Limited'. BAE agreed to make an ex gratia payment of £30 million for the benefit of the people of Tanzania less a court fine.[119] BAE was fined £500,000 and ordered to pay the SFO £225,000 in legal costs.[120]

An American company making dubious pay-offs at that time in Africa got exemplary punishment. Titan Corporation, a military intelligence and communications company, pleaded guilty to bribery in Benin and was fined $13 million under the Foreign Corrupt Practices Act.[121] Titan had made 'social payments' to its agent, believing the money was used to pay for electoral campaigning, such as T-shirts instructing Beninese citizens to vote for President Mathieu Kérékou, who was up for re-election. In March 2001 Kérékou won the Presidential Election. Four days later, Titan was permitted to increase its contract price by more than $6 million. American prosecutors were unable to discover if Kérékou knew about the payments.

On 1 March 2010, BAE pleaded guilty[122] to conspiring to defraud the United States by impairing and impeding its lawful functions, making false statements about its Foreign Corrupt Practices Act compliance programme, and violating the Arms Export Control Act and International Traffic in Arms Regulations by failing to disclose commissions when applying for export licences. BAE was fined $400 million because 'the actions of BAE Systems impeded U.S. efforts to ensure international trade is free of corruption and to maintain control over sensitive U.S. technology' said the Acting Deputy Attorney General. The OECD was[123] 'disappointed that the UK did not consider re-opening the Al Yamamah investigation' and argued that 'the UK should have reassessed the national security issues surrounding the discontinuance [of the SFO investigation into Al Yamamah] before BAE's settlement with the US authorities'.

In May 2011, BAE agreed to settle 2,591 violations of the Arms Export Control Act and International Traffic in Arms Regulations in connection with, among other things, 'failure to report the payment of fees or commissions'. BAE was fined another $79 million, this time by the State Department.[124] The Americans could prosecute BAE and levy heavy fines because of the Arms Export Control Act that had been passed in 1976 in the wake of the Lockheed and Northrop scandals.

Because Geoffrey Edwards's litigation against Associated Electrical Industries had been hushed up by the British Government, there was no equivalent law in Britain, making it far more difficult for the SFO to prosecute BAE for its actions.

The 2011 conviction also related to BAE's conduct in South Africa. In the 1990s, a democratic government came to power in post-apartheid South Africa promising to reduce military spending in order to focus resources on healing the deep socio-economic wounds apartheid had left on South African society. However, the ruling African National Congress, which took office in 1994, decided to spend billions of rand on modern weapons. Although the South African Defence Forces' equipment was ageing, in 1994 South Africa still accounted for over 70 per cent of all defence spending in Southern Africa and had vastly more military equipment than its neighbours.[125]

In this new arms deal, signed in 1999, South Africa purchased four corvettes and three submarines from German companies, thirty light helicopters from the Italian company Agusta, 24 Hawk trainer jets from BAE, and 26 Gripen combat aircraft from BAE and Saab.

The procurement of Hawk and Gripen was curious. Neither aircraft made the final shortlist in 1995, but Defence Minister Joe Modise later changed the procurement system. In 1998 Modise told his colleagues on the selection committee that a 'visionary approach' should exclude cost from the selection criteria in South Africa's largest post-apartheid procurement and despite the great economic challenges facing the country. Hawk and Gripen were eventually selected.

According to the SFO,[126] BAE paid £115 million in commissions on the deal to a variety of different companies, some, according to American prosecutors, via Red Diamond.

One recipient of BAE money was Fana Hlongwane, Modise's political adviser from 1994 until Modise's retirement in 1999 (after the arms deal had been signed). Hlongwane received a salary from the Department of Defence, and hence was a public official. Between 2003 and 2007 BAE paid £10 million to his company, Hlongwane Consulting.[127] The SFO said[128] BAE had not provided 'any written report to justify the size of these payments'.

One SFO investigator wrote:[129]

I believe that the varied ways in which Fana Hlongwane has received payments in relation to the Hawk/Gripen contract is highly suspicious.

BAe operated a covert method of payment through the Red Diamond system, however, it appears that even this system was insufficiently opaque to disguise payments to Fana Hlongwane. As such, BAe chose to use Red Diamond and Arstow [a company registered in the British Virgin Islands] to transfer money to Mr. Hlongwane.

I suspect that this secretive arrangement was designed to facilitate any or all of the following:

(a) The onward payment of monies by Fana Hlongwane to South African government officials who could influence the decision making process on the selection of Hawk and Gripen; and/or

(b) Payments to Mr. Hlongwane himself for influence brought by him whilst he was special adviser to the Minister of Defence; and/or

(c) The onward payments of monies to Mr. Hlongwane to South African government officials to ensure that the tranching arrangements were honoured.

Although the Judicial Review action aimed at reopening the Al Yamamah investigation failed, in Britain a new Bribery Act was finally passed by Parliament in 2010, entering into force on 1 July 2011. The new Act created four new offences of corruption, including the offence of bribery of a foreign official, and contains very severe sanctions.

But will this change British corporate behaviour? It seems unlikely without vigorous law enforcement. In February 2002, the Anti-terrorism, Crime and Security Act, which extended the reach of Britain's old corruption laws overseas, became law. However, in December 2011, almost ten years later, Britain informed the OECD[130] it had convicted only three individuals and two companies for bribery overseas, with one other company convicted of an offence related to foreign bribery. The SFO's budget is forecast to be 40 per cent lower in 2014–15 than in 2008–09, without accounting for inflation. Further, notes the OECD,[131] 'police resources available to the SFO have also decreased', and it is[132] 'concerned about the SFO's resources and staff turnover'.

The SFO Investigates Another British Arms Deal with Saudi Arabia

The SFO investigation into Al Yamamah ended in 2006, but in 2012 it opened a new investigation into another British arms deal with Saudi

Arabia, known as the Saudi Arabian National Guard Communications (SANGCOM) project. This was another Government-to-Government deal, between the British Ministry of Defence and the Saudi Arabian National Guard, run until late 2010 by King Abdullah.

Like Al Yamamah, the roots of the SANGCOM project are deep in the past. The first Memorandum of Understanding was signed in 1978. The original prime contractor was Cable & Wireless, but currently GPT Special Project Management Ltd, a UK-registered company which is ultimately a subsidiary of the European aerospace conglomerate Airbus Group, supplies the fixed and mobile communications equipment. The Ministry of Defence has a team in Saudi Arabia managing this project, as it has done for Al Yamamah.

Like Al Yamamah, within the framework of the Memorandum of Understanding are a series of agreements known as Letters of Offer and Assistance, each of which deal with a particular part of the SANGCOM project.

In May 2012, *Private Eye* and *Exaro News* published[133] a schedule of payments made between 2007 and 2010 by GPT to two offshore companies. The schedule, said to have been compiled by a financial officer of GPT, shows that a total of around £14.5 million was paid to two Cayman Islands-registered companies: Simec International and Duranton International. The payments were made to HSBC accounts in London and New York.

As we saw earlier, in 1976 Ministry of Defence Permanent Secretary Frank Cooper had approved[134] the inclusion of a 3 per cent commission to a company called SIMEC International in the price of the SANGCOM project.[135] DSO officials thought[136] the commissions Cooper approved, 'although described as "technical consultancy", [amount] in practice to the exertion of influence to sway decisions in favour of the client'.

SIMEC International was a Liechtenstein 'anstalt', founded on 23 October 1975. The directors were Bryan Somerfield and Peter Austin. That month, according to then Head of Defence Sales Lester Suffield,[137] Cable & Wireless had, with Ministry of Defence approval, submitted detailed proposals for the SANGCOM project to the National Guard.

Born in 1919, Bryan Somerfield was an Arabist[138] and former RAF Intelligence Officer.[139] In 1964 he retired from the RAF and later moved to Beirut, entering the commercial world. His business partner, Peter Austin, was described by one diplomat[140] as a young 'whizz-kid'.

Somerfield was familiar with National Guard contracts. In the late 1960s, Somerfield acted for Hadsphaltic,[141] a company offering to build an underground power station for the National Guard. Somerfield was the businessman, mentioned in Chapter 3, who had been taken to the office of METICO, Fustuq's firm, and assured he would win the contract.[142]

Somerfield was well known to Ministry of Defence officials by the end of the 1960s. Then Head of Defence Sales, Raymond Brown, at his request, had endorsed[143] the Hadsphaltic offer to the National Guard. Ambassador Willie Morris was told[144] that Somerfield 'also had a special pull with the [Saudi] Royal Family'.

SIMEC advised British Leyland on agency arrangements for specialised military Land Rovers for Saudi Arabia.[145] In 1975, British Leyland won a contract to supply Land Rovers to the National Guard,[146] and the Ryder report said[147] their agent was Abdullah's brother-in-law N. Fustok.

SIMEC were then included as an agent, with Ministry of Defence approval, for the SANGCOM project. The other agent approved by Cooper was the Engineering and Trading Operations Company Beirut,[148] managed by Mahmoud Fustok.[149]

In 1978, less than three weeks after the Saudi Government had issued a new circular banning agents in arms deals and Government-to-Government deals,[150] DSO officials considered using SIMEC to sell an artillery system to the Saudi Army.[151] SIMEC had approached a DSO official in Saudi Arabia and asked for the agency, but the official 'did not ask how much of that fee was to lubricate wheels'. DSO officials were wary[152] of flying 'in the face of Saudi regulations, especially after the Randel case' when the Shah of Iran had accused the British of paying commissions to Shapoor Reporter without his knowledge. Diplomats were uneasy about approving the use of SIMEC, and suggested[153] SIMEC be described as a 'sub-contractor' rather than agent. They wryly observed that 'the law might well be honoured more in the breach than in the observance, and the Saudi's [sic] might well turn a blind eye to it in the case of honourable defence sales arrangements with the British [Ministry of Defence]'.

Ambassador John Wilton in Jedda advised[154] that the interpretation of the law would be a 'political' rather than 'a strictly legal matter'. He claimed there would be no discussion of SIMEC's role unless they were caught influence peddling (banned under the Saudi law). Diplomats told the DSO[155] they could use SIMEC if their activities 'keep them out of any trouble with the Saudis'.

In November 1980, SIMEC purchased a company called Duranton. Somerfield became Duranton's chairman, and Austin one of the other directors. Duranton were 'agents, advisers and consultants in particular to persons and institutions interested in trade between Europe and the Middle East'.[156] Two Cayman Island companies called SIMEC and Duranton were founded in 1982.[157] Austin, who bought his own Caribbean island, Little Whale Cay, in 1985, ran the companies for decades.[158]

Somerfield and Austin continued to be involved in National Guard contracts. In May 1981, Britain won another big Government-to-Government deal with the National Guard, this time a contract to provide medical services, known as SANGMED.[159] The contractor was the International Hospitals Group, but one person involved in setting up the deal was Peter Austin of Simec International,[160] who was so well-connected he negotiated personally with Abdullah. International Hospitals Group, a private healthcare company, built and managed two hospitals for the National Guard with the help of 20 Royal Engineers and a medical advisory team.[161] The contract ended in 1993. Somerfield died in February 2004.

In 2010, Ian Foxley, a former British Army officer, was appointed by GPT as Programme Director. Foxley claims[162] at least some of the Ministry of Defence SANGCOM team knew of and acquiesced in the bribes he says GPT paid. And, as we have just seen, the Ministry of Defence were aware of Somerfield's activities from the late 1960s, and knew of SIMEC's role in three National Guard contracts.

On 7 August 2012, the Director of the SFO, now David Green QC, announced[163] a criminal investigation into the 'allegations concerning GPT and aspects of the conduct of their business in the Kingdom of Saudi Arabia'.

In 2012, my MP, Stephen Pound, asked the Ministry of Defence to explain their anti-bribery procedures. Gerald Howarth, the Parliamentary Under Secretary of State (International Security Strategy) at the Ministry of Defence, replied:[164]

the Ministry of Defence is committed to the prevention, deterrence and detection of bribery. Contracts supervised by the Saudi Armed Forces Project Office are therefore subject to the same procedures and processes as all other Ministry of Defence (MOD) contracts. Additionally, as part of the verification of supplier processes and prices, and with the support of the Saudi Arabian Government, senior officials within the Project Office seek assurances from the project prime contractor that procedures are in place for the prevention of bribery, in accordance with the detailed guidance published by the Ministry of Justice.

It was a remarkable answer. At the time Howarth gave it, BAE had been convicted in America of making misleading statements to the American authorities about Al Yamamah, and fined $400 million. But the Ministry of Defence appeared not to have undertaken any serious review of the decades-old policy of relying on 'assurances' following this conviction or the revelations about the Travellers World programme. This suggests the Ministry of Defence does not take bribery much more seriously than it did decades ago.

So, given the low number of convictions achieved in the decade since Britain could prosecute companies for overseas bribery, the real test of the British Government's anti-bribery credentials will come when the SFO nears the end of its GPT investigation.

Will the Saudi Royal Family threaten the British Government again? Will the Ministry of Defence try and shut down the investigation, as it did with Al Yamamah? Will the SFO be able to prosecute?

Conclusion

Defence sales offer tempting opportunities for the unprincipled the world over.

So wrote Britain's High Commissioner to Malaysia, Sir Eric Norris, in 1976.[1] The inevitably incomplete documentary evidence from British and American arms deals reviewed in this book demonstrates, in my view, that this statement still holds true today.

Statistics about the prevalence of any illicit activity are naturally uncertain, but in 2000 the Trade Promotion Coordinating Committee of the American Government claimed[2] that about half of the bribe offers reported to it between mid 1994 and April 1999 were for arms deals. It seems likely that, as Joe Roeber claimed,[3] the arms trade is 'the most corrupt of all legal trades'. The non-governmental organisation Trace International reviewed international anti-corruption enforcement activity between 1997 and 2011 (dominated by America) and found[4] the 'aerospace/defense/security' sector was second only to 'extractive industries' in terms of the number of enforcement actions.

So arms trade corruption is almost certainly widespread today. But, you may ask, what is the problem?

Many British Government officials dislike corruption, but do not necessarily see it as harmful. Take James Craig, who served as Willie Morris's deputy at the British Embassy in Jedda from 1967 to 1970, and later as Ambassador to Saudi Arabia from 1979 to 1984. Along with Morris, he found the corruption in Saudi arms deals repugnant, and wanted to steer well clear of it. However, when Ambassador, he told London[5] that

in the particular system of corruption followed here it is hard to see that anyone is harmed. Six firms bid for a contract. Each one builds into his tender a percentage for his [CENSORED] sponsor – fixer. The contract is awarded either on merit or because it is one particular sponsor – fixer's turn for a perk. The firms are all competing on an equal basis. The commission they offer costs them nothing: if they don't win the contract, they don't pay; if they do win, the Government pays because the price is inflated. Thus Government money passes from the Government to the fixer – sponsor who becomes rich and in his turn makes other people better off (managers, clerks, drivers, servants, henchmen, clients). It is a kind of unstructured social service benefit. It wouldn't suit you or me; but you and I have Western consciences and standards.

He wrote that 'corruption in the Arab world is not regarded as the heinous offence it is in the West'. I single out Craig's comments merely because they illustrate a way of thinking expressed by many at the time the Serious Fraud Office halted its Al Yamamah investigation.

In grand corruption, those taking bribes betray their nation. Even in the oil-rich countries of the Persian Gulf, such as Saudi Arabia, where direct taxation is non-existent, the substantial revenues siphoned off by corruption are still resources that could have been used for the benefit of the population. Further, though it is easy to forget, now the Gulf states have been oil-rich for decades, their oil reserves, which provide over half of Government revenues in most Gulf states,[6] are finite. Thus revenues lost through corruption are a permanent cost to the people of these countries.

In the many countries which are not as well endowed with natural resources, there are huge direct human costs to corruption. In South Africa, for example, the Government claimed in 1999 the arms deal described in Chapter 9 would cost $5 billion.[7] At the same time President Thabo Mbeki said South Africa could not afford anti-retroviral medication for the more than 5 million South Africans living with HIV/AIDS (Human Immunodeficiency Virus/Acquired Immunodeficiency Syndrome).[8] A Harvard University study[9] estimates that between 2000 and 2005, more than 330,000 South Africans died because they could not afford anti-HIV therapies. They further estimate that the lack of medication also resulted in 35,000 babies being born with HIV. Eventually the South African Government agreed to subsidise anti-HIV therapies but by 2008 still spent 7.63 rand on the arms deal for every rand spent on anti-HIV therapies.[10]

Between 2000 and 2008, the amount spent on the arms deal exceeded South Africa's housing budget, and was equivalent to 64 per cent of the education budget and 84 per cent of the health budget.[11] This was a great betrayal of a people who had hoped their lives would be transformed for the better in post-apartheid South Africa.

Grand corruption sets the tone for everyone else. It encourages, or at least legitimises, petty corruption, or the 'everyday abuse of entrusted power by low- and mid-level public officials in their interactions with ordinary citizens'.[12] Laurence Cockcroft shows in his book *Global Corruption: Money, Power and Ethics in the Modern World*[13] the profound and malign everyday impacts of corruption on the lives of ordinary people in the developing world.

The notion that that those in the developing world see corruption as part of their way of life is, in the West, a self-serving lazy cliché that cannot be sustained by the evidence. In the mid 1970s most developing countries had laws banning corruption. Even in Saudi Arabia, decrees banning corruption were issued in 1968, 1975 and 1978. Why would the elites in these countries do that if they believed their populations thought corruption was acceptable? Why have the elites in the developing world always gone to such great lengths to keep their own corrupt behaviour secret?

Most British diplomats were alive to the reality of public opinion. Morris wrote in 1970[14] that were there a revolution in Saudi Arabia, he was 'quite sure that a main subject of revolutionary interest and fervour would be past arms purchases and the corrupt dealings surrounding them'. He described corruption as a 'time bomb under the regime'.

Would those Britons who believe that 'it is hard to see that anyone is harmed' by bribes paid by British companies overseas be able to accept the following? Suppose Lockheed Martin, in their attempt to sell F-35 Joint Strike Fighters to the British Armed Forces, had set up a £8 million per year 'slush fund' for the Commander of the Royal Air Force, and operated it for the lifetime of a 20-year contract. Would they look upon this with equanimity? Would they accept an American argument that the corruption was harmless, and that, in any event, the Americans needed the high-tech jobs the deal provided? The argument that some bribery overseas by big business is 'harmless' or unimportant is, self-evidently, hypocrisy and has no substance or validity.

Books of this kind, which describe an important problem in some detail, usually find difficulty in describing a convincing solution or alternative. One can tackle bribery by looking at the 'demand' side and the 'supply' side.

However, we must accept that corruption can never be totally eradicated. Like other forms of theft, such as burglary, it will always be with us. For a significant proportion of humanity infidelity will always be tempting. Great temptations, especially those provided by high office and vast sums, make infidelity more likely. No law or other initiative can change this reality. But, as with burglary, it is in humanity's interests to devise laws, institutions and cultures that minimise the prevalence and impact of this very damaging misdemeanour.

As it is impossible to change human nature, tackling the demand side will not, on its own, be sufficient to reduce significantly the prevalence of bribery in the arms trade or other areas of international trade. Technical measures, such as those promoted by Transparency International's Defence and Security Programme,[15] to reduce the risk of corruption within customer Governments, are worthwhile and should be whole-heartedly supported, but are unlikely on their own to have much impact. Nor should we suppose that the current trend towards democratisation in the developing world, welcome though it is, will automatically reduce corrupt behaviour.

Thus action on the 'supply side' is vital. What I hope this book has clearly shown is that companies will pay bribes where they are tempted by large contracts and face ineffective (or non-existent) laws (or enforcement of laws) against overseas corruption. In democracies such as Britain and America, Governments try and steer clear of involvement in corruption because they are accountable to legislatures which are responsive to an extent to public opinion. Large companies are instead accountable to shareholders, in practice the small number of individuals who control the main institutional shareholdings.

We should not suppose that voluntary 'ethical' corporate policies will solve the problem. In 1978 the Chairman of British Aerospace (BAe), Lord Frank Beswick, sent a draft BAe statement on 'business ethics' to the Department of Industry. It said:[16] 'under no circumstances will the Corporation countenance corrupt practices including payments or other inducements being given by Corporation employees to political parties, Government officials or a customer's executives'. I hope this book has provided the evidence you need to evaluate the effectiveness of that statement.

The first requirement for effective supply-side action against corruption is strict laws in importing countries, but also, more importantly, in the countries of major exporters too. This will not solve the problem but it will help. The Lockheed scandal in the 1970s led to the passing of the Foreign Corrupt Practices Act, yet the Lockheed Corporation still paid bribes in the late 1980s in Egypt.

At least Lockheed was caught and punished. The fact that laws will not eradicate a problem is not an argument for failing to introduce effective laws. Only the perverse would argue that because burglary is still present in Britain we should weaken or abandon burglary laws.

Equally important is that all countries enforce anti-bribery laws. The Organisation for Economic Co-operation and Development (OECD) Working Group on Bribery must rely largely on peer review and scrutiny of countries which have signed the Anti-Bribery Convention, to apply pressure on countries to adopt and enforce effective laws. In a recent (2011) Annual Report of the Working Group, the OECD Secretary-General says the Convention 'has been quite effective'.[17] In the first twelve years, 14 countries convicted 90 companies and nearly 210 individuals for bribery. At the end of 2011 there were approximately 300 investigations into overseas bribery underway in 26 countries.

Unfortunately, though the Working Group's peer review work has been extremely important and led to many worthwhile changes, the OECD's existing tools have not enabled it to ensure the Convention is being implemented and enforced the same everywhere. In 2011 the OECD produced summaries of the steps each country had taken to implement and enforce the Convention since 1998. A comparison of the reports about America and Britain is revealing. The report about America runs to 136 pages; Britain's to a mere five pages. It seems that to make the Convention more effective, other means are needed so that countries who are not fully complying face real sanctions.

Another enforcement requirement is that companies that are convicted of corruption or corruption-related offences face severe sanction. For its actions in the Czech Republic, Hungary and Saudi Arabia, BAE was fined $400 million in America by the Department of Justice and $79 million by the Department of State. In Britain, BAE was fined £500,000 for its actions in Tanzania (as well as having to make an ex gratia payment to Tanzania of £29.5 million). For a company which earned over $33 billion from military contracts in 2010,[18] these penalties (of just over $500 million) are not trivial, but neither are they a serious financial problem (just over 1.5 per cent of BAE's military revenues for 2010). Further, BAE has not been barred at all from the public procurement process in Britain and America (and, needless to say, Saudi Arabia), the company's most lucrative markets.

Penalties for corporate corruption or corruption-related offences need to be more than something that can be written off or managed as just another business risk. The penalty needs to cause serious prejudice to the current financial health of the business, or the company's future chances of winning business for a certain period, just as a conviction for a serious crime for an individual seriously prejudices their future employment and other prospects. If this happens, it is much less likely that guilty corporate leaders will be able to keep their jobs or find alternative executive employment. They will have a powerful incentive to stay clean.

Transparency is another key issue. One reason arms trade and other grand corruption flourishes is secrecy. This is greatly aided by the offshore financial system, which is very difficult even for law enforcement officials to penetrate, and a substantial part of which is located in British-connected jurisdictions. Britain has a huge disincentive to undermine this offshore system, as the enormous amounts of money held offshore are very valuable to the British economy. For example, Cockcroft points out the British Treasury published a report in 2009 estimating the Crown Dependencies 'had contributed "net financing" of \$332.5 billion to [British] banks in the second quarter of 2009'.[19] The necessary changes which would make it as easy for law enforcement authorities to investigate financial crimes in offshore jurisdictions as it is in Britain or America, would, one imagines, make the offshore jurisdictions less attractive places for illicit money. Thus until, for some other reasons, flows from offshore financial centres become less important to the British financial system, it is hard to see the British Government dismantling the secrecy that surrounds the offshore system.

Transparency would not just make it easier to convict companies that pay bribes overseas. It might also make it easier to recover the proceeds. Currently, officials and their associates can extort bribes from foreign companies knowing that even if the company is convicted of bribery, they will in all likelihood still keep their ill-gotten gains. However, much of the money paid out in bribes is held in the financial system of OECD countries, or offshore secrecy jurisdictions under the ambit of OECD countries (because most wealthy people prefer the legal certainty that holding money in Western or Western-oriented jurisdictions brings with it). If transparency makes it easier to recover the proceeds of bribery from the recipients, then extortion may become a much less attractive practice for foreign rulers, politicians, officials and their associates.

Undoubtedly, a great deal of progress has been made over the last 50 years. The British Government no longer actively facilitates arms trade corruption, and indeed Britain now has one of the strongest anti-bribery laws in the world. Those changes have been mainly caused by external pressures, rather than a real desire of British Governments to stamp out corruption.

Impunity and secrecy are two key problems that still need to be overcome. Thus, despite British arms companies now claiming that they have reformed and the problem of corruption is in the past, we are only at the start of the road to reducing arms trade corruption significantly. All countries need to emulate the Americans and step up their enforcement efforts, and impose penalties on companies that bribe that would constitute exemplary punishment and a real deterrent to paying bribes. But to assist these law enforcement efforts, reform of the offshore system is needed. Achieving these goals is far from straightforward, and will likely take many years.

Notes

Where Uniform Resource Locators (website addresses) are given, all were last accessed on 27 February 2013.

Introduction

1. Frank Vogl, *Waging War on Corruption: Inside the Movement Fighting the Abuse of Power*, Plymouth: Rowman & Littlefield, 2012, p. 114.
2. OECD, *Corruption: A Glossary of International Standards in Criminal Law*, Paris: OECD, 2008, pp. 34–6.
3. OECD, *Corruption*, op cit., p. 22.
4. http://www.transparency.org/whoweare/organisation/faqs_on_corruption.
5. Department of Justice, Press Release, 1 March 2010.
6. Rachel Stohl and Suzette Grillot, *The International Arms Trade*, Cambridge: Polity Press, 2009, p. 17.
7. Ibid., p. 34.
8. Ibid., pp. 18–20.
9. Ibid., p. 14.
10. Anthony Sampson, *The Arms Bazaar: The Companies, the Dealers, the Bribes: From Vickers to Lockheed*, Sevenoaks: Hodder and Stoughton, 1983.
11. Ibid., p. 54.
12. 'Witness Statement of Joe Roeber', paragraphs 47–51, *Gilby* v *IC* [2008] UKIT EA_2007_0071.
13. *Gilby* v *IC* [2008] UKIT EA_2007_0071.
14. At the end of the 1980s, the Foreign and Commonwealth Office received around 40,000 secret reports per year, two thirds from GCHQ and one third from SIS (Richard Norton-Taylor, *Truth is a Difficult Concept: Inside the Scott Inquiry*, London: Fourth Estate, 1995, p. 100). Frank Brenchley, who was the Head of the Arabian Department at the Foreign and Commonwealth Office from 1963 to 1967 and Assistant Under Secretary for the Middle East from 1967 to 1969, confirmed that 'quite often' the SIS and GCHQ provided 'extremely valuable information' about Middle Eastern Governments (Frank Brenchley, *Britain, The Six-Day War and Its Aftermath*, London: I.B. Tauris, 2005, p. xxii).
15. Lockheed Aircraft Corporation, *Report of the Special Review Committee of the Board of Directors Lockheed Aircraft Corporation*, Burbank: Lockheed Aircraft Corporation, 1977, p. 14.
16. Ibid.

Chapter 1

1. M.C.G. Man to M. Stewart, 'Mr. Man's First Impressions on returning to Saudi Arabia', 15 March 1965, FO 371/179885, The National Archives (hereafter TNA).

2. C.T. Crowe to A.F. Douglas-Home, 22 July 1963, FO 371/168869, TNA.

3. M.C.G. Man to M. Stewart, 'Mr. Man's First Impressions on returning to Saudi Arabia', 15 March 1965, FO 371/179885, TNA.

4. C.T. Crowe to R.A. Butler, 'Sir Colin Crowe's Valedictory Despatch', 14 October 1964, FO 371/174676, TNA.

5. W. Morris to A.F. Douglas-Home, 'On leaving Saudi Arabia', 13 May 1972, FCO 8/1907, TNA.

6. C.T. Crowe to A.F. Douglas-Home, 30 June 1963, FO 371/168869, TNA.

7. C.T. Crowe to A.F. Douglas-Home, 31 August 1963, FO 371/168869, TNA.

8. C.T. Crowe to A.F. Douglas-Home, 30 June 1963, FO 371/168869, TNA.

9. Gerald De Gaury, Faisal: King of Saudi Arabia, Louisville: Fons Vitae, 2007, p. 95.

10. Frank Brenchley, Britain and the Middle East: An Economic History, 1945–87, London: Lester Crook Academic Publishing, 1989, p. 82.

11. C.T. Crowe to A.F. Douglas-Home, 30 June 1963, FO 371/168869, TNA.

12. M.C.G. Man to M. Stewart, 'Mr. Man's First Impressions on returning to Saudi Arabia', 15 March 1965, FO 371/179885, TNA.

13. 'Third Report of the British Military Mission to the Saudi Arabian National Guard', FCO 8/783, TNA.

14. A.J.M. Craig to M. Stewart, 'The Jedda Scene', 31 July 1969, FCO 8/1203, TNA.

15. C.T. Crowe to R.A. Butler, 'Sir Colin Crowe's Valedictory Despatch', 14 October 1964, FO 371/174676, TNA.

16. JIC(65)90 (Final), 9 May 1966, CAB 158/60, TNA.

17. H.R. Hubert to D.N. Brinson, 2 February 1967, FCO 46/190, TNA.

18. Daily Express, 25 July 1966 and R. Stevens to Arabian Department, 7 August 1963, FO 371/168887, TNA.

19. G.E. Knight to G. Edwards, 17 February 1964, SC/MSS/165/1/2/1/9, Caldecote Papers, The Institution for Engineering and Technology (hereafter IET).

20. G. Edwards to P.A.R. Carrington, 24 August 1971, DEFE 13/649, TNA.

21. Alan Whicker, Journey of a Lifetime, London: HarperCollins, 2009, pp. 172–3.

22. E. Carr, 'Middle East Report No.2/64. Saudi Arabia', 19 June 1964, SC/MSS/165/1/2/1/9, Caldecote Papers, IET.

23. M.A. Marshall to F.C. Mason, 15 May 1963, FO 371/168882, TNA.

24. Ibid.

25. R. Stevens to Arabian Department, 7 August 1963, FO 371/168887, TNA.

26. R.S. Crawford to Arabian Department, 29 June 1962, FO 371/163018, TNA.

27. M.A. Marshall, 'Conversation with Mr. Samson and Mr. Pett-Ridge of B.A.C.', 16 May 1963, FO 371/168886, TNA.

28. L.A. Sanson to F.W. Higginson, 12 August 1963, SC/MSS/165/1/2/1/9, Caldecote Papers, IET.

29. *Who's Who in Saudi Arabia 1983-84: Third Edition*, Jeddah: Tihama, 1983–1984, p. 249.

30. L.A. Sanson to F.W. Higginson, 12 August 1963, SC/MSS/165/1/2/1/9, Caldecote Papers, IET.

31. Ibid.

32. Ibid.

33. Ibid.

34. G.E. Knight to Prince Sultaan, 28 August 1963, SC/MSS/165/1/2/1/9, Caldecote Papers, IET.

35. W. Morris to M. Stewart, 'Saudi Arabian Foreign Policy', 10 April 1969, FCO 8/1172, TNA.

36. M.C.G. Man to M. Stewart, 'Mr. Man's First Impressions on returning to Saudi Arabia', 15 March 1965, FO 371/179885, TNA.

37. De Gaury, op cit., p. 95.

38. F. Legh to D.I. Morphet, 'King FAISAL bin Abdul Aziz', 20 June 1967, FCO 8/821, TNA.

39. De Gaury, op cit., p. 96.

40. C.T. Crowe to A.F. Douglas-Home, 31 July 1963, FO 371/168878, TNA.

41. L.A. Sanson to Lord Caldecote, 12 December 1963, SC/MSS/165/1/2/1/9, Caldecote Papers, IET.

42. 'Record of Conversation. Arms for Saudi Arabia', 12 February 1964, FO 371/174682, TNA.

43. C.T. Crowe, 'Lightning', 9 February 1964, FO 371/174682, TNA.

44. 'Record of Conversation. Arms for Saudi Arabia', 12 February 1964, FO 371/174682, TNA.

45. A.G. Duguid to Lord Caldecote, 11 February 1964, SC/MSS/165/1/2/1/9, Caldecote Papers, IET.

46. G.E. Knight to G. Edwards, 17 February 1964, SC/MSS/165/1/2/1/9, Caldecote Papers, IET.

47. Ibid.

48. 'Report on a Visit to Saudi Arabia by the Sales and Service Director 8th to 13th, March 1965.', SC/MSS/165/1/2/1/9, Caldecote Papers, IET.

49. L.A. Sanson to F.W. Higginson, 12 August 1963, SC/MSS/165/1/2/1/9, Caldecote Papers, IET.

50. 'Saudi Arabia Report No. 10', 18 October 1967, SC/MSS/165/1/2/1/3, Caldecote Papers, IET.

51. W. Morris to D.J. McCarthy, 7 November 1968, FCO 8/1190, TNA.

52. G. Edwards to A.G. Duguid, 7 August 1964, SC/MSS/165/1/2/1/9, Caldecote Papers, IET.

53. 'Re-amended Statement of Claim', paragraph 1, *Geoffrey Edwards* v *Associated Electrical Industries Ltd* (hereafter *Edwards* v *AEI*), 8 March 1974, FCO 8/2347, TNA.

54. 'Statement of Claim', paragraph 3, *Abdul Rahman Bin Abdul Aziz Al Saud* v. *Associated Electrical Industries Ltd* (hereafter *Abdul Rahman* v *AEI*), 6 October 1970, FCO 8/2347, TNA.

55. Ibid.

56. Airwork, 'Air Defence Project. Building Requirement', 22 November 1966, SC/MSS/165/1/2/1/3, Caldecote Papers, IET.

57. G.M. Hobday, 'Visit Report', 24 December 1965, SC/MSS/165/1/2/1/9, Caldecote Papers, IET.

58. C.T. Crowe, 'Lightning', 9 February 1964, FO 371/174682, TNA.

59. G. Edwards to A.G. Duguid, 7 August 1964, SC/MSS/165/1/2/1/9, Caldecote Papers, IET.

60. Jedda Telegram No.306 to Foreign Office, 11 May 1964, FO 371/174683, TNA.

61. A.G. Duguid to B. Cookson, 17 June 1964, SC/MSS/165/1/2/1/9, Caldecote Papers, IET.

62. Ibid.

63. B. Cookson to A.G. Duguid, 18 June 1964, SC/MSS/165/1/2/1/9, Caldecote Papers, IET.

64. A.G. Duguid to B. Cookson, 17 June 1964, SC/MSS/165/1/2/1/9, Caldecote Papers, IET.

65. G. Edwards to Lord Caldecote, 15 March 1964, SC/MSS/165/1/2/1/9, Caldecote Papers, IET and G. Edwards, 'Report. Position in Saudi Arabia as at 30th January 1965', FO 371/179888, TNA.

66. G. Edwards, 'Report. Position in Saudi Arabia as at 30th January 1965', FO 371/179888, TNA.

67. G. Edwards to A.G. Duguid, 7 August 1964, SC/MSS/165/1/2/1/9, Caldecote Papers, IET.

68. *Foreign Relations of the United States, 1964–1968: Volume XXI, Near East Region; Arabian Peninsula*, Washington: US Government Printing Office, 2000, Document 240, p. 464.

69. Lord Caldecote to N. Marten, 7 November 1963, FO 371/168898, TNA.

70. G. Edwards, 'Report. Position in Saudi Arabia as at 30th January 1965', FO 371/179888, TNA.

71. Ibid.

72. G.M. Hobday to F.W. Page, 11 March 1965, SC/MSS/165/1/2/1/9, Caldecote Papers, IET.

73. Ibid.

74. G.M. Hobday to Lord Caldecote, 3 March 1965, SC/MSS/165/1/2/1/9, Caldecote Papers, IET.

75. G.M. Hobday to F.W. Page, 5 April 1965, SC/MSS/165/1/2/1/9, Caldecote Papers, IET.

76. 'The Anglo-American Arms Deal: A Chronological Summary', FO 371/185493, TNA.

77. H.A. Copeman to A.J. Gower Isaac, 10 February 1966, T 225/2004, TNA.

78. 'Statement of Claim', paragraph 11, *Abdul Rahman v AEI*, 6 October 1970, FCO 8/2347, TNA.

79. M.C.G. Man to M. Stewart, 13 December 1965, FO 371/179886, TNA.

80. W. Morris to H.J.L. Suffield, 11 February 1970, FCO 8/1498, TNA.

81. John Stonehouse, *Death of an Idealist*, London: W.H. Allen, 1975, p. 48.

82. Ibid., p. 49.

83. Foreign Office Telegram No.728 to Jedda, 31 July 1964, FO 371/174683, TNA.

84. D.W. Healey to Prince Sultan, 23 December 1964, FO 371/174683, TNA.

85. Stonehouse, op cit., pp. 52–3.

86. Ibid., p. 50.

87. Ibid., p. 53.

88. R. Jenkins to H. Wilson, 24 November 1965, T 312/1135, TNA.

89. H. Wilson to R. Jenkins, 24 November 1965, T 312/1135, TNA.

90. Stonehouse, op cit., p. 77.

91. J.W. Adderley to J.P. Sheen, 19 December 1966, FCO 8/792, TNA.

92. R.J. Raff to F.W. Higginson, 1 July 1965, SC/MSS/165/1/2/1/9, Caldecote Papers, IET.

93. GEN 90(78)1, 23 February 1978, CAB 130/1016, TNA and M.J. Kerry to F.R. Mingay, 3 March 1978, PJ 1/55, TNA. As explained in Chapter 9, this view of the Prevention of Corruption Act 1906 differed from that given by the British Government to the OECD in the 2000s. However, what matters here is how the law was perceived at around the time Edwards was making payments.

94. Patrick Bannerman of the Foreign and Commonwealth Office saw the documents showing which 'influential Saudis' Edwards had paid money to. See J.P. Bannerman to T.J. Clark, 27 June 1975, FCO 8/2586, TNA.

95. H.J. Lee, 'Development of a Saudi Arabian Navy, Brief for Chairman', July 1968, File 871, Vickers Archive, Cambridge University Library (hereafter VA).

96. L. Redshaw to Messrs G. Gatti & Co., 24 July 1968, File 871, VA.

97. L. Redshaw to H.E. Bell, 1 August 1968, File 871, VA.

98. H.E. Bell to L. Redshaw, 13 August 1968, File 871, VA.

99. H.E. Bell to L. Redshaw, 14 August 1968, File 871, VA.

100. Wingetac Telex No.567 to L. Redshaw, 15 August 1968, File 871, VA.

101. L. Redshaw to R.P.H. Yapp, 20 August 1968, File 871, VA.

102. P. Sabersky to R.P.H. Yapp, 23 August 1968, File 871, VA.

103. L. Redshaw to Dr Erwin Haymann, 2 September 1968, File 871, VA.

104. 'The Royal Saudi Arabian Navy', NISUM N/7484/73, DEFE 63/25, TNA.

105. United States Senate, *Hearings before the Subcommittee on Multinational Corporations of the Committee on Foreign Relations, 94th Congress., 2nd Session., Part 14*, Washington: U.S. Government Printing Office, 1976, p. 91.

106. Ibid.

107. David Boulton, *The Lockheed Papers*, London: Jonathan Cape, 1978, p. 7.

108. United States Senate, *Hearings, 94th Congress., 2nd Session., Part 14*, op cit., pp. 343–7, 349–50 and 353.

109. Ibid.

110. Report by Commissie van Drie, 26 August 1976, Chapter 2, p. 11, FCO 33/3014, TNA.

111. Mark Phythian, *The Politics of British Arms Sales Since 1964*, Manchester: Manchester University Press, 2000, p. 3.

112. Ibid., p. 61.

113. *Export of Defence Equipment: Report of an Inquiry by Sir Donald Stokes*, 12 November 1965, Appendix A, AVIA 65/1690, TNA.

114. 'Note of a Meeting between The Minister (RAF) and Sir Donald Stokes on 7th July', WO 32/21301, TNA.

115. 'Extract from minutes of Defence Perm Sec's mtg. on 14 July 1965', AVIA 65/1690, TNA.

116. *Export of Defence Equipment: Report of an Inquiry by Sir Donald Stokes*, 12 November 1965, p. 10, AVIA 65/1690, TNA.

117. Ibid., p. 35.

118. *Hansard*, House of Commons, Vol. 723, 1965–66, 25 January 1966, Col. 64.

119. P.H. Gore-Booth to All Heads of Mission in Foreign Countries, 27 October 1966, DEFE 13/509, TNA.

Chapter 2

1. M.S. Weir to J.M. Brown, 26 May 1965, FO 371/179889, TNA.

2. D.I. Morphet to J.M. Brown, 11 August 1965, FO 371/179890, TNA.

3. J.M. Brown to D.I. Morphet, 25 August 1965, FO 371/179890, TNA.

4. C.D. Wiggin to W. Morris, 13 March 1965, FO 371/180660, TNA.

5. H.R. Hubert to I.R. Courtney, 5 March 1965, FO 371/180660, TNA.

6. Ibid.

7. Ibid.

8. W. Morris, 'Appointment of a Lebanese agent to sell British Arms in the Middle East', 17 March 1965, FO 371/180660, TNA.

9. H.R. Hubert to W. Morris, 24 March 1965, FO 371/180660, TNA.

10. C.D. Wiggin to W. Morris, 10 April 1965, FO 371/180660, TNA.

11. R.S. Crawford to H.A. Caccia, 18 March 1965, FO 371/180660, TNA.

12. W. Morris to C.D. Wiggin, 8 October 1965, FO 371/180660, TNA.

13. D.N. Brinson to L.C.W. Figg, 18 January 1967, FCO 46/190, TNA.

14. H.R. Hubert to D.N. Brinson, 2 February 1967, FCO 46/190, TNA.
15. L.C.W. Figg to D.N. Brinson, 22 February 1967, FCO 46/190, TNA.
16. C. Hewertson to J.A. Patterson, 4 May 1967, T 225/2918, TNA.
17. 'Agents', DEFE 68/96, TNA.
18. J. Moreton to J. Patterson, 5 September 1967, T 225/2918, TNA.
19. R.F. Brown to D.W. Healey, 15 October 1969, DEFE 23/68, TNA.
20. 'Agreement between the United Kingdom Ministry of Defence (Directorate of Army Sales) and The Commercial and Industrial Company Limited, Amman, represented by Mr Shehadah Twal', 24 November 1969, DEFE 68/96, TNA.
21. T.E. Nissen to C. Hewertson, 4 August 1969, DEFE 68/96, TNA.
22. Ibid.
23. R.F. Brown to D.W. Healey, 15 October 1969, DEFE 23/68, TNA.
24. T.E. Nissen to H.R. Hubert, 4 December 1970, DEFE 68/96, TNA.
25. T.E. Nissen to H.R. Braden, 10 July 1972, DEFE 68/96, TNA.
26. C.D. Wiggin to W. Morris, 10 April 1965, FO 371/180660, TNA.
27. Memorandum, 'Visit to Saudi Arabia by Commander R.G. Gaunt, DSC, RN. 5th–13th April 1968', FCO 8/787, TNA.
28. Ibid.
29. 'Country Assessment Sheet. Lebanon', June 1971, FCO 17/1446, TNA.
30. C.E. King to M. Stewart, 'Lebanon: Annual Review for 1969', 5 February 1970, FCO 17/1104, TNA.
31. P.H.G. Wright to A.F. Douglas-Home, 'First Impressions of Lebanon', 4 March 1972, FCO 17/1711, TNA.
32. D.A. Keown-Boyd to R.Y. Birley, 4 June 1971, FCO 17/1450, TNA.
33. C.E. King to J.P. Tripp, 1 April 1970, FCO 17/1119, TNA.
34. D.A. Keown-Boyd to R.Y. Birley, 4 June 1971, FCO 17/1450, TNA.
35. C.E. King to J.P. Tripp, 1 April 1970, FCO 17/1119, TNA.
36. D.A. Keown-Boyd to R.Y. Birley, 4 June 1971, FCO 17/1450, TNA.
37. J.A. Davidson to T.L. Crosthwait, 10 December 1968, FCO 8/1200, TNA.
38. D.A. Keown-Boyd to R.Y. Birley, 4 June 1971, FCO 17/1450, TNA.
39. Beirut Telegram OYO/052 to Ministry of Defence, 11 February 1971, FCO 17/1449, TNA.
40. H.R. Hubert, 'Visit to Beirut 13–18 February 1971', 19 February 1971, FCO 17/1449, TNA.
41. Ibid.
42. D.A. Keown-Boyd to R.Y. Birley, 4 June 1971, FCO 17/1450, TNA.
43. Ibid.
44. H.R. Hubert, 'Visit to Beirut 13–18 February 1971', 19 February 1971, FCO 17/1449, TNA.
45. H.R. Hubert to V.E. Beckett, 25 March 1971, FCO 17/1449, TNA.
46. H.R. Hubert to S.A.R. Cawston, 24 February 1971, FCO 17/1449, TNA.
47. H.R. Hubert to V.E. Beckett, 25 March 1971, FCO 17/1449, TNA.

48. A.J. Sindall to V.E. Beckett, 21 May 1971, FCO 17/1449, TNA.

49. Beirut Telegram OYQ/EBR 188 to Ministry of Defence, 5 June 1971, FCO 17/1449, TNA.

50. H.R. Hubert to APS/Minister of State (DP), 21 June 1971, FCO 17/1450, TNA.

51. D. Sales(1), 'Visit to the Lebanon 16–20 May 1971', FCO 17/1449, TNA.

52. Coopers & Lybrand, 'Interim Report on Millbank Technical Services Limited', March 1975, p. 3, CAOG 18/676, TNA.

53. R.F. Brown to D.W. Healey, 15 October 1969, DEFE 23/68, TNA.

54. D.A. Keown-Boyd to J.A. Kershaw, 27 July 1971, FCO 17/1450, TNA.

55. H.R. Hubert to APS/Minister of State (DP), 21 June 1971, FCO 17/1450, TNA.

56. Ministry of Defence Telegram DIG OYQ to Beirut, 13 August 1971, FCO 17/1450, TNA.

57. Beirut Telegram OYQ 234 to Ministry of Defence, 5 August 1971, FCO 17/1450, TNA.

58. Ministry of Defence Telegram DIG OYQ to Beirut, 13 August 1971, FCO 17/1450, TNA.

59. Beirut Telegram OYQ to Ministry of Defence, 15 August 1971, FCO 17/1450, TNA.

60. Ministry of Defence Telegram DIG OYQ to Beirut, 13 August 1971, FCO 17/1450, TNA.

61. Beirut Telegram No.414 to Foreign and Commonwealth Office, 21 September 1971, FCO 17/1451, TNA.

62. Beirut Telegram No.434 to Foreign and Commonwealth Office, 28 September 1971, FCO 17/1451, TNA.

63. Beirut Telegram OYQ303 to Ministry of Defence, 4 October 1971, FCO 17/1451, TNA.

64. B.G. Dove to H.J.L. Suffield, 18 October 1971, FCO 17/1451, TNA.

65. Beirut Telegram OYQ 348 to Ministry of Defence, 5 November 1971, FCO 17/1451, TNA.

66. Beirut Telegram OYQ 361 to Ministry of Defence, 25 November 1971, FCO 17/1451, TNA.

67. Beirut Telegram to Ministry of Defence, 29 November 1971, FCO 17/1451, TNA.

68. P.H.G. Wright to R.M. Evans, 4 December 1971, FCO 17/1451, TNA.

69. Beirut Telegram OYQ 389 to Ministry of Defence, 23 December 1971, FCO 17/1451, TNA.

70. I.R. Callan to V.E. Beckett, 22 July 1972, FCO 17/1714, TNA.

71. J.F. Doble to M.L.H. Hope, 18 December 1972, FCO 17/1714, TNA.

72. Beirut Telegram EDQ23 to Ministry of Defence, 19 January 1973, FCO 93/107, TNA.

73. P.H.G. Wright to A.D. Parsons, 28 March 1973, FCO 93/107, TNA.

74. Beirut Telegram No.727 to Foreign and Commonwealth Office, 11 October 1973, FCO 93/107, TNA.

75. Arms Working Party, 'Extract of Minutes of a Meeting held on Tuesday, 23rd July 1963', FO 371/168887, TNA.

76. War Office Telegram No.927 to Jedda, 20 February 1964, FO 371/174682, TNA and Ministry of Defence Telegram ONR 0861 to Jedda, 3 June 1966, FO 371/185493, TNA.

77. Paris Telegram No.204 to Foreign Office, 27 February 1968, FCO 8/781, TNA.

78. T.N. Bromage to SO to MD/HDS, 3 May 1968, WO 32/20242, TNA.

79. Ministry of Defence Telegram OYQ to Jedda, 13 September 1968, FCO 8/782, TNA.

80. W. Morris to A.J.D. Stirling, 6 November 1968, FCO 8/1187, TNA.

81. A.J.M. Craig to W.H. Fullerton, 12 February 1969, FCO 8/1187, TNA.

82. A.J.D. Stirling to T.F. Brenchley, 'Tanks for Saudi Arabia', 19 December 1967, FCO 8/780, TNA.

83. J.H. Robbie to The Director of Procurement, Saudi Arabian Defence Forces, 11 March 1968, File 871, VA.

84. Memorandum, 'Prices of Vickers Offer for 175 Tanks', DEFE 68/136, TNA.

85. Jedda Telegram DA/83 to Foreign and Commonwealth Office, 22 April 1968, FCO 8/781, TNA.

86. J.H. Robbie to T.L. Rowan, 21 October 1968, File 871, VA.

87. B.S. Heath to J.H. Robbie, 'Visit to Saudi Arabia by Colonel B.S.Heath 4th – 6th August 1968', 8 August 1968, File 871, VA.

88. D.J. McCarthy to R.A. Burroughs, 'Tanks for Saudi Arabia', 25 September 1968, FCO 8/782, TNA.

89. Jedda Telegram No.54 to Foreign Office, 24 January 1968, FCO 8/780, TNA.

90. Jedda Telegram No.624 to Foreign and Commonwealth Office, 17 October 1968, FCO 8/1187, TNA.

91. J.H. Robbie to T.L. Rowan, 21 October 1968, File 871, VA.

92. Jedda Telegram No.636 to Foreign and Commonwealth Office, 28 October 1968, FCO 8/1187, TNA.

93. D.J. McCarthy to W. Morris, 18 October 1968, FCO 8/1187, TNA.

94. W. Morris to D.J. McCarthy, 31 October 1968, FCO 8/1187, TNA.

95. B.S. Heath to T.L. Rowan, 'Visit to Saudi Arabia – 22nd to 26th September 1969. Report by Col. B.S. Heath', 29 September 1969, File 871, VA.

96. Ibid.

97. W.M. Wingate Gray to DIS, MoD, 10 December 1971, TNA, FCO 8/1754.

98. W.G. Neilson, 'Report for February/March 1970', 8 April 1970, FCO 8/1501, TNA.

99. W. Morris to H.J.L. Suffield, 11 February 1970, FCO 8/1498, TNA.

100. W. Morris to A.J.D. Stirling, 22 January 1969, FCO 8/1200, TNA.

101. W. Morris to R. McGregor, 16 February 1969, FCO 8/1191, TNA.

102. Author's calculations from *BP Statistical Review of World Energy June 2012*, 'Oil Production – barrels (from 1965)'.

Chapter 3

1. DO(O)(S)(64)13, 6 August 1964, CAB 148/8, TNA.
2. C.J. Treadwell to T.F. Brenchley, 2 October 1963, FO 371/168892, TNA.
3. Beirut Telegram PYO/189 to Ministry of Defence, 27 November 1968, FCO 8/1200, TNA.
4. R.F. Brown to T.F. Brenchley, 30 May 1968, FCO 8/788, TNA.
5. A.F. Douglas-Home to M.H. Macmillan, 10 May 1963, PREM 11/4447, TNA.
6. 'Report by Mr Symons', FO 371/174671, TNA.
7. Jedda Telegram No.17 to Foreign and Commonwealth Office, 16 January 1969, FCO 8/1200, TNA and Foreign and Commonwealth Office Telegram No.14 to Jedda, 16 January 1969, FCO 8/1200, TNA.
8. Jedda Telegram No.53 to Foreign and Commonwealth Office, 2 February 1969, FCO 8/1200, TNA.
9. Ibid.
10. Jedda Telegram No.68 to Foreign and Commonwealth Office, 10 February 1969, FCO 8/1200, TNA.
11. W.M.L. Adler to H.R. Hubert, 11 February 1969, FCO 8/1200, TNA.
12. Bahrain Telegram No.4 to Jedda, 18 February 1969, FCO 8/1200, TNA.
13. Annex C, W. Morris to A.D. Parsons, 4 August 1971, FCO 8/1753, TNA.
14. W. Morris to H.J.L. Suffield, 11 February 1970, FCO 8/1498, TNA.
15. W. Morris to D.J. McCarthy, 12 February 1969, FCO 8/1200, TNA.
16. Foreign and Commonwealth Office Telegram No.58 to Jedda, 24 February 1969, FCO 8/1200, TNA.
17. Ibid., and W.H. Fullerton to D.J. McCarthy, 5 March 1969, FCO 8/1200, TNA.
18. Foreign and Commonwealth Office Telegram No.58 to Jedda, 24 February 1969, FCO 8/1200, TNA.
19. Beirut Telegram No.97 to Foreign and Commonwealth Office, 19 February 1969, FCO 8/1200, TNA and Foreign and Commonwealth Office Telegram No.124 to Beirut, 7 March 1969, FCO 8/1200, TNA.
20. W. Morris to D.J. McCarthy, 12 February 1969, FCO 8/1200, TNA.
21. W.H. Fullerton to D.J. McCarthy, 5 March 1969, FCO 8/1200, TNA.
22. D.J. McCarthy to A.J.M. Craig, 8 July 1969, FCO 8/1200, TNA.
23. Ibid.
24. Ibid.
25. [CENSORED] to General Manager, Millbank Technical Services, 25 May 1970, FCO 8/1503, TNA.
26. D.J. McCarthy to A.J.M. Craig, 8 July 1969, FCO 8/1200, TNA.

27. Ibid.
28. H.St.J.B. Armitage to A.J.M. Craig, 17 July 1969, FCO 8/1200, TNA.
29. A.J.M. Craig to D.J. McCarthy, 7 August 1969, FCO 8/1198, TNA.
30. W.H. Fullerton to A.J.M. Craig, 14 August 1969, FCO 8/1187, TNA.
31. H.R. Hubert to W.G. Neilson, 29 September 1969, FCO 8/1195, TNA.
32. W. Morris to H.J.L. Suffield, 11 February 1970, FCO 8/1498, TNA.
33. H.St.J.B. Armitage to A.B. Milne, 6 November 1969, FCO 8/1999, TNA.
34. W. Morris to A.D. Parsons, 9 February 1972, FCO 8/1914, TNA.
35. H.St.J.B. Armitage to A.B. Milne, 6 November 1969, FCO 8/1999, TNA.
36. W.H. Fullerton to H.St.J.B. Armitage, 1 January 1970, FCO 8/1503, TNA.
37. W.H. Fullerton to H.St.J.B. Armitage, 11 February 1970, FCO 8/1502, TNA.
38. W.H. Fullerton to A.A. Acland, 23 February 1970, FCO 8/1502, TNA.
39. W.H. Fullerton to H.St.J.B. Armitage, 11 February 1970, FCO 8/1502, TNA.
40. A.A. Acland to W.H. Fullerton, 23 February 1970, FCO 8/1502, TNA.
41. A.A. Acland to W. Morris, 6 March 1970, FCO 8/1502, TNA.
42. Ibid.
43. Ministry of Defence Telegram 171350 MAR to Jedda, 17 March 1970, FCO 8/1502, TNA.
44. Foreign and Commonwealth Office Telegram No.116 to Jedda, 6 May 1970, FCO 8/1503, TNA and Letter D.G.H. Jarvis to [CENSORED], 4 June 1970, FCO 8/1503, TNA.
45. M.H. Tallboys to A.A. Acland, May 1970, FCO 8/1503, TNA.
46. Ibid.
47. H.J.L. Suffield to Private Secretary/P.A.R. Carrington, 3 March 1972, FCO 8/1914, TNA.
48. M.H. Tallboys to A.A. Acland, May 1970, FCO 8/1503, TNA.
49. Foreign and Commonwealth Office Telegram No.121 to Jedda, 11 May 1970, FCO 8/1503, TNA.
50. Letter D.G.H. Jarvis to [CENSORED], 4 June 1970, FCO 8/1503, TNA.
51. Letter D.G.H. Jarvis to I.A. Roberts, 15 June 1970, FCO 8/1503, TNA.
52. Letter A.A. Acland to W. Morris, 16 June 1970, FCO 8/1503, TNA.
53. J.M. Moss to J.A.N. Graham, 17 June 1970, FCO 8/1503, TNA.
54. J.M. Moss, 'Note of a Meeting between Lord Winterbottom and [CENSORED]', 17 June 1970, FCO 8/1503, TNA.
55. H.St.J.B. Armitage to I.A. Roberts, 22 June 1970, FCO 8/1503, TNA.
56. H.St.J.B. Armitage to H.R. Hubert, 17 October 1970, FCO 8/1504, TNA.
57. H.R. Hubert, 'Visit to Saudi Arabia to discuss the build-up of the National Guard. 9–15 October 1970', 16 October 1970, FCO 8/1504, TNA.
58. 'Presentation to His Royal Highness Prince Abdullah Bin Abdul Aziz, Commander, Saudi Arabian National Guard', DEFE 68/239, TNA.
59. H.J.L. Suffield to Private Secretary/P.A.R. Carrington, 3 March 1972, FCO 8/1914, TNA.

60. R. Anderson, 'Visit to Saudi Arabia. 2nd–4th August 1971', 5 August 1971, DEFE 13/797, TNA.

61. Annex C, W. Morris to A.D. Parsons, 4 August 1971, FCO 8/1753, TNA.

62. R. Anderson, 'Visit to Saudi Arabia. 2nd–4th August 1971', 5 August 1971, DEFE 13/797, TNA.

63. Annex C, W. Morris to A.D. Parsons, 4 August 1971, FCO 8/1753, TNA.

64. I.J.H.L. Gilmour to M.V. Macmillan, 24 November 1971, T 225/3863, TNA.

65. H.J.L. Suffield to Private Secretary/P.A.R. Carrington, 3 March 1972, FCO 8/1914, TNA.

66. Simon C. Smith, *Britain's Revival and Fall in the Gulf: Kuwait, Bahrain, Qatar and the Trucial States, 1950–1971*, London: RoutledgeCurzon, 2004, pp. 103–4.

67. W. Morris to A.D. Parsons, 8 March 1972, FCO 8/1910, TNA.

68. Jedda Telegram No.26 to Foreign and Commonwealth Office, 11 January 1972, FCO 8/1914, TNA.

69. H.R. Hubert, 'Saudi National Guard and Saudi Navy. Visit by Mr. H.R. Hubert to Jedda 7–9 January 72', 11 January 1972, FCO 8/1914, TNA.

70. H.R. Hubert to R. Anderson, 20 January 1972, FCO 8/1914, TNA.

71. Ibid.

72. Jedda Telegram No.85 to Foreign and Commonwealth Office, 8 February 1972, FCO 8/1914, TNA.

73. Ministry of Defence Telegram DIG/EDQ to Jedda, 18 February 1972, FCO 8/1914, TNA.

74. R.G. Woodhouse, 'Report by Defence Attaché, Jedda', 16 June 1973, FCO 8/2118, TNA.

Chapter 4

1. Christopher de Bellaigue, *Patriot of Persia: Muhammad Mossadegh and a Very British Coup*, London: The Bodley Head, 2012, p. 117.

2. Donald N. Wilber, *Regime Change in Iran*, Nottingham: Spokesman, 2006, p. 37.

3. De Bellaigue, op cit., pp. 230–2.

4. N.W. Browne, 'British Policy on Iran, 1974–1978', p. 42, FCO 8/4029, TNA.

5. Ibid, p. 40.

6. Ibid, p. 44.

7. A. Reeve, 'Conventional Arms Transfer Policy', Tables II and III, FCO 66/1423, TNA.

8. Coopers & Lybrand, 'Interim Report on Millbank Technical Services Limited', March 1975, Appendix E1, CAOG 18/676, TNA.

9. 'Leading Personalities in Iran, 1979', FCO 8/3349, TNA.

10. Tehran Telegram WWW/EDQ 201 to Ministry of Defence, 23 November 1970, FO 248/1694, TNA.

11. Ibid.

12. 'Certificate of Nationalisation. Shapoor Ardeshirji Reporter', 5 August 1955, HO 334/391, TNA.

13. Abbas Milani, *The Shah*, Basingstoke: Palgrave Macmillan, 2011, p. 172.

14. A.M. Palliser to D.A.L. Owen, 13 February 1978, DEFE 23/198, TNA.

15. 'Certificate of Nationalisation. Shapoor Ardeshirji Reporter', 5 August 1955, HO 334/391, TNA.

16. Tehran Telegram WWW/EDQ 201 to Ministry of Defence, 23 November 1970, FO 248/1694, TNA.

17. Ministry of Defence Telegram RTT 241010Z to Tehran, 24 November 1970, FO 248/1694, TNA.

18. Tehran Telegram WWW/RTT 207 to Ministry of Defence, 25 November 1970, FO 248/1694, TNA.

19. Foreign and Commonwealth Office Telegram No.594 to Tehran, 4 December 1970, FO 248/1694, TNA.

20. R.G. Roe to S.A. Reporter, 4 December 1970, DEFE 24/1691, TNA.

21. P.A.R. Carrington to the Shah of Iran, 4 December 1970, DEFE 24/1691, TNA.

22. Tehran Telegram WWW/OYQ 254 to Ministry of Defence, 10 December 1970, FO 248/1694, TNA.

23. Tehran Telegram WWW/EDQ 298 to Ministry of Defence, 23 December 1970, FO 248/1694, TNA.

24. Coopers & Lybrand, 'Interim Report on Millbank Technical Services Limited', March 1975, p. 9 and Appendix E1, CAOG 18/676, TNA.

25. F.W. Mulley to D.W. Healey, 27 April 1978, PREM 16/2130, TNA.

26. Coopers & Lybrand, 'Interim Report on Millbank Technical Services Limited', March 1975, p. 5, CAOG 18/676, TNA.

27. Ibid., p. 10, and Appendix A.

28. *Supplement to The London Gazette*, London: HMSO, 1 January 1973, p. 17.

29. Tehran Telegram No.671 to Foreign and Commonwealth Office, 14 November 1977, DEFE 24/1690, TNA and J.E.D. Street to PS/F.W. Mulley, 11 July 1977, DEFE 24/1317, TNA.

30. S.A. Reporter to H.J.L. Suffield, 18 January 1975, DEFE 23/217, TNA.

31. Tehran Telegram 7652 to Washington, 31 October 1973 (http://aad.archives.gov/aad/series-description.jsp?s=4073&cat=all&bc=sl).

32. Tehran Telegram 6191 to State Department, 25 July 1974 (http://aad.archives.gov/aad/series-description.jsp?s=4073&cat=all&bc=sl).

33. Tehran Telegram 1096 to State Department, 3 February 1976 (http://aad.archives.gov/aad/series-description.jsp?s=4073&cat=all&bc=sl).

34. 'Visit of the Secretary of State for Foreign and Commonwealth Affairs to Iran. 4-8 March 1976. UK Defence Sales to Iran', DEFE 13/1123, TNA.

35. A. Sharman to F.R. Mingay, 23 March 1977, PJ 1/47, TNA.

36. J.E.D. Street to PS/F.W. Mulley, 11 July 1977, DEFE 24/1317, TNA.

37. 'Brief B7. Brief for Foreign and Commonwealth Secretary's visit to Iran 13-15 May', DEFE 23/149, TNA.

38. Asadollah Alam, *The Shah and I: The Confidential Diary of Iran's Royal Court, 1968–77*, London: I.B. Tauris & Co., 2008, p. 421.

39. Tehran Telegram No.671 to Foreign and Commonwealth Office, 14 November 1977, DEFE 24/1690, TNA.

40. Ibid.

41. F.W Mulley to L.J. Callaghan, 28 October 1977, DEFE 24/1690, TNA.

42. D.O. Henley to F. Cooper, 12 January 1977, DEFE 68/110, TNA.

43. A.D. Osborne to J.E.D. Street, 21 February 1977, DEFE 23/149, TNA.

44. 'Aide Memoire on the Randel Case: Implications for HMG', 26 October 1977, DEFE 23/217, TNA.

45. J.E.D. Street to PS/F.W. Mulley, 24 October 1977, DEFE 13/1176, TNA.

46. F.W Mulley to L.J. Callaghan, 28 October 1977, DEFE 24/1690, TNA.

47. *London Evening News*, 14 April 1976.

48. 'Aide Memoire on the Randel Case: Implications for HMG', 26 October 1977, DEFE 23/217, TNA.

49. F.W Mulley to L.J. Callaghan, 28 October 1977, DEFE 24/1690, TNA.

50. N.W. Browne, 'British Policy on Iran, 1974–1978', pp. 3–5, FCO 8/4029, TNA.

51. State Department Telegram 212238 to Tehran, 26 August 1976 (http://aad. archives.gov/aad/series-description.jsp?s=4073&cat=all&bc=sl).

52. J.E.D. Street to PS/F.W. Mulley, 11 July 1977, DEFE 24/1317, TNA.

53. D.E. Tatham to I.T.M. Lucas, undated draft, FCO 8/2867, TNA.

54. 'Aide Memoire on the Randel Case: Implications for HMG', 26 October 1977, DEFE 23/217, TNA.

55. Anthony Parsons, *The Pride & the Fall: Iran 1974–1979*, London: Jonathan Cape, 1984, p. 29.

56. 'Sir Leicester SUFFIELD. Re-examined by MR RICHARDSON', *Regina* v *Wellburn & Ors*, 9 November 1977, DEFE 24/1690, TNA.

57. *Hansard*, House of Commons, Vol. 939, 1977–78, 17 November 1977, Col. 368W.

58. Parsons, op cit., p. 53.

59. Tehran Telegram No.671 to Foreign and Commonwealth Office, 14 November 1977, DEFE 24/1690, TNA.

60. Foreign and Commonwealth Office Telegram No.531 to Tehran, 25 November 1977, DEFE 23/217, TNA.

61. Tehran Telegram No.675 to Foreign and Commonwealth Office, 20 November 1977, DEFE 24/1690, TNA.

62. Tehran Telegram No.713 to Foreign and Commonwealth Office, 30 November 1977, DEFE 23/217, TNA.

63. A.M. Palliser to F. Cooper, 21 December 1977, DEFE 23/217, TNA.
64. R. Anderson to F. Cooper, 3 January 1978, DEFE 23/217, TNA.
65. A.M. Palliser to D.A.L. Owen, 13 February 1978, DEFE 23/198, TNA.
66. F.W. Mulley to D.W. Healey, 27 April 1978, PREM 16/2130, TNA.
67. A.M. Palliser to D.A.L. Owen, 13 February 1978, DEFE 23/198, TNA.
68. A.M. Palliser to F. Cooper, 16 January 1978, DEFE 23/217, TNA.
69. R. Anderson to PS/F. Cooper, 26 January 1978, DEFE 23/217, TNA.
70. A.P. Hockaday to F. Cooper, 18 January 1978, DEFE 23/217, TNA.
71. R.G. Roe to S.A. Reporter, 4 December 1970, DEFE 24/1691, TNA.
72. N.W. Browne, 'British Policy on Iran, 1974–1978', p. 5, FCO 8/4029, TNA.
73. Tehran Telegram No.154 to Foreign and Commonwealth Office, 21 February 1978, FCO 8/3210, TNA.
74. R. Ellis to F. Cooper, 1 March 1978, DEFE 23/198, TNA.
75. R. Anderson to AUS(Sales Admin), 14 February 1978, DEFE 23/198, TNA.
76. R. Ellis to F. Cooper, 16 March 1978, DEFE 23/198, TNA.
77. A.M. Palliser to D.A.L. Owen, 13 February 1978, DEFE 23/198, TNA.
78. Alam, op cit., p. 56.
79. R. Anderson to F. Cooper, 3 January 1978, DEFE 23/217, TNA.
80. R. Anderson to F. Cooper, 8 February 1978, DEFE 23/198, TNA.
81. Alan Munro, *Keep the Flag Flying: A Diplomatic Memoir*, London: Gilgamesh Publishing, 2012, p. 124.
82. S.A. Reporter to R. Ellis, 1 June 1979, DEFE 23/198, TNA.
83. R.S. Gorham to PUSD, 10 April 1979, FCO 8/3349, TNA.
84. EY(79)15, 16 March 1979, CAB 134/4358, TNA.
85. EY(79)16, 15 March 1979, CAB 134/4358, TNA.
86. *Report of the Inquiry into the Export of Defence Equipment and Dual-Use Goods to Iraq and Related Prosecutions*, London: HMSO, 15 February 1996, Volume 1, p. 286.
87. EY(79)5th Meeting, 21 March 1979, CAB 134/4358, TNA.
88. OD(79)6, 6 June 1979, CAB 148/183, TNA.
89. EY(79)5th Meeting, 21 March 1979, CAB 134/4358, TNA.
90. F.L. Pym to M.H. Thatcher, 22 November 1979, FCO 93/1979, TNA.
91. N.W. Browne, 'British Policy on Iran, 1974–1978', p. 25, FCO 8/4029, TNA.

Chapter 5

1.   E.L. Richardson to G.R. Ford, 8 June 1976, http://www.sechistorical. org/collection/papers/1970/1976_0608_RichardsonScowcroftT.pdf   and 'Report on National Laws Penalizing Bribery', http://www.sechistorical.org/ collection/papers/1970/1976_1231_LawsBribery.pdf.
2.   P.R.H. Wright, 'Note of a Meeting after lunch at Chequers on Sunday, 22 May 1977', 22 May 1977, FV 22/117, TNA.

3. House of Representatives, *Unlawful Corporate Payments Act of 1977*, 95th Congress, 1st Session, Report No. 95–640, 28 September 1977.

4. U.S. General Accounting Office, *Impact of Foreign Corrupt Practices Act on U.S.Business* (Publication No. AFMD-81-34), March 1981.

5. U.S. Securities and Exchange Commission, 'Report of the Securities and Exchange Commission on Questionable and Illegal Corporate Payments and Practices', in *Securities Regulation & Law Report*, Special Supplement, No. 353, 19 May 1976.

6. Boulton, op cit., p. 257.

7. Ibid., p. 261.

8. Ibid., p. 262.

9. United States Senate, *Hearings before the Subcommittee on Multinational Corporations of the Committee on Foreign Relations, 94th Congress, 1st Session, Part 12*, Washington: U.S. Government Printing Office, 1975, p. 107.

10. Ibid., pp. 160 and 166.

11. Boulton, op cit., p. 264.

12. United States Senate, *Hearings before the Committee on Banking, Housing and Urban Affairs, 94th Congress, 1st Session*, Washington: U.S. Government Printing Office, 1975, p. 52.

13. Ibid., p. 40.

14. Lockheed Aircraft Corporation, op cit., p. 14.

15. Report by Commissie van Drie, 26 August 1976, Chapter 2, p. 1, FCO 33/3014, TNA.

16. Ibid., Chapter 1, p. 1.

17. E.J.W. Barnes to C.A.R. Crosland, 'Prince Bernhard and the Lockheed Affair', 28 September 1976, FCO 33/3014, TNA.

18. Report by Commissie van Drie, 26 August 1976, Foreword, p. 6, FCO 33/3014, TNA.

19. Ibid., Foreword, p. 2.

20. E.J.W. Barnes to C.A.R. Crosland, 'Prince Bernhard and the Lockheed Affair', 28 September 1976, FCO 33/3014, TNA.

21. Ibid.

22. Boulton, op cit., p. 141.

23. United States Senate, *Hearings, 94th Congress, 2nd Session, Part 14*, op cit., p. 30.

24. Ibid., p. 378.

25. Ibid., pp. 36 and 383.

26. A.M. Layden to C. Hulse, 2 March 1976, FCO 33/2941, TNA.

27. A.D.S. Goodall to R.A. Hibbert, 19 March 1976, FCO 33/2941, TNA.

28. M.E. Pellew to P.G. Harborne, 5 March 1979, FCO 33/4047, TNA and Case of European Court of Human Rights, 18 December 1980 (CASE CROCIANI, PALMIOTTI, TANASSI, LEFEBVRE D'OVIDIO V. ITALY) Appeal Nbr: 8603/79; 8722/79; 8723/79; 8729/79.

29. Case of European Court of Human Rights, 18 December 1980 (CASE CROCIANI, PALMIOTTI, TANASSI, LEFEBVRE D'OVIDIO V. ITALY) Appeal Nbr: 8603/79; 8722/79; 8723/79; 8729/79.

30. Boulton, op cit., p. 242.

31. Ibid., p. 248.

32. Ibid., p. 250.

33. Ibid.

34. James Babb, *Tanaka: The Making of Postwar Japan*, Harlow: Longman, 2000, pp. 94–5.

35. Peter J. Hertzog, *Japan's Pseudo-Democracy*, Folkestone: Japan Library, 1993, p. 164.

36. Babb, op cit., p. 99.

37. Hertzog, op cit., pp. 166–7.

38. Boulton, op cit., p. 13.

39. Lockheed Aircraft Corporation, op cit., pp. 21–2.

40. J.R. Garson to General Counsel, Department of Commerce, undated, http://www.sechistorical.org/collection/papers/1970/1976_0331_GarsonLawT.pdf.

41. U.S. Securities and Exchange Commission, op cit.

42. Ibid.

43. U.S. General Accounting Office, *Impact of Foreign Corrupt Practices Act on U.S. Business*, op cit.

44. 'Statement of the Honourable Roderick M. Hills Chairman, Securities and Exchange Commission, before the Subcommittee on Consumer Protection and Finance of the House of Representatives Committee on Interstate and Foreign Commerce', 21 September 1976, http://www.sechistorical.org/collection/papers/1970/1976_0921_HillsStatementT.pdf.

45. Acting Commissioner of Internal Revenue to Acting General Counsel, 'Corporate Slush Funds – Illegal Foreign Payments', 9 March 1977, http://www.sechistorical.org/collection/papers/1970/1977_0309_IRSCorporate.pdf.

46. Ibid.

47. 'U.S. Government Agency Actions regarding Illicit Foreign Payments', November 1975, http://www.sechistorical.org/collection/papers/1970/1975_1101_USForeign.pdf.

48. U.S. General Accounting Office, *Lockheed's Commission Payments to Obtain Foreign Sales* (Publication No. PSAD-77-85), March 1977.

49. *Gaines v. Haughton*, 645 F.2D 761 (9th Cir. 1981) (hereafter *Gaines v Haughton*).

50. Lockheed Aircraft Corporation, op cit., p. 3.

51. Ibid., p. 10.

52. G.R. Ford to H.A. Kissinger, 31 March 1976, http://www.sechistorical.org/collection/papers/1970/1976_0331_WebbRichardsonT.pdf.

53. The White House, 'Statement by the President', 14 June 1976, http://www. sechistorical.org/collection/papers/1970/1976_0614_PresidentQuestionableT.pdf.

54. J.E. Carter to W. Proxmire, 20 June 1977, http://www.sechistorical.org/ collection/papers/1970/1977_0620_CarterFCPA.pdf.

55. House of Representatives, op cit.

56. U.S. Securities and Exchange Commission, op cit.

57. Public Law 94-329, 30 June 1976, http://www.gpo.gov/fdsys/pkg/ STATUTE-90/pdf/STATUTE-90-Pg729.pdf.

58. T.F. Brenchley, 'Saudi Arms Deal', 1 September 1966, FO 371/185498, TNA.

59. Prince Sultan to Saudi Arabian Air Defence Consortium, 7 December 1965, FO 371/185493, TNA.

60. F.W. Page to J.R. Christie, 30 July 1969, FCO 8/1194, TNA.

61. T.F. Brenchley, 'Saudi Arms Deal', 1 September 1966, FO 371/185498, TNA.

62. Jedda Telegram No.586 to Foreign Office, 18 October 1966, FO 371/185499, TNA.

63. T.F. Brenchley, 'Saudi Arms Deal', 1 September 1966, FO 371/185498, TNA.

64. 'Note of a Meeting with Prince Sultan in Riyadh on 26 November, 1966', FCO 8/2586, TNA.

65. 'Re-amended Statement of Claim', paragraph 4, *Edwards v AEI*, 8 March 1974, FCO 8/2347, TNA.

66. W. Morris to D.J. McCarthy, 20 June 1969, FCO 8/1193, TNA.

67. 'Saudi Arabia Report No. 10', 18 October 1967, SC/MSS/165/1/2/1/3, Caldecote Papers, IET.

68. 'Re-amended Statement of Claim', paragraph 9, *Edwards v AEI*, 8 March 1974, FCO 8/2347, TNA.

69. W. Morris to D.J. McCarthy, 20 June 1969, FCO 8/1193, TNA.

70. Lord Caldecote to G. Edwards, 22 November 1967, SC/MSS/165/1/2/1/3, Caldecote Papers, IET.

71. G. Edwards to Lord Caldecote, 11 December 1967, SC/MSS/165/1/2/1/3, Caldecote Papers, IET.

72. G. Edwards to Lord Caldecote, 24 January 1968, SC/MSS/165/1/2/1/4, Caldecote Papers, IET.

73. J.W. Adderley to Lord Caldecote, 19 July 1968, SC/MSS/165/1/2/1/4, Caldecote Papers, IET.

74. 'Amended Statement of Claim', paragraph 7, *Edwards v AEI*, 19 November 1969, FCO 8/2347, TNA.

75. 'Re-amended Statement of Claim', paragraph 12, *Edwards v AEI*, 8 March 1974, FCO 8/2347, TNA.

76. J.R. Young to J.H. Wilkinson, 23 September 1974, FCO 8/2347, TNA.

77. W. Morris to D.J. McCarthy, 20 June 1969, FCO 8/1193, TNA.

78. B. Cookson to D. Lewis, 5 June 1969, SC/MSS/165/1/2/1/5, Caldecote Papers, IET.

79. Handwritten note of Lord Caldecote, January 1969, SC/MSS/165/5/2/4, Caldecote papers, IET.
80. C.B. Benjamin to US/EIR, 'Saudi Arabian Air Defence Scheme: Brief for Minister' Visit: 21–26 January', 13 January 1971, Appendix V, FCO 8/1746, TNA.
81. 'Statement of Claim', *Abdul Rahman v AEI*, 6 October 1970, FCO 8/2347, TNA.
82. 'Country Assessment Sheet: Saudi Arabia', April 1974, FCO 8/2340, TNA.
83. P.R.H. Wright to M.S. Weir, 3 September 1974, FCO 8/2347, TNA.
84. Goodman, Derrick & Co., Solicitors to The Treasury Solicitor, 2 October 1974, FCO 8/2347, TNA.
85. L.J.R. Dando to J.R. Young, 19 February 1974, FCO 8/2346, TNA.
86. P.R.H. Wright to M.S. Weir, 3 September 1974, FCO 8/2347, TNA.
87. Ibid.
88. L.J.R. Dando to T.J. Clark, 6 August 1974, FCO 8/2347, TNA.
89. J.R. Young to P.R.H. Wright, 5 September 1974, FCO 8/2347, TNA.
90. Goodman, Derrick & Co., Solicitors to The Treasury Solicitor, 1 November 1974, FCO 8/2347, TNA.
91. Jedda Telegram No.300 to Foreign and Commonwealth Office, 8 May 1975, FCO 8/2586, TNA and Jedda Telegram No.5 Saving to Foreign and Commonwealth Office, 17 May 1975, FCO 8/2586, TNA.
92. R.K. Batstone to T.J. Clark, 21 May 1975, FCO 8/2586, TNA.
93. J.P. Bannerman to T.J. Clark, 27 June 1975, FCO 8/2586, TNA.
94. *Northrop Corp. v. Triad Financial Establishment*, 593 F.Supp. 928, 942 (C.D.Cal.1984) (hereafter *Northrop v Triad*).
95. Ibid.
96. Ibid.
97. Harry T. Drury and Peter J. Glenboski, *Peace Hawk: A Case Study of a Foreign Military Sales Program and its Management*, June 1977, http://www.dtic.mil/cgi-bin/GetTRDoc?Location=U2&doc=GetTRDoc.pdf&AD=ADA044210.
98. *Northrop v Triad*.
99. Ibid.
100. Ibid.
101. Ibid.
102. State Department Telegram 129755 to Jidda, 3 June 1975 (http://aad.archives.gov/aad/series-description.jsp?s=4073&cat=all&bc=sl).
103. *Northrop v Triad*.
104. Ibid.
105. Jidda Telegram 3541 to State Department, 19 May 1975 (http://aad.archives.gov/aad/series-description.jsp?s=4073&cat=all&bc=sl).
106. State Department Telegram 129755 to Jidda, 3 June 1975, (http://aad.archives.gov/aad/series-description.jsp?s=4073&cat=all&bc=sl).

107. Jidda Telegram 3940 to State Department, 2 June 1975 (http://aad.archives. gov/aad/series-description.jsp?s=4073&cat=all&bc=sl).

108. Ibid.

109. Cairo Telegram 5516 to State Department, 3 June 1975 (http://aad.archives. gov/aad/series-description.jsp?s=4073&cat=all&bc=sl).

110. State Department Telegram 129754 to Jidda, 3 June 1975 (http://aad. archives.gov/aad/series-description.jsp?s=4073&cat=all&bc=sl).

111. State Department Telegram 129795 to Cairo, 4 June 1975 (http://aad. archives.gov/aad/series-description.jsp?s=4073&cat=all&bc=sl).

112. State Department Telegram 129800 to Cairo, 4 June 1975 (http://aad. archives.gov/aad/series-description.jsp?s=4073&cat=all&bc=sl).

113. J.P. Bannerman to T.J. Clark, 27 June 1975, FCO 8/2586, TNA.

114. Ibid.

115. State Department Telegram 133578 to Jidda, 7 June 1975 (http://aad.archives. gov/aad/series-description.jsp?s=4073&cat=all&bc=sl) and United States Senate, *Hearings, 94th Congress, 1st Session, Part 12*, op cit., pp. 112–3.

116. State Department Telegram 137147 to OECD, 12 June 1975 (http:// aad.archives.gov/aad/series-description.jsp?s=4073&cat=all&bc=sl)   and United States Senate, *Hearings, 94th Congress, 1st Session, Part 12*, op cit., pp. 182, 435 and 437–8.

117. J.P. Bannerman to T.J. Clark, 27 June 1975, FCO 8/2586, TNA.

118. Ibid.

119. Ibid.

120. Jidda Telegram 4317 to State Department, 16 June 1975 (http://aad.archives. gov/aad/series-description.jsp?s=4073&cat=all&bc=sl).

121. J.P. Bannerman to T.J. Clark, 27 June 1975, FCO 8/2586, TNA.

122. Ibid.

123. Ibid.

124. Ibid.

125. I.T.M. Lucas to E.E. Orchard, 18 July 1975, FCO 8/2586, TNA.

126. H.R. Braden to J.P. Bannerman, 7 July 1975, FCO 8/2586, TNA.

127. *Northrop v Triad*.

128. *Northrop v Triad* and Lewis D. Solomon and Leslie G. Linville, 'Transnational Conduct of American Multinational Corporations: Questionable Payments Abroad', *Boston College Industrial and Commercial Law Review*, Vol. XVII, No. 3 (March 1976).

129. *Northrop v Triad*.

130. Ibid.

131. United States Senate, *Hearings, 94th Congress, 1st Session, Part 12*, op cit., p. 349.

132. Ibid., pp. 351 and 1088.

133. *Northrop v Triad*.

134. State Department Telegram 218786 to Jidda, 13 September 1975 (http://aad. archives.gov/aad/series-description.jsp?s=4073&cat=all&bc=sl).

135. State Department Telegram 299348 to Doha, 19 December 1975 (http://aad. archives.gov/aad/series-description.jsp?s=4073&cat=all&bc=sl).

136. U.S. Securities and Exchange Commission, op cit.

137. *Northrop v Triad.*

138. *Northrop Corporation* v. *Triad International Marketing, S.A., and Triad Financial Establishment,* 108 S.Ct.261, 484 U.S. 914, No. 87-349.

139. Sampson, op cit., p. 161.

140. Ibid., p. 304.

141. Whicker, op cit., pp. 172–3.

142. 'Visit by Foreign and Commonwealth Secretary to Saudi Arabia 25–27 August', Brief E4, FCO 8/3752, TNA.

143. W. Morris, 'Saudi Defence Procurement, and the Air Defence contracts in particular', 1 May 1971, DEFE 13/797, TNA.

144. *Who's Who in Saudi Arabia 1983–84,* op cit., p. 249.

Chapter 6

1. D.W.G. Wass to J.L. Rampton, 5 April 1976, CAB 197/49, TNA.

2. J.J.B. Hunt to N.L. Wicks, 9 April 1976, PREM 16/909, TNA.

3. *The Sunday Times,* 11 April 1976.

4. GEN 11(76)2, 26 April 1976, CAB 130/859, TNA.

5. GEN 11(76)1st Meeting, 28 April 1976, CAB 130/859, TNA.

6. *Hansard,* House of Commons, Vol. 911, 1975–76, 18 May 1976, Cols. 1213–14.

7. GEN 11(76)1st Meeting, 28 April 1976, CAB 130/859, TNA.

8. R.N. Dales to P.R.H. Wright, 19 May 1976, PREM 16/2271, TNA.

9. P.R.H. Wright to R.N. Dales, 17 May 1976, PREM 16/2271, TNA.

10. R.N. Dales to P.R.H. Wright, 19 May 1976, PREM 16/2271, TNA.

11. C.W. France to D.W.G. Wass, 11 June 1976, T 364/29, TNA and F.D. Evans to P.R.H. Wright, 10 June 1976, FCO 8/2824, TNA.

12. C.W. France to D.W.G. Wass, 11 June 1976, T 364/29, TNA.

13. Ibid.

14. F.D. Evans to P.R.H. Wright, 8 June 1976, PREM 16/2271, TNA.

15. S.L. Egerton to P. Dimond, 8 June 1976, T 364/29, TNA.

16. Jedda Telegram No.319 to Foreign and Commonwealth Office, 9 June 1976, FCO 8/2824, TNA.

17. C.W. France to D.W.G. Wass, 11 June 1976, T 364/29, TNA.

18. Jedda Telegram CREDA 235 to Department of Trade, 14 June 1975, FCO 8/2824, TNA.

19. F.D. Evans to P.R.H. Wright, 10 June 1976, FCO 8/2824, TNA.

20. P.R.H. Wright to F.D. Evans, 10 June 1976, PREM 16/2271, TNA.

21. L.J. Callaghan to E.E. Dell, 11 June 1976, PREM 16/2271, TNA.
22. Ibid.
23. F.D. Evans to P.R.H. Wright, 10 June 1976, FCO 8/2824, TNA.
24. 'Background Note: BP/Saudi Arabia Bribery Allegations', FCO 58/1514, TNA.
25. I.T.M. Lucas to D.F. Murray, 8 November 1977, DEFE 24/1690, TNA.
26. A.J. Wilton to P.D. Brittain, 14 March 1973, FCO 8/1999, TNA and R.A.Kealy to J.R. Young, 10 July 1973, FCO 8/2001, TNA.
27. A.J. Wilton to P.D. Brittain, 14 March 1973, FCO 8/1999, TNA.
28. R.A. Kealy to J.R. Young, 10 July 1973, FCO 8/2001, TNA.
29. D.E. Tatham to I.T.M. Lucas, undated draft, FCO 8/2867, TNA.
30. J.H. Wilkinson to J.E.D. Street, 4 November 1977, DEFE 24/1690, TNA.
31. *Guardian*, 20 January 1978.
32. I.T.M. Lucas to D.F. Murray, 8 November 1977, DEFE 24/1690, TNA.
33. F.P. Nurdin to H.J.L. Suffield, 7 January 1974, DEFE 24/1690, TNA.
34. F.W. Mulley to L.J. Callaghan, 28 October 1977, DEFE 24/1690, TNA.
35. 'Sir Leicester SUFFIELD. Cross-examined by MR HOWARD', *Regina* v *Wellburn & Ors*, 9 November 1977, DEFE 24/1690, TNA.
36. *Guardian*, 10 November 1977.
37. R.Ellis to F. Cooper, 21 December 1976, DEFE 68/109, TNA.
38. D.O. Henley to F. Cooper, 1 September 1976, PJ 1/43, TNA.
39. F. Cooper to D.O. Henley, 3 November 1976, DEFE 68/109, TNA.
40. Ibid.
41. A.J. Wilton to P.R.H. Wright, 28 February 1973, FCO 8/1999, TNA.
42. Phythian, op cit., p. 238.
43. F.W. Mulley to L.J. Callaghan, 28 October 1977, DEFE 24/1690, TNA.
44. R. Ellis to F. Cooper, 21 December 1976, DEFE 68/109, TNA.
45. C. Hewertson to J.A. Patterson, 4 May 1967, T 225/2918, TNA.
46. F. Cooper to H.J.L. Suffield, 9 June 1976, DEFE 68/110, TNA.
47. *Daily Mail*, 19 May 1977.
48. J.L. Beaven to H.B. Formstone, 12 May 1977, FCO 65/1930, TNA, Lagos Telegram CREDA 269 to Department of Trade, 23 May 1977, FCO 65/1930, TNA, and M.A. Holding to P.R.A. Mansfield, 27 May 1977, FCO 65/1930, TNA.
49. Foreign and Commonwealth Office Telegram No.379 to Lagos, 27 May 1977, FCO 65/1930, TNA.
50. *Hansard*, House of Commons, Vol. 932, 1976–77, 19 May 1977, Col. 693.
51. Ibid., Col. 692.
52. *Daily Mail*, 21 May 1977.
53. *Daily Telegraph*, 29 July 2008.
54. R.S. Faber to J.O. Kerr, 20 May 1977, FCO 69/592, TNA.
55. J.J.B. Hunt to N.L.Wicks, 20 May 1977, PREM 16/1287, TNA.

56. P.R.H. Wright, 'Note of a Meeting after lunch at Chequers on Sunday, 22 May 1977', 22 May 1977, FV 22/117, TNA.

57. National Enterprise Board, 'Allegations in the Daily Mail of 19 and 20 May 1977 about British Leyland Limited', 13 June 1977, DEFE 24/1316, TNA.

58. SAMV(75)10A, 15 October 1975, FCO 8/2605, TNA.

59. *Daily Mail*, 19 May 1977.

60. National Enterprise Board, 'Allegations in the Daily Mail of 19 and 20 May 1977 about British Leyland Limited', 13 June 1977, DEFE 24/1316, TNA.

61. Ibid.

62. D.J. Plumbly to R.A. Kealy, 27 September 1975, FCO 8/2405, TNA.

63. National Enterprise Board, 'Allegations in the Daily Mail of 19 and 20 May 1977 about British Leyland Limited', 13 June 1977, DEFE 24/1316, TNA.

64. R.H.W. Bullock to E.E. Dell, 28 June 1977, FV 22/118, TNA.

65. Ibid.

66. *Gaines v Haughton*.

67. GEN 90(77)1st Meeting, 6 July 1977, CAB 130/978, TNA.

68. N.L. Wicks to L.J. Callaghan, 6 July 1977, PREM 16/1287, TNA.

69. Ibid.

70. K.R. Stowe, 'Meeting between the Prime Minister and Mr. Varley. 10 Downing Street on Tuesday 12 July at 4.45 p.m.', 12 July 1977, PREM 16/1287, TNA.

71. GEN 90(77)2nd Meeting, 27 July 1977, CAB 130/978, TNA.

72. GEN 90(77)3rd Meeting, 27 October 1977, CAB 130/978, TNA.

73. GEN 90(77)4th Meeting, 9 November 1977, CAB 130/978, TNA.

74. D.M.D. Thomas to PS/D.A.L. Owen, 7 July 1978, FCO 69/603, TNA.

75. R. Anderson to F. Cooper, 18 April 1978, DEFE 23/198, TNA.

76. Jedda Telegram No.93 to Foreign and Commonwealth Office, 6 February 1978, FCO 69/602, TNA.

77. D.M.D. Thomas to PS/D.A.L. Owen, 25 July 1978, FCO 69/603, TNA.

78. G. Feast to Heads of Post, 17 August 1978, FCO 69/604, TNA.

79. D.O. Henley to F. Cooper, 12 January 1977, DEFE 68/110, TNA.

80. H.J.L. Suffield to F. Cooper, 23 June 1976, DEFE 23/149, TNA.

81. Ibid.

82. Ibid.

83. F. Cooper to H.J.L. Suffield, 23 June 1976, DEFE 23/149, TNA.

84. J.C. Kay to D.A.L. Owen, 'Visit to Saudi Arabia by the Secretary of State for Defence: 20–25 September, 1977', 2 October 1977, FCO 8/3049, TNA.

85. A.J. Wilton to D.A.L. Owen, 23 March 1978, FCO 8/3126, TNA.

86. H.J.L. Suffield to F. Cooper, undated draft, DEFE 68/319, TNA.

87. *Annuaire Des Societies Libanaises A Responsabilite Limitee*, 3rd edition, Beirut: MECICO, 1977, p. 213.

88. Ibid.

89. Jedda Telegram No.85 to Foreign and Commonwealth Office, 8 February 1972, FCO 8/1914, TNA and Ministry of Defence Telegram DIG/EDQ to Jedda, 18 February 1972, FCO 8/1914, TNA.

90. D.O. Henley to F. Cooper, 12 January 1977, DEFE 68/110, TNA.

91. Ibid.

92. Ibid.

93. Ibid.

94. Ibid.

95. F. Cooper to D.O. Henley, 2 May 1977, DEFE 68/110, TNA.

96. D.O. Henley to F. Cooper, 21 July 1977, DEFE 68/110, TNA.

97. D.O. Henley to F. Cooper, 2 June 1977, DEFE 68/110, TNA.

98. F. Cooper to D.O. Henley, 27 June 1977, DEFE 68/110, TNA.

99. F. Cooper to D.O. Henley, 10 August 1977, DEFE 68/110, TNA.

100. J.F. Howe to R. Ellis, 23 August 1977, DEFE 68/110, TNA.

101. *New York Times*, 2 April 1982.

102. J.P. Bannerman to D.E. Tatham, 11 July 1973, FCO 8/2125, TNA.

103. Associated Press, 10 February 2006.

104. *Report of the Tribunal of Inquiry into Payments to Politicians and Related Matters Part I*, Dublin: The Stationery Office, Prn. A6/1834, p. 104, paragraph 6-25.

105. Ibid., p. 103, paragraph 6-22 and p. 104, paragraph 6-24.

106. Ibid., p. 106, paragraph 6-34.

107. *Report of the Tribunal of Inquiry into Payments to Politicians*, op cit., p. 104, paragraph 6-24.

108. Associated Press, 10 February 2006.

109. J.W.D. Gray to R.E. Palmer, 23 March 1981, FCO 8/3820, TNA.

Chapter 7

1. S.Res.265, 94th Congress (1975).

2. GEN 90(77)2, July 1977, CAB 130/978, TNA.

3. 'Entry into force of a Convention and Pre-Conditions to signing/ratification and Reservations and Amendment', September 1978, PJ 1/59, TNA.

4. GEN 11(76)1, 26 April 1976, CAB 130/859, TNA.

5. D.E. Tatham to I.T.M. Lucas, 2 February 1978, FCO 69/606, TNA.

6. GEN 11(76)1, 26 April 1976, CAB 130/859, TNA.

7. Ibid.

8. GEN 11(76)1st Meeting, 28 April 1976, CAB 130/859, TNA.

9. GEN 11(76)1, 26 April 1976, CAB 130/859, TNA.

10. *Hansard*, House of Commons, Vol. 911, 1975–76, 18 May 1976, Col. 1214.

11. 'Minutes of 62nd meeting of the British Overseas Trade Board held on Tuesday 21st June 1977 at 1 Victoria Street, London, SW1', FV 78/21, TNA.

12. N.D. Peace to F.R. Mingay, 8 February 1977, PJ 1/44, TNA.

13. H.F.R. Catherwood to E.E. Dell, 19 July 1977, PJ 1/50, TNA.
14. *Hansard*, House of Commons, Vol. 911, 1975–76, 18 May 1976, Col. 1214.
15. M.M. Baker to R.W. Gray, 6 July 1977, PJ 1/49, TNA.
16. R.W. Gray to M.M. Baker, 8 July 1977, PJ 1/49, TNA.
17. GEN 90(77)2, July 1977, CAB 130/978, TNA.
18. GEN 90(77)3, 22 July 1977, CAB 130/978, TNA.
19. GEN 90(77)2nd Meeting, 27 July 1977, CAB 130/978, TNA.
20. W. Morris to D.A.L. Owen, 'Corruption in Egypt', 26 February 1979, FCO 93/1967, TNA.
21. M.S. Weir to A.M. Palliser, 26 January 1976, FCO 8/2629, TNA.
22. A.J. Wilton to D.A.L. Owen, 'British Export Performance to Saudi Arabia', 3 May 1977, FV 22/117, TNA.
23. K. Keith to A.M. Palliser, 13 February 1979, FCO 8/3413, TNA.
24. Ibid.
25. M.E. Hunt to K. Keith, 1 March 1979, FCO 8/3413, TNA.
26. J.A. Ford to L.J. Callaghan, 'Indonesia: The Anatomy of Corruption', 5 April 1976, FCO 15/2172, TNA.
27. E.G. Norris to A.M. Simons, 21 June 1976, FCO 15/2145, TNA.
28. A. Mueller to S. Abramson, 17 March 1976, PJ 1/41, TNA.
29. The White House, 'Statement by the President', 14 June 1976, http://www.sechistorical.org/collection/papers/1970/1976_0614_PresidentQuestionableT.pdf.
30. IOC(76)50, 9 July 1976, PJ 1/42, TNA.
31. United Nations Economic and Social Council, E/5883, 4 August 1976, PJ 1/42, TNA.
32. The White House, 'Statement by the President', 14 June 1976, http://www.sechistorical.org/collection/papers/1970/1976_0614_President QuestionableT.pdf.
33. E.L. Richardson to G.R. Ford, 19 January 1977, http://www.sechistorical.org/collection/papers/1970/1977_0119_RichardsonPresident.pdf.
34. F.R. Mingay to M.G.D. Evans, 24 November 1976, PJ 1/43, TNA.
35. F.R. Mingay, 'UN ECOSOC Ad Hoc Working Group on Corrupt Practices', 20 January 1977, PJ 1/44, TNA.
36. F.R. Mingay to R.M. Allott, 18 February 1977, PJ 1/46, TNA.
37. Ibid.
38. PMVE(77)42, 3 March 1977, PJ 1/46, TNA.
39. E.L. Richardson to G.R. Ford, 19 January 1977, http://www.sechistorical.org/collection/papers/1970/1977_0119_RichardsonPresident.pdf.
40. Office of Senator William Proxmire, Press Release, 12 March 1976, http://www.sechistorical.org/collection/papers/1970/1976_0312_Proxmire Release.pdf.

41. E.L. Richardson to G.R. Ford, 19 January 1977, http://www.sechistorical. org/collection/papers/1970/1977_0119_RichardsonPresident.pdf.

42. P.M. Wald to H.O. Staggers, 20 April 1977, http://www.sechistorical.org/ collection/papers/1970/1977_0420_WaldStaggers.pdf.

43. Department of Trade, 'UN ECOSOC Ad Hoc Intergovernmental Working Group on the Problem of Corrupt Practices. Third Session: 28 March–8 April 1977', April 1977, PJ 1/47, TNA.

44. GEN 11(76)1st Meeting, 28 April 1976, CAB 130/859, TNA.

45. BOTB(77)20, 10 June 1977, FV 78/22, TNA.

46. W.K. Prendergast to B.G. Cartledge, 29 November 1978, PREM 16/2130, TNA.

47. Ibid.

48. A.M. Palliser to R.T. Armstrong, 25 July 1980, FCO 8/3734, TNA.

49. R. Williams to DS5, 'Saudi Arabian Defence Relations', 3 November 1980, FCO 8/3753, TNA.

50. General Division 3, 'ECOSOC Ad Hoc Intergovernmental Working Group on the Problem of Corrupt Practices. Third (Resumed) Session Geneva 27 June–1 July 1977', 6 July 1977, PJ 1/49, TNA.

51. Ibid.

52. G7, 'Appendix to Downing Street Summit Declaration. London, England, May 8, 1977', http://www.g8.utoronto.ca/summit/1977london/appendix. html.

53. P.R.H. Wright, 'Note of a Meeting after lunch at Chequers on Sunday, 22 May 1977', 22 May 1977, FV 22/117, TNA.

54. United Nations Economic and Social Council, E/AC.6/L.606, 29 July 1977, PJ 1/51, TNA.

55. R.W. Gray to R.A. Burrows, 6 July 1977, PJ 1/49, TNA.

56. GEN 90(77)2nd Meeting, 27 July 1977, CAB 130/978, TNA.

57. General Division 3, 'Supplementary Brief on International Action, for the Secretary of State for Trade', 14 July 1977, PJ 1/50, TNA.

58. J.G. Pilling to F.R. Mingay, 10 August 1977, PJ 1/51, TNA.

59. E.E. Dell to L.J. Callaghan, 14 October 1977, PREM 16/1287, TNA.

60. D.W. Healey to L.J. Callaghan, 27 October 1977, DEFE 13/1176, TNA.

61. GEN 90(77)3rd Meeting, 27 October 1977, CAB 130/978, TNA.

62. GEN 90(77)6, 7 November 1977, CAB 130/978, TNA.

63. I.B. Nichol to R.M. Malbey, 6 January 1978, PJ 1/54, TNA.

64. M.W. Hunt to F.R. Mingay, December 1977, PJ 1/53, TNA.

65. M.K.O. Simpson-Orlebar to D.M.D. Thomas, 'Proposed International Agreement to Combat Bribery and Extortion in International Trade', 23 May 1978, FCO 58/1259, TNA.

66. F.R. Mingay to L. Pliatzky, 4 July 1978, PJ 1/58, TNA.

67. M.K.O. Simpson-Orlebar to D.M.D. Thomas, 'Proposed International Agreement to Combat Bribery and Extortion in International Trade', 23 May 1978, FCO 58/1259, TNA.

68. W.A.J. Ekins-Daukes to G. Lanchin, 14 December 1978, PJ 1/61, TNA.

69. W.A.J. Ekins-Daukes to L. Pliatzky, 28 November 1978, PJ 1/97, TNA.

70. W.B. Sinton to Mr Fell, 9 June 1978, FCO 58/1259, TNA.

71. F.R. Mingay to L. Pliatzky, 4 July 1978, PJ 1/58, TNA.

72. Ibid.

73. E.E. Dell to L.J. Callaghan, 14 July 1978, PJ 1/97, TNA.

74. J. Smith to L.J. Callaghan, 2 January 1979, PJ 1/61, TNA.

75. S.C. Silkin to L.J. Callaghan, 9 January 1979, PJ 1/61, TNA.

76. J. Smith to S.C. Silkin, 17 January 1979, PJ 1/61, TNA.

77. M. Rees to L.J. Callaghan, 22 January 1979, PJ 1/61, TNA.

78. S.C. Silkin to J. Smith, 22 January 1979, PJ 1/61, TNA.

79. B.G. Cartledge to T.G. Harris, 29 January 1979, PJ 1/61, TNA.

80. R.F. Stimson to PS/Mr Judd, 14 February 1979, FCO 58/1513, TNA.

81. 'Record of a Meeting between Mr Silkin and Mr Judd: 1600 hours, Thursday, 15th February 1979: Room 11, House of Commons', 15 February 1979, FCO 58/1513, TNA.

82. GEN 90(79)1, 26 March 1979, CAB 130/1075, TNA.

83. GEN 90(79)1st Meeting, 28 March 1979, CAB 130/1075, TNA.

84. GEN 90(79)1, 26 March 1979, CAB 130/1075, TNA.

85. GEN 90(79)1st Meeting, 28 March 1979, CAB 130/1075, TNA.

86. United Nations Economic and Social Council, E/1979/104, 25 May 1979, PJ 1/66, TNA.

87. W.A.J. Ekins-Daukes to Q.J. Thomas, 4 June 1979, PJ 1/66, TNA.

88. D. Mellor to W.B. Sinton, 10 January 1978, FCO 58/1257, TNA.

89. F.R. Mingay to E.E. Dell, 6 June 1978, PJ 1/57, TNA.

90. W.A.J. Ekins-Daukes to F.R. Mingay, 12 July 1979, PJ 1/67, TNA.

91. *Hansard*, House of Commons, Vol. 911, 1975–76, 18 May 1976, Col. 1214.

92. W.A.J. Ekins-Daukes to G. Lanchin, 26 June 1979, PJ 1/66, TNA.

93. T.G. Harris to W.A.J.Ekins-Daukes, 3 July 1979, PJ 1/66, TNA.

94. C. Parkinson to D.R. Hurd, 30 August 1979, PJ 1/67, TNA.

95. Lord Strathcona to C. Parkinson, 17 October 1979, PJ 1/67, TNA.

96. S.C. Rhodes to R.J. Ayling, 18 January 1980, PJ 1/68, TNA.

97. M.G.D. Evans to R. Ralph, 24 July 1980, PJ 1/69, TNA.

98. M.G.D. Evans to P. Gent, 3 October 1980, PJ 1/69, TNA.

99. M.J. Lackey to C. Parkinson, 21 October 1980, PJ 1/69, TNA.

100. 'Report on Export Disincentives. Report of the Working Party V to the Chairman of the Interagency Export Disincentives Task Force', February 1980, http://digitalcollections.library.cmu.edu/awweb/awarchive?type=file &item=470964.

101. U.S. General Accounting Office, *Impact of Foreign Corrupt Practices Act on U.S. Business*, op cit.

Chapter 8

1. H.D.A.C. Miers to J.C. Moberly, 11 February 1980, FCO 8/3443, TNA.
2. 'Visit of the Secretary of State for Defence to Oman. 21–23 April 1975. Oman. I. Political', FCO 8/2403, TNA.
3. 'Visit of S of S for Defence to Saudi Arabia and the Gulf. Oman. Leading Personalities. 35 Qais Abdul Mun'im Al-Zawawi', FCO 8/3828, TNA.
4. H.D.A.C. Miers to J.C. Moberly, 11 February 1980, FCO 8/3443, TNA.
5. H.D.A.C. Miers to A.J.M. Craig, 6 February 1981, FCO 8/4221, TNA.
6. OD(80)25th Meeting, 3 December 1980, CAB 148/189, TNA.
7. J.W.F. Nott to M.H. Thatcher, 2 April 1981, PREM 19/467, TNA.
8. A. Reeve, 'Conventional Arms Transfer Policy', Table IX, FCO 66/1423, TNA.
9. Charles Gardner, *British Aircraft Corporation: A History*, London: Batsford, 1981, p. 249.
10. Ibid.
11. J.C. Kay to D.A.L. Owen, 'Visit to Saudi Arabia by the Secretary of State for Defence: 20–25 September, 1977', 2 October 1977, FCO 8/3049, TNA.
12. British Aerospace, News Release, 10 August 1982.
13. R. Anderson to PS/R. Mason, 17 December 1975, FCO 8/2591, TNA and Lord Strathcona to F.L. Pym, 10 December 1980, DEFE 13/1362, TNA.
14. A.W. Pearce to M.H. Thatcher, 8 April 1981, PREM 19/467, TNA.
15. A.J. Coker to C. Lee, 2 February 1978, FCO 8/3130, TNA.
16. I.T.M. Lucas to A.J. Wilton, 7 December 1976, FCO 8/2813, TNA.
17. William Simpson, *The Prince: The Secret Story of the Word's Most Intriguing Royal Prince Bandar bin Sultan*, New York: Regan Books, 2006, p. 13.
18. David B. Ottaway, *The King's Messenger: Prince Bandar Bin Sultan and America's Tangled Relationship with Saudi Arabia*, New York: Walker & Company, 2008, pp. 23–4.
19. PBS Frontline, *Transcript: Black Money*, http://www.pbs.org/wgbh/pages/frontline/blackmoney/etc/script.html.
20. Ottaway, op cit., pp. 41–3.
21. Simpson, op cit., p. 132.
22. Jedda Telegram EDQ 170 to Ministry of Defence, 30 March 1972, DEFE 68/133, TNA.
23. F.E. Rosier to A.J.M. Craig, 8 July 1980, FCO 8/3740, TNA.
24. R.O. Miles to H.D.A.C. Miers, 18 December 1980, FCO 8/3758, TNA.
25. R.C. Mottram to C.D. Powell, 25 September 1985, PJ 5/39, TNA.
26. Ibid.

27. Simpson, op cit., p. 138.
28. R.C. Mottram to C.D. Powell, 25 September 1985, PJ 5/39, TNA.
29. PBS Frontline, *Transcript: Black Money*, http://www.pbs.org/wgbh/pages/frontline/blackmoney/etc/script.html.
30. Simpson, op cit., p. 144.
31. 'Memorandum of Understanding for the Provision of Equipment and Services for the Royal Saudi Air Force', PJ 5/39, TNA.
32. R.C. Mottram to C.D. Powell, 26 September 1985, PJ 5/39, TNA.
33. T. Knapp to P. Mountfield, 21 October 1985, PJ 5/39, TNA.
34. A.J.M. Craig to P.A.R. Carrington, 25 January 1981, FCO 8/4200, TNA.
35. P.F. Ricketts to C.D. Powell, 10 October 1985, http://image.guardian.co.uk/sys-files/Guardian/documents/2007/06/01/ch07doc05.pdf.
36. Chrissie Hirst, *The Arabian Connection: the UK Arms Trade to Saudi Arabia*, London: Campaign Against Arms Trade, May 2000, p. 9.
37. 'Witness Statement of Stephen Pollard', paragraph 11, *Campaign Against Arms Trade v Information Commissioner* [2008] UKIT EA_2006_0040 (hereafter *CAAT v IC*), Campaign Against Arms Trade (hereafter CAAT).
38. Ibid.
39. D.C. Hole to W.H. Fullerton, 18 February 1969, FCO 8/1191, TNA.
40. J.E. Petersen, *Oman's Insurgencies: The Sultanate's Struggle for Supremacy*, London: Saqi Books, 2007, p. 217.
41. I.S. Winchester to A.A. Acland, 5 September 1970, FCO 8/1454, TNA.
42. A.J.M. Craig to D.J. McCarthy, 11 September 1969, FCO 8/1194, TNA.
43. M.S. Weir to P.R.H. Wright, 'Airwork and the Saudi Air Defence Scheme', 23 March 1967, FCO 8/792, TNA.
44. 'Aide Memoire', 20 February 1967, SC/MSS/165/5/2/11, Caldecote papers, IET.
45. D.J. McCarthy to P.T. Hayman, 'Saudi use of British contract pilots?', 2 December 1969, FCO 8/1110, TNA.
46. W. Morris to D.J. McCarthy, 9 December 1969, FCO 8/1110, TNA.
47. W. Morris to M. Stewart, 'Saudi Arabia/People's Republic of South Yemen: The Wadi'a Border Clash', 20 January 1970, FCO 8/1459, TNA.
48. P.W. Gardiner to J.H.A. Winship, 2 November 1989, Gardiner papers, CAAT.
49. P.W. Gardiner, 'Witness Statement', 23 June 2006, pp. 4–5, Gardiner papers, CAAT.
50. Ibid., p. 6.
51. Ibid., p. 2.
52. Ibid., p. 15.
53. Ibid.
54. Ibid., p .14.
55. Ibid.
56. Ibid., p. 27.
57. Ibid., pp. 26–9.

58. Ibid., p. 24.

59. Ibid., p. 26.

60. Ibid., pp. 26–30.

61. Ibid.

62. Ibid.

63. Ibid., pp. 34 and 47.

64. *Daily Mail*, 7 April 2007.

65. P.W. Gardiner, 'Witness Statement', 23 June 2006, p. 47, Gardiner papers, CAAT.

66. Ibid., p. 49.

67. Ibid., p. 40.

68. Ibid., p. 43.

69. Ibid., p. 45.

70. Ibid., p. 39.

71. Ibid., p. 40.

72. Ibid., p. 43.

73. Ibid., p. 35.

74. Ibid., p. 36.

75. Ibid., p. 33.

76. Ibid., p. 34.

77. Ibid., p. 23.

78. H.J.L. Suffield to F. Cooper, 23 June 1976, DEFE 23/149, TNA and D.O. Henley to F. Cooper, 12 January 1977, DEFE 68/110, TNA.

79. H.J.L. Suffield to F. Cooper, undated draft, DEFE 68/319, TNA.

80. *Hansard*, House of Commons, Vol. 199, 1991–92, 27 November 1991, Col. 560W.

81. *Hansard*, House of Commons, Vol. 308, 1997–98, 16 March 1998, Col. 446W.

82. 'Background', Draft Parliamentary answer to Allan Rogers MP, 22 November 1991, Ministry of Defence Freedom of Information disclosure to the author.

83. National Audit Office Freedom of Information disclosure to the author.

84. Ibid.

85. J. Parsons to L.H. Hughes, 9 September 1991, National Audit Office Freedom of Information disclosure to the author.

86. 'Statement of Nicholas Martin Prest', paragraph 18, *Chan U Seek* v *Alvis Vehicles Limited* (Claim No. HC02C01157) (hereafter *Chan U Seek* v *Alvis*), CAAT.

87. Ibid., paragraph 60.

88. Ibid., paragraph 6.

89. 'Amended Particulars of Claim', paragraph 6 (3), *Chan U Seek* v *Alvis*, CAAT.

90. 'Re-amended Defence', paragraph 6.1, *Chan U Seek* v *Alvis*, CAAT.

91. 'Amended Particulars of Claim', paragraph 7, *Chan U Seek* v *Alvis*, CAAT.

92. 'Statement of Nicholas Martin Prest', paragraph 12, *Chan U Seek* v *Alvis*, CAAT.

93. Ibid., paragraph 31.

94. Ibid., paragraphs 34–5.

95. Ibid., paragraph 51.

96. Ibid., paragraph 44.

97. 'Deposition by Witness Rini Soewondho', paragraph 20, *Chan U Seek* v *Alvis*, CAAT.

98. 'Witness Statement of Lionel Wilfred Steele', paragraph 20, *Chan U Seek* v *Alvis*, CAAT.

99. Ibid., paragraph 16.

100. 'Statement of Nicholas Martin Prest', paragraph 44, *Chan U Seek* v *Alvis*, CAAT.

101. Ibid., paragraph 53.

102. 'Witness Statement of Lionel Wilfred Steele', paragraph 30, *Chan U Seek* v *Alvis*, CAAT.

103. 'Statement of Nicholas Martin Prest', paragraph 57, *Chan U Seek* v *Alvis*, CAAT.

104. *Guardian*, 7 December 2004.

105. Ibid.

106. V. New to S. Hawley, 23 March 2005, CAAT.

107. J. Thorpe to N.J. Gilby, 22 March 2005, CAAT.

108. V. New to S. Hawley, 23 March 2005, CAAT.

109. J. Thorpe to N.J. Gilby, 22 March 2005, CAAT.

110. http://amabhungane.co.za/article/2011-06-24-the-arms-deal-cache.

111. 'Note for Opening', *Regina* v *BAE Systems plc*, p. 4.

112. Ibid., p. 5.

113. http://dl.dropbox.com/u/29088336/arms cache share/ x960000_BAE plans covert offshore payment system.pdf.

114. Ibid.

115. Ibid.

116. Ibid.

117. US State Department to D. Parkes, May 2011, http://www.pmddtc.state.gov/compliance/consent_agreements/pdf/BAES_PCL.pdf.

118. 'Note for Opening', *Regina* v *BAE Systems plc*, p. 5.

119. U.S. Department of Justice. U.S.Attorney. Northern District of Georgia, 'News Release', 27 January 1995, http://www.justice.gov/criminal/fraud/fcpa/cases/lockheed/1995-01-27-lockheed-press-release-(plea-as-to-lock-heed-love).pdf.

120. Ibid.

121. OECD, *United States: Phase 2: Report on Application of the Convention on Combating Bribery of Foreign Public Officials in International Business*

Transactions and the 1997 Recommendation on Combating Bribery in International Business Transactions, Paris: OECD, 2002, p. 16.

122. 'Information', *U.S. v General Electric Company*: Docket No. 92-CR-087, http://www.justice.gov/criminal/fraud/fcpa/cases/general-electric/1992-07-22-general-electric-information.pdf and 'Statement of Facts in Support of Guilty Plea', *U.S. v Herbert B. Steindler*, et al: Court Docket Number: 94-CR-068; 94-CR-029, http://www.justice.gov/criminal/fraud/fcpa/cases/steindlerh-et-al/1994-07-18-steindlerh-et-al-statement-of-facts-(as-to-steindler).pdf.

123. Michael V. Seitzinger, *Foreign Corrupt Practices Act: A Legal Overview*, Congressional Research Service Report RS21925, 2 September 2004, pp. CRS-4 to CRS-5.

124. Public Law No. 100-418, 23 August 1988, http://www.justice.gov/criminal/fraud/fcpa/history/1988/houserpt-100-418.pdf.

125. Mark Pieth, Lucinda A. Low, Peter J. Cullen, *The OECD Convention on Bribery: A Commentary*, Cambridge: Cambridge University Press, 2007, p. 11.

126. OECD, *Recommendation of the Council on Bribery in International Business Transactions* (adopted by the Council 27 May 1994).

127. Pieth et al, op cit., p. 13.

128. Ibid., p. 14.

129. Ibid., p. 15.

130. Ibid., p. 18.

131. *SIPRI Yearbook 2001: Armaments, Disarmament and International Security*, Stockholm: SIPRI, p. 223.

132. BAE Systems, *Annual Report 2000*, Farnborough: BAE Systems, 2001, p. 43.

133. J. Weston to W.S. Cohen, 16 November 2000, in Appendix A, 'Statement of Offense', *U.S. v BAE Systems plc*: Docket No. 10-CR-035-JDB (hereafter *U.S. v BAE*), http://www.justice.gov/criminal/fraud/fcpa/cases/bae-system/03-01-10baesystems-plea-agree.pdf.

134. P.W. Gardiner, 'Witness Statement', 23 June 2006, p. 59, Gardiner papers, CAAT.

135. Ibid., pp. 60–1.

136. Blake-Turner & Co to S. Fordyce and P.W. Gardiner, 19 February 2002, Gardiner papers, CAAT.

137. Blake-Turner & Co to P.W. Gardiner, 15 April 2002, Gardiner papers, CAAT.

138. P.W. Gardiner to P.J.S. Wilson, 30 May 2002, Gardiner papers, CAAT.

139. P.W. Gardiner, 'Witness Statement', 23 June 2006, p. 68, Gardiner papers, CAAT.

140. Ibid., pp. 72–3.

141. P.W. Gardiner to J.H.A. Winship, 18 April 2002, Gardiner papers, CAAT.

142. P.W. Gardiner to P.J.S. Wilson, 30 May 2002, Gardiner papers, CAAT.

143. P.W. Gardiner, 'Witness Statement', 23 June 2006, pp. 83–5, Gardiner papers, CAAT.

144. Ibid., p. 86.

145. Ibid., p. 90.

146. OECD, *United Kingdom Phase 2bis Report on the Application of the Convention on Combating Bribery of Foreign Public Officials in International Business Transactions and the 1997 Recommendation on Combating Bribery in International Business Transactions*, Paris: OECD, October 2008, p. 50.

147. OECD, *United Kingdom Phase 2 Report on the Application of the Convention on Combating Bribery of Foreign Public Officials in International Business Transactions and the 1997 Recommendation on Combating Bribery in International Business Transactions*, Paris: OECD, March 2005, pp. 48–9.

148. OECD, *United Kingdom Phase 2bis Report*, op cit., p. 50.

149. OECD, *United Kingdom Phase 2 Report*, op cit., p. 49.

150. 'Witness Statement of Robert Wardle', 17 December 2007, paragraph 4, *Corner House Research & Campaign Against Arms Trade, R (on the application of) v Director of the Serious Fraud Office & Anor* [2008] EWHC 714 (Admin) (hereafter *Corner House v SFO*).

151. M. Cowie to L. Charalambous, 11 October 2004, Gardiner papers, CAAT.

Chapter 9

1. *Hansard*, House of Commons, Vol. 475, Part 2, 2007–08, 1 May 2008, Col. 573W, and 'Witness statement of Robert Wardle', 31 January 2008, paragraph 27, *Corner House v SFO*.

2. Author's calculations from OECD, *Steps taken to implement and enforce the OECD Convention on Combating Bribery of Foreign Public Officials in International Business Transactions: United States*, Paris: OECD, 31 May 2011.

3. OECD, *United Kingdom Phase 2 Report*, op cit., p. 40.

4. Ibid., p. 48.

5. Ibid., p. 80.

6. M. Lester to P.H. Goldsmith, 7 November 2005 in 'Exhibit RW4', 'Witness Statement of Robert Wardle', *Corner House v SFO*.

7. J. G. Jones to A.T. O'Donnell, 6 December 2005 in 'Exhibit RW2', 'Witness Statement of Robert Wardle', *Corner House v SFO*

8. M. Lester to P.H. Goldsmith, 7 November 2005 in 'Exhibit RW4', 'Witness Statement of Robert Wardle', *Corner House v SFO*.

9. Ibid.

10. Agence France Press, 3 October 2005.

11. M. Lester to P.H. Goldsmith, 7 November 2005 in 'Exhibit RW4', 'Witness Statement of Robert Wardle', *Corner House v SFO*.

12. Ibid.

13. Reuters, 10 September 2006.

14. J. Hitchin to M. Cowie, 8 December 2005 in 'Exhibit RW4', 'Witness Statement of Robert Wardle', *Corner House v SFO*.

15. *Financial Times*, 4 April 2007.

16. 'Witness Statement of Robert Wardle', 17 December 2007, paragraphs 8 and 11, *Corner House v SFO*.

17. Ibid., paragraphs 12 and 14–15.

18. A.T. O'Donnell to J.G. Jones, 16 December 2005 in 'Exhibit RW2', 'Witness Statement of Robert Wardle', *Corner House v SFO*.

19. Ministry of Defence, Press Release, 22 December 2005.

20. J.G. Jones to A.T. O'Donnell, 25 January 2006 in 'Exhibit RW2', 'Witness Statement of Robert Wardle', *Corner House v SFO*.

21. *Financial Times*, 26 February 2007.

22. House of Commons, Constitutional Affairs Committee, Session 2006–07, Fifth Report, *Constitutional Role of the Attorney General*, London: TSO, 19 July 2007, Ev 34.

23. *Financial Times*, 26 February 2007.

24. *Corner House v SFO*, paragraph 4.

25. House of Commons, Constitutional Affairs Committee, op cit., Ev 34.

26. *Financial Times*, 26 February 2007.

27. A.T. O'Donnell to J.G. Jones, 29 September 2006 in 'Exhibit RW2', 'Witness Statement of Robert Wardle', *Corner House v SFO*.

28. J.G. Jones to A.T. O'Donnell, 3 October 2006 in 'Exhibit RW2', 'Witness Statement of Robert Wardle', *Corner House v SFO*.

29. H. Garlick to J.G. Jones, 27 October 2006, in 'Exhibit RW4', 'Witness Statement of Robert Wardle' in *Corner House v SFO* and 'Helen Garlick' in *Corner House Research & Ors, R (On The Application of) v The Serious Fraud Office* [2008] UKHL 60.

30. 'Memorandum of Understanding for the Provision of Equipment and Services for the Royal Saudi Air Force', PJ 5/39, TNA.

31. House of Commons, Defence Committee, Session 1989–90, First Report, *The Appointment of the Head of Defence Export Services*, London: HMSO, 22 November 1989, Ev 30.

32. Riyadh Telegram ZMC/ZDK/ZBG/A2P to Ministry of Defence, 6 January 1986, PJ 5/40, TNA.

33. Ibid.

34. *Guardian*, 28 October 2006.

35. Transcript, 4 March 2008, p. 88, *CAAT v IC*, CAAT.

36. 'Witness Statement of Stephen Pollard', paragraph 15, *CAAT v IC*, CAAT.

37. 'Witness Statement of Paul Inman', paragraph 18, *CAAT v IC*, CAAT.

38. 'Second Witness Statement of Simon Marsh', paragraph 7, in *Campaign Against Arms Trade v. IC* (Freedom of Information Act 2000) [2011] UKFTT EA_2011_0109 (GRC), CAAT.

39. *CAAT v IC*, paragraph 84.

40. *Daily Mail*, 25 November 2006.

41. *Hansard*, House of Commons, Vol. 453, Part 1, 2006–07, 30 November 2006, Col. 1222.

42. *Daily Telegraph*, 29 November 2006.

43. K. Hartley, *The Industrial and Economic Benefits of Eurofighter Typhoon*, Hallbergmoos: Eurofighter, 16 June 2006, p. 21. This figure is derived by taking the jobs total for the Saudi export order and applying the British work share percentage for the Typhoon programme.

44. 'Statement of Facts and Issues', paragraph 26, in *Corner House Research & Ors, R (On The Application of) v The Serious Fraud Office* [2008] UKHL 60.

45. 'Witness Statement of Robert Wardle', 17 December 2007, paragraph 28, *Corner House v SFO*.

46. A.C.L. Blair to P.H. Goldsmith, 8 December 2006 in 'Exhibit RW2', 'Witness Statement of Robert Wardle', *Corner House v SFO*.

47. 'Witness Statement of Robert Wardle', 17 December 2007, paragraph 34, *Corner House v SFO*.

48. A.C.L. Blair to P.H. Goldsmith, 8 December 2006 in 'Exhibit RW2', 'Witness Statement of Robert Wardle', *Corner House v SFO*.

49. O. Robbins to J.G. Jones, 12 December 2006 in 'Exhibit RW2', 'Witness Statement of Robert Wardle', *Corner House v SFO*.

50. 'Witness Statement of Robert Wardle', 17 December 2007, paragraph 39, *Corner House v SFO*.

51. *Intelligence and Security Committee Annual Report 2006–2007*, Cm 7299, London: TSO, January 2008, paragraph 107.

52. 'Witness Statement of Robert Wardle', 17 December 2007, paragraph 51, *Corner House v SFO*.

53. *Hansard*, House of Lords, Vol. 687, 2006–07, 14 December 2006, Cols 1711–3.

54. OECD, *United Kingdom Phase 2 Report*, op cit., p. 80.

55. OECD, *United Kingdom Phase 2bis Report*, op cit., p. 5.

56. OECD, Press Release, 14 March 2007.

57. Monty Raphael, *Blackstone's Guide to The Bribery Act 2010*, Oxford: Oxford University Press, 2010, pp. 23–4.

58. OECD, *United Kingdom Phase 2 Follow-up Report on the Implementation of the Phase 2 Recommendations*, Paris: OECD, June 2007, p. 6.

59. Raphael, op cit., p. 25.

60. OECD, *United Kingdom Phase 2bis Report*, op cit., p. 41.

61. Ibid., p. 70.

62. Raphael, op cit., p. 27.

63. https://www.wikileaks.org/plusd/cables/07PARIS829_a.html.

64. 'Serious Fraud Office Investigation into BAE Systems/Saudi Arabia. Further note to OECD from United Kingdom', 8 March 2007, paragraph 8, CAAT.

65. https://www.wikileaks.org/plusd/cables/07PARIS829_a.html.

66. 'Serious Fraud Office Investigation into BAE Systems/Saudi Arabia. Further note to OECD from United Kingdom', 8 March 2007, paragraph 6, CAAT.

67. Transcript, 4 March 2008, p. 26, *CAAT v IC*, CAAT.
68. *Hansard*, House of Commons, Vol. 489, Part 2, 2008–09, 10 March 2009, Col. 400W.
69. https://www.wikileaks.org/plusd/cables/07PARIS829_a.html.
70. OECD, *United Kingdom Phase 2bis Report*, op cit., p. 12.
71. Ibid., p. 13.
72. Ibid., p. 12.
73. Ibid., p. 35.
74. Mark Hollingsworth with Sandy Mitchell, *Saudi Babylon: Torture, Corruption and Cover-Up Inside the House of Saud*, Edinburgh: Mainstream Publishing Company, 2006.
75. House of Lords and House of Commons, Joint Committee on Human Rights, Session 2008–09, Twenty-third Report, *Allegations of UK Complicity in Torture*, London: TSO, 4 August 2009, HC 230, summary.
76. *Exaro News*, 24 April 2012.
77. *Financial Times*, 30 April 2007.
78. http://www.saudiembassy.net/archive/2007/news/page784.aspx.
79. Ministry of Defence, Press Release, 17 September 2007.
80. Reuters, 17 September 2007.
81. *Hansard*, House of Commons, Vol. 457, Part 2, 2006–07, 27 February 2007, Col. 1149W.
82. *Corner House Research & Campaign Against Arms Trade, R (on the application of) v Director of the Serious Fraud Office & Anor* [2008] EWHC 714 (Admin).
83. *Corner House Research & Ors, R (On The Application of) v The Serious Fraud Office* [2008] UKHL 60.
84. *Guardian*, 18 February 2011.
85. 'Statement of Offense', *U.S. v BAE*, http://www.justice.gov/criminal/fraud/fcpa/cases/bae-system/03-01-10baesystems-plea-agree.pdf.
86. Ibid.
87. Woolf Committee, *Ethical business conduct in BAE Systems plc – the way forward: Executive Summary*, London: Woolf Committee, May 2008, p. 4.
88. Ibid.
89. Lockheed Aircraft Corporation, op cit., p. 3.
90. Woolf Committee, op cit., pp. 5–6.
91. *Jane's Defence Weekly*, 13 May 1998.
92. *Financial Times*, 18 October 2000.
93. *Air Forces Monthly*, July 2001.
94. 'Statement of Offense', *U.S. v BAE*, http://www.justice.gov/criminal/fraud/fcpa/cases/bae-system/03-01-10baesystems-plea-agree.pdf.
95. *Financial Times*, 11 December 2001.
96. Statement of Offense', *U.S. v BAE*, http://www.justice.gov/criminal/fraud/fcpa/cases/bae-system/03-01-10baesystems-plea-agree.pdf.
97. *Guardian*, 30 September 2008 and 2 March 2009.

98. Statement of Offense', *U.S.* v *BAE*, http://www.justice.gov/criminal/fraud/fcpa/cases/bae-system/03-01-10baesystems-plea-agree.pdf.

99. *Flight International*, 18–24 September 2001.

100. Ibid., 11–17 February 2003 and Gripen International, Press Release, 3 February 2003.

101. Statement of Offense', *U.S.* v *BAE*, http://www.justice.gov/criminal/fraud/fcpa/cases/bae-system/03-01-10baesystems-plea-agree.pdf.

102. Serious Fraud Office, Press Release, 29 January 2010.

103. *Guardian*, 7 February 2010.

104. Notes by Rob Evans of hearing at Highbury magistrates court, 28 January 2010, CAAT.

105. Notes by Rob Evans of hearing at Westminster magistrates court, 3 February 2010, CAAT.

106. 'Settlement Agreement between the Serious Fraud Office and BAE Systems plc', February 2010.

107. 'Note for Opening', *Regina* v *BAE Systems plc*, p. 5.

108. Ibid., p. 6.

109. Ibid.

110. Ibid., p. 7.

111. Ibid.

112. Ibid.

113. Ibid.

114. Ibid., p. 10.

115. 'Settlement Agreement between the Serious Fraud Office and BAE Systems plc', February 2010.

116. *Regina* v *BAE Systems plc*, paragraph 15.

117. Serious Fraud Office, Press Release, 5 February 2010.

118. 'Statement of Offence', *Regina* v *BAE Systems plc*.

119. 'Settlement Agreement between the Serious Fraud Office and BAE Systems plc', February 2010.

120. *Regina* v *BAE Systems plc*, paragraph 19.

121. Office of the United States Attorney Southern District of California, News Release, 1 March 2005, and 'Information', *U.S.* v *Titan Corporation*: Docket No. 05-CR-314-BEN, http://www.justice.gov/criminal/fraud/fcpa/cases/titan-corp.html.

122. Department of Justice, Press Release, 1 March 2010.

123. OECD, *Phase 3 Report on Implementing the OECD Anti-Bribery Convention in the United Kingdom*, Paris: OECD, March 2012, p. 38.

124. State Department, Press Release, 17 May 2011.

125. Paul Holden and Hennie van Vuuren, *The Devil in the Detail: How the Arms Deal changed everything*, Jeppestown, Jonathan Ball Publishers, 2011, p. 99.

126. Holden and van Vuuren, op cit., pp. 191 and 208. The author possesses a copy of the SFO affidavit quoted by Holden and van Vuuren to which this and the following three endnotes refer. The author was passed a copy after

it was leaked to a South African newspaper and widely circulated in the media.

127. Ibid., p. 195.
128. Ibid., p. 196.
129. Ibid., pp. 196–7.
130. OECD, *OECD Working Group on Bribery Annual Report 2011*, Paris: OECD, pp. 14 and 17.
131. OECD, *Phase 3 Report*, op cit., p. 39.
132. Ibid., p. 40.
133. *Private Eye*, Issue 1314, and *Exaro News*, 15 May 2012.
134. F. Cooper to H.J.L. Suffield, 23 June 1976, DEFE 23/149, TNA.
135. H.J.L. Suffield to F. Cooper, 23 July 1976, DEFE 23/149, TNA.
136. H.J.L. Suffield to F. Cooper, undated draft, DEFE 68/319, TNA.
137. H.J.L. Suffield to F. Cooper, 23 July 1976, DEFE 23/149, TNA.
138. H.J. Amery to P.A.R. Carrington, 22 May 1980, FCO 8/3738, TNA.
139. I.T.M. Lucas to M.S. Weir, 'Agency arrangements for Saudi Arabia', 21 February 1978, FCO 8/3118, TNA.
140. Ibid.
141. H.St.J.B. Armitage to A.B. Milne, 6 November 1969, FCO 8/1999, TNA.
142. Ibid.
143. H.J.St.B. Armitage to A.B. Milne, 29 November 1969, FCO 8/1999, TNA.
144. W. Morris to I.S. Winchester, 8 February 1972, FCO 8/1914, TNA.
145. D.J. McCarthy to C.S., 18 November 1976, FCO 8/2633, TNA.
146. SAMV(75)10A, 15 October 1975, FCO 8/2605, TNA.
147. National Enterprise Board, 'Allegations in the Daily Mail of 19 and 20 May 1977 about British Leyland Limited', 13 June 1977, DEFE 24/1316, TNA.
148. F. Cooper to H.J.L. Suffield, 23 June 1976, DEFE 23/149, TNA and H.J.L. Suffield to F. Cooper, 23 June 1976, DEFE 23/149, TNA.
149. *Annuaire Des Societies Libanaises A Responsabilite Limitee*, op cit., p. 213.
150. H.V.B. Brown to M.W. Hunt, 22 January 1978, FCO 8/3118, TNA.
151. J.E.D. Street to M.S. Weir, 8 February 1978, FCO 8/3118, TNA.
152. I.T.M. Lucas to M.S. Weir, 'Agency arrangements for Saudi Arabia', 21 February 1978, FCO 8/3118, TNA.
153. B.A. Major to D.I. Lewty, 12 April 1978, FCO 8/3118, TNA.
154. Jedda Telegram No.255 to Foreign and Commonwealth Office, 23 April 1978, FCO 8/3118, TNA.
155. B.A. Major to H.R. Braden, 25 April 1978, FCO 8/3118, TNA.
156. 1980 Annual Report of Duranton Limited (No.1022377), available at http://www.companieshouse.gov.uk.
157. *Private Eye*, Issue 1330.
158. Ibid.
159. J.D.S. Dawson to M.O'D.B. Alexander, 1 July 1981, PREM 19/1126, TNA.
160. H.J. Amery to P.A.R. Carrington, 22 May 1980, FCO 8/3738, TNA.
161. *Exaro News*, 30 October 2012.

162. *Exaro News*, 29 May 2012.
163. Serious Fraud Office, Press Release, 7 August 2012.
164. *Hansard*, House of Commons, Vol. 549, Part 2, 2012–13, 3 September 2012, Col. 69W.

Conclusion

1. E.G. Norris to A.M. Simons, 21 June 1976, FCO 15/2145, TNA.
2. William M. Daley, *The National Export Strategy: Working for America, Seventh Annual Report to the United States Congress*, Washington: Trade Promotion Coordinating Committee, March 2000, p. 11.
3. 'Witness Statement of Joe Roeber', paragraph 45, *Gilby* v *IC* [2008] UKIT EA_2007_0071.
4. *Global Enforcement Report 2011*, Annapolis: TRACE International, 2011, Figure VII.
5. A.J.M. Craig to H.D.A.C. Miers, 24 March 1980, FCO 8/3443, TNA.
6. See *CIA World Factbook* at https://www.cia.gov/library/publications/the-world-factbook.
7. Andrew Feinstein, Paul Holden and Barnaby Pace, *Corruption and the arms trade: sins of commission* in *SIPRI Yearbook 2011: Armaments, Disarmament and International Security*, Stockholm: SIPRI, p. 26.
8. Ibid.
9. Pride Chigwedere et al., 'Estimating the Lost Benefits of Antiretroviral Drug Use in South Africa', *Journal of Acquired Immune Deficiency Syndromes*, Vol. 49, Issue 4 (December 2008).
10. Feinstein et al., op cit., p. 26.
11. Holden and van Vuuren, op cit., p. 354.
12. http://www.transparency.org/whoweare/organisation/faqs_on_corruption.
13. Laurence Cockcroft, *Global Corruption: Money, Power and Ethics in the Modern World*, London: I.B. Tauris, 2012, chapter 4.
14. W. Morris to H.J.L. Suffield, 11 February 1970, FCO 8/1498, TNA.
15. http://www.ti-defence.org/what-we-do/govmil.
16. Lord Beswick to R.E. Dearing, 14 February 1978, FV 22/119, TNA.
17. OECD, *OECD Working Group on Bribery Annual Report 2011*, op cit., p. 3.
18. See the *Defense News* Top 100 for 2011 at http://special.defensenews.com/top-100.
19. Cockcroft, op cit., p. 175.

Index

Abdullah, Prince (Commander of Saudi
    Arabian National Guard, later Crown
    Prince then King, Saudi Arabia) 38,
    40, 86, 109, 141, 167, 175
  desire for Government-to-Government
    deal 50
  negotiation with British Government
    51–4, 106, 109
  refusal to use agents 40–1
  relations with Austin, Peter 177
  relations with British Military Mission
    42
  relations with Fustok, N. 102, 105, 176
  relations with Fustuq 43, 49, 105
Abdul Aziz bin Abdullah, Prince
  BAe benefits programme 141
Abdul Rahman, Prince (businessman,
    later Deputy Minister of Defence
    and Aviation, Saudi Arabia) 5, 91
  agreement with Associated Electrical
    Industries (AEI) 9, 13
  agreement with Geoffrey Edwards 9,
    82–4
  commissions 7, 9, 82–4
  legal action against Associated
    Electrical Industries (AEI) 83–4
  relations with Geoffrey Edwards 5,
    12–13, 40, 82–4
Abeer bin Turki, Princess
  BAe benefits programme 141
Acland, Antony (Head of Arabian
    Department, Foreign and
    Commonwealth Office) 49–52
Aden 137
Adham, Kamal (Head of Saudi
    Intelligence) 46
  owner of Pennway Investment
    Corporation and consultant for
    Rolls-Royce 115–16
  Scicon bid for Saudi Ministry of the
    Interior contract 94–5
Administration of Justice Act 1970 84
Africa 101, 118, 123, 172–3
African National Congress 173
Agency fee see Reporter, Shapoor
Agents (general)
  role in business deals 4, 19, 30, 46

Agusta 173
air defence system see Saudi Arabian Air
    Defence (SAAD) scheme
Airbus Group see GPT Special Project
    Management Limited
Airwork
  commissions 9, 80, 88
  see also Edwards, Geoffrey; Saudi
    Arabian Air Defence (SAAD)
    scheme; Winship, Tony
Akins, James (American Ambassador to
    Saudi Arabia) 86
Al Haggar, Colonel Fahad 97
  commissions 97
  see also Kuwait
Al Salam 166, 168
Al Yamamah x, 134–7, 142–3, 152–64,
    166–7, 172, 174–5
  initial Serious Fraud Office
    investigation 153
  investigation by American Department
    of Justice 167, 178
  see also BAe benefits programme;
    Serious Fraud Office investigation of
    BAE Systems
Alam, Asadollah (Iranian Minister of
    Court) 62, 68
Alamuddin, Najeeb 26
Alamuddin, Sulayman (Managing
    Director, Near East Resources)
  friend of Hubert, Harold 26
  sales to Lebanon 26, 30, 31
  sales to Saudi Arabia 44, 47, 49
Alderman, Richard (Director, Serious
    Fraud Office) 166
Al-Helaissi, Abdurrahman (Saudi
    Ambassador to London) 33, 46
Ali Reza, Abdullah 98
  commissions 98
Ali Reza, Ali 35–7
  commissions 35–7
All Nippon Airways (ANA) 75
Alvis
  commissions 45, 51, 91, 143–4, 146
  negotiation of deal in Indonesia 143–6
  negotiation of deal with Saudi Arabian
    National Guard 41–6, 49–52

Alvis *continued*
    negotiation of deal with Saudi Army 33
    use of Near East Resources as agent in
        Lebanon 26, 31
    use of Near East Resources as agent in
        Saudi Arabia 44–5, 49
Al-Zawawi, Qais (Minister of State for
        Foreign Affairs, Oman)
    corruption 129
American Government 151, 166
    action against corruption 77, 89
    attempting to prevent disclosures about
        corruption 87, 90
    knowledge of commissions 85, 91
    OECD Anti-Bribery Convention 150
    proposals for international agreement
        against corruption 112, 117–20, 122,
        124–7
    see also Trade Promotion Coordinating
        Committee
AMX-30 tanks 37
Anglo-Persian Oil Company *see* British
        Petroleum (BP)
Anglo-Iranian Oil Company *see* British
        Petroleum (BP)
Anti-terrorism, Crime and Security Act
        2001 151–2, 154, 163–4, 174
    convictions secured under 154, 174
antitrust laws 76
Arabian American Oil Company
        (ARAMCO) 12
Arabian Electronic Projects of Jedda
        (AEP) 94
    see also Adham, Kamal
arbitration 84
Arms Export Control Act (America) 79
    conviction under 172
Arstow 174
Associated Electrical Industries (AEI) 82
    commissions 9, 80–1, 87, 91
    see also Abdul Rahman, Prince;
        Edwards, Geoffrey; Freedom of
        Information Act; Saudi Arabian Air
        Defence (SAAD) scheme;
        Thunderbird missile system
Austin, Peter 175, 177
Austria 169

BAE Systems (BAE) 150, 154, 183
    benefits programme *see* Abeer bin
        Turki, Princess; Abdul Aziz bin
        Abdullah, Prince; Behery, General;
        Gardiner, Peter; Faisal bin Turki,

        Prince; Haifa bin Turki, Princess;
        Noura, Princess; Saudi Royal Family;
        Travellers World; Turki bin Nasser,
        Prince; Winship, Tony
    commissions 151, 169–71, 173
    compliance with Foreign Corrupt
        Practices Act 150–1, 167
    investigation/conviction/fine by
        American Department of Justice x,
        148, 167, 169–70, 172–3, 178, 183
    sale of Eurofighter Typhoon to Saudi
        Arabia 155–7, 161, 166
    sales to Czech Republic 169–70, 183
    sales to Hungary 169–70, 183
    sales to South Africa 172–4
    sales to Tanzania 170–1
    use of agents 164, 168–72
    see also British Aerospace; British
        Aircraft Corporation; Serious Fraud
        Office investigation of BAE Systems;
        Woolf Committee
Bahrain 53, 57, 130
Baldwin, Jack 82
Bandar bin Sultan, Prince 132, 167
    Al Yamamah 134
Bank of England Exchange Control 69,
        102, 111–12, 114
Bannerman, Patrick 88
Barger, Tom (Director, Northrop) 86
Barnett, Joel (Chief Secretary to the
        Treasury) 94, 112, 114, 117, 126
Barton, Graham 101, 103, 105
Basque 146
Bean, Mr Justice 171
Beherey, General
    BAe benefits programme 139–40
Benin 172
Bernhard, Prince 18, 74, 79
Beswick, Frank (Chairman, British
        Aerospace) 182
Blair, Tony (British Prime Minister)
        155–6, 161
Bolton-Lee, Anouska 141
Bourn, Sir John (Comptroller and
        Auditor General) 143
Brandt's *see* William Brandt's Sons and
        Company Ltd
bribe
    definition ix
    general mentions of/euphemisms for 9,
        10, 12, 19, 21–2, 24, 26, 31, 36–7, 40,
        46, 49, 54, 58, 72–4, 77–9, 85, 93, 97,

102–5, 107, 109–20, 122–6, 128, 136, 151, 163, 168, 174, 178–80, 182, 184–5
bribery
definition ix
Bribery Act 2010 174
British Aerospace (BAe) 69, 150
    benefits programme *see* Abeer bin Turki, Princess; Abdul Aziz bin Abdullah, Prince; Behery, General; Gardiner, Peter; Faisal bin Turki, Prince; Haifa bin Turki, Princess; Noura, Princess; Saudi Royal Family; Travellers World; Turki bin Nasser, Prince; Winship, Tony
    commissions 142–3, 148, 171
    draft statement on business ethics 182
    involvement in Saudi Arabian Air Defence Assistance Project (SADAP) 142
    role of fixers 130
    use of agents 147–8
    see also Al Yamamah; Gardiner, Peter; Red Diamond Trading Ltd; Reporter, Shapoor; Siemens Plessey Electronic Systems; Winship, Tony
British Aerospace Defence Systems Limited *see* Siemens Plessey Electronic Systems
British Aerospace (Operations) Limited *see* British Aerospace (BAe)
British Aircraft Corporation (BAC), the 4, 16, 19, 80
    attempts to settle *Edwards* v *AEI* 83–4
    commissions 7, 9–11, 13, 15, 80, 82, 88, 91, 106–8
    involvement in Saudi Arabian Air Defence Assistance Project (SADAP) 106, 108, 131–2
    sales to Kuwait 98
    use of Near East Resources as agent in Lebanon 26
    see also Edwards, Geoffrey; Reporter, Shapoor; Saudi Arabian Air Defence (SAAD) scheme; Thunderbird missile system
British Government 42, 173
    Al Yamamah 134, 142, 163
    assurances about BAC 14
    attitudes to corruption in international trade 101, 104, 110, 112, 114–15, 153
    attitudes to proposed agreement against corruption in international trade 112–13, 117–19, 121–7

British Leyland scandal 99, 101, 103
    involvement in arms sales 19–20, 22, 24, 71, 155, 159, 166
    knowledge of commissions 13, 19, 31, 71, 80, 82–3, 91, 96–8, 104, 111, 131, 142
    Ministers 61, 64, 70–1, 94, 101, 104–5, 109–10, 112–15, 117, 119, 121–3, 125, 156
    OECD Anti-Bribery Convention 150, 163, 165
    Randel case 63–4, 98
    relations with Saudi Arabia 132, 156–8, 160–2, 165–6
    see also diplomats; Ministerial Group on Improper Trade Practices; Ministerial Group on Special Commissions and Similar Payments; Shah of Iran
British Hovercraft Corporation 47
    commissions 47
British Leyland 176
    commissions 102, 105
    problems for investigators xv
    scandal 99–103, 105, 108, 112, 114, 121
British Overseas Trade Board
    discussions about corruption in international trade 113
British Petroleum (BP) 56, 92
    payments in Italy and other countries 92–4, 110, 112, 126
    see also Scicon
British Shipbuilders *see* Nigeria
British Virgin Islands 148, 174
Brown, Raymond (Head of Defence Sales) 20, 21, 23, 33, 41, 176
Buckingham Palace 167
Buqshan 47
    commissions 47
Burnand, Peter 25–7, 30
    commissions 25–7

C-130 aircraft 74, 149
Cabinet Secretary 93, 101, 156–8
Cable & Wireless 175
    commissions 106
    see also Engineering and Trading Operations Company Beirut; SIMEC International
Caldecote, Lord (Director, the British Aircraft Corporation)
    attempts to settle *Edwards* v *AEI* 83
    knowledge of activities of Geoffrey Edwards 7, 12, 81–2

Caldecote, Lord *continued*
    knowledge of commissions 6–7, 81–2
    personal papers xiii, 13
    see also Thunderbird missile system
California 75
Callaghan, Jim (British Prime Minister)
    70, 72
    British Leyland scandal 101, 103
    decisions about BP payments in Italy 93
    discussions about corruption in
        international trade 104, 114
    knowledge of commissions 98
    proposals for international agreement
        against corruption 118, 121, 123–4
    Scicon bid for Saudi Ministry of the
        Interior contract 94–6
Campaign Against Arms Trade 162
Carr, Edgar 11
Carrington, Lord (Peter) 7, 60, 132
Carter, Jimmy (American President) 78,
    118, 127, 132
Catherwood, Sir Frederick (Chairman,
    British Overseas Trade Board) 113–14
Cawston, Colonel Antony (British
    Defence Attaché, Beirut) 26–7, 32
Cayman Islands 114, 175, 177
Central Intelligence Agency (CIA)
    financing of Italian political parties 75
    1953 coup in Iran with the Secret
        Intelligence Service (SIS) 56, 65, 68
Central Policy Review Staff 114–15
Central Treaty Organisation 56
Centurion tank 24
Chalabi 29, 31–2
Chamoun, Camile 25
    commissions 28, 30–2
    see also Millbank Technical Services;
        Suffield, Sir Lester
Chan U Seek 143–5
    commissions 144
Chandler, Colin 159
Chidiac
    commissions 27, 29, 30
Chieftain tank
    attempted sale to the Netherlands 23
    sale to Iran 58–60, 63–4, 66, 70
    sale to Jordan 71
    sale to Kuwait 97–8
    use in Iran 67
Church Committee
    documents xiii, 89
    hearings 73–5, 79, 85–6, 87, 89–90
    investigation 73–6, 91, 110

Church, Senator Frank 73, 89
Churchill, Winston (British Prime
    Minister) 56
Civil Service 113
Code of Conduct for Transnational
    Corporations 125, 127
Cohen, William (American Defense
    Secretary) 150, 167
'Commissie van drie' 74
commissions (general) 4, 16, 22–4, 33,
    46–8, 76–7, 79, 85, 93, 99, 102, 104,
    108, 111, 114–16, 118, 121, 130, 142–3,
    172, 179
    ban in Iran 61
    bans in Saudi Arabia 16, 33, 35, 38,
        40–2, 46, 54, 89, 103, 107, 176, 181
    see also Abdul Rahman, Prince;
        Airwork; Al Haggar, Colonel Fahad;
        Ali Reza, Abdullah; Ali Reza, Ali;
        Alvis; Arms Export Control Act;
        Associated Electrical Industries
        (AEI); British Aerospace (BAe);
        British Aircraft Corporation (BAC);
        British Hovercraft Corporation;
        British Leyland; Buqshan; Burnand,
        Peter; Chamoun, Camile; Chan U
        Seek; Chidiac; Edwards, Geoffrey;
        Engineering and Trading Operations
        Company Beirut; Fahd, Prince;
        Fustok, Mr N.; Fustuq; Habre,
        Abdullah; Kamouh, Antoine; Khalid
        bin Abdullah, Prince; Khashoggi,
        Adnan; Lockheed Aircraft
        Corporation; Malik, Adam;
        Marubeni Corporation; Matthew,
        John (QC); Millbank Technical
        Services (MTS); Near East
        Resources; Northrop Corporation;
        Redshaw, Leonard; Scicon; SIMEC
        International; Tanaka, Kakuei; Twal,
        Shehadah; Vickers; Vithlani,
        Shailesh; Wingetac
Companies Act 1985 171
Confederation of British Industry 113
Congress 76, 78–9, 110, 118, 134, 149
conventions used xvi
Cookson, Brian (Company Secretary, the
    British Aircraft Corporation) 83
Cooper, Sir Frank (Permanent Secretary,
    Ministry of Defence)
    directives on commissions in arms
        deals 99, 106, 109, 143

discussions about BAC commissions 108

discussions about Shapoor Reporter 65

sales to Kuwait 98

sales to Saudi Arabia 106–7, 175

corruption

arguments 181–2

definitions ix, 181

evidence xiv

extent of 72, 129

impact of 180–1

role in arms trade xi, 22

see also bribe

Council of Europe Criminal Law Convention against Corruption ix

Cowper-Coles, Sir Sherard (British Ambassador to Saudi Arabia) 161–2, 165, 167

Craig, James (Deputy to, later British Ambassador to Saudi Arabia) 47, 134, 179–80

meeting with fixer in Lebanon 51

Criminal Justice Act 1987 155

Crociani, Camillo (President, Finmeccanica) 75

Crotale surface-to-air missile deal 32

Crowe, Sir Colin (British Ambassador to Saudi Arabia) 7, 9

Crown Agents 26, 46, 71

Crown Dependencies 184cumshaw *see* bribe

Czech Republic 154, 169

Daily Mail 99–102, 105, 121, 160

Daily Telegraph 160

Daimler *see* Near East Resources

Dassault 9, 11

see also Edwards, Geoffrey

Defence Sales Organisation (DSO) 19–20, 21, 89, 101, 154

agent in Jordan 23

agent in the Netherlands 23

approving commissions 91, 96–9, 106, 142, 175

dealings with agents 33, 48, 65–6, 97, 176

policy on use of agents 22–3, 51, 68, 99, 106, 176–7

sales campaign in Lebanon 24–8, 30

sales to Iran 59–60, 63, 66–7, 69

sales to Kuwait 96–8

sales to Saudi Arabia 106, 142, 159

sales to Saudi Arabian National Guard 43, 45, 50–1, 55, 105, 175

discussions about corruption in international trade 101, 104, 110, 114

proposals for international agreement against corruption 121–3

Scicon bid for Saudi Ministry of the Interior contract 95–6

see also Brown, Raymond; Cooper, Sir Frank; Prest, Nicholas; Randel, Lieutenant Colonel David; Suffield, LesterDell, Edmund (Trade Secretary)

den Uyl, Joop (Dutch Prime Minister) 74

Department of Defence (South Africa) 173

Department of Defense (America) *see* Pentagon

Department of Industry 182

Department of Trade 95, 110

Department of Trade and Industry 158

developing countries

attitudes to proposed agreement against corruption in international trade 118, 123, 125, 127

Diplomatic Conference 120, 122–3, 125, 127

diplomats

attitudes to agents 21–2, 176–7

attitudes to corruption allegations 64–5, 111, 129, 136, 181

decision-making about the use of agents 42, 44, 49–50, 54, 59, 71

discussions about possible official involvement in bribery 47–8

involvement in *Edwards* v *AEI* and *Abdul Rahman* v *AEI* 83–4, 88–9

proposals for international agreement against corruption 124, 127

Scicon bid for Saudi Ministry of the Interior contract 94–5

Dixson, Dr Maurice (Commercial Director, Military Aircraft Division, British Aerospace) 159

Donaldson, Brigadier Adrian (Commander, British Military Mission, Saudi Arabian National Guard) 42–4, 54

enquiries about fixers 42–3

see also Saudi Arabian National Guard

Douglas-Home, Alec (Foreign Secretary) 42

Dove, Basil (Manager, Millbank
    Technical Services) 28
Duguid, Gordon (salesman, the British
    Aircraft Corporation) 7
    discussion of commissions 9–10
    see also Edwards, Geoffrey
Duranton International 175, 177

ECOSOC *see* UN Economic and Social
    Council (ECOSOC)
Edwards, Geoffrey 4, 14, 16, 90
    agreement with Associated Electrical
        Industries (AEI) 9
    agreement with the British Aircraft
        Corporation (BAC) 7, 11
    commissions 7, 9, 13, 14–16, 80–2, 84,
        87–8
    influential contacts 12, 16, 88
    legal action against Associated
        Electrical Industries (AEI) 82–4,
        87–9, 173
    mercenary organisation 137
    relations with Airwork 9
    relations with Associated Electrical
        Industries (AEI) 5, 9, 81–2
    relations with Defence Sales
        Organisation (DSO) 33
    relations with Duguid, Gordon 11–12
    relations with Saudi Royal Family 4, 5,
        119
    relations with the British Aircraft
        Corporation (BAC) 5–16
    see also Abdul Rahman, Prince;
        Freedom of Information Act; Harold,
        Hubert; Saudi Arabian Air Defence
        (SAAD) scheme; Thunderbird
        missile system
Egypt 149, 182
Eisenhower, Dwight D. (American
    President) 56
Ellis, Ron (Head of Defence Sales) 67, 69,
    98
Embassies 115
    American, Jedda 86
    British, Beirut
        British Defence Attaché 40–1, 43–4
        view of local commercial practices
            25
        views of arms deals 25, 27, 32–3
    British, Cairo
        view of local commercial practices
            115
    British, Caracas
        enquiry about agents 22–3

British, Jedda 49, 54, 105
    bribery reports 21, 37
    discussions about official
        involvement in bribery 47–8
    recommendations about agents 35,
        43, 52, 94–5, 116
    reports about bans on commissions
        33, 40
British, Riyadh 165
British, Rome 75
British, Tehran 71
    attitude towards agents 21, 24
    reports about Shapoor Reporter
        58–60
Emergency Loan Guarantee Board 77
Engineering and Trading Operations
    Company Beirut 176
    commissions 106
    see also Cable & Wireless; Fustok,
        Mahmoud; SIMEC International
Envers Trading Corporation *see* Vithlani,
    Shailesh
Ernst and Ernst 73, 86
Eurofighter consortium 160
Eurofighter Typhoon *see* BAE Systems
    (BAE)
Europe 118–19, 126, 148, 150, 169–70, 177
Evans, Rob 159
Evans, Sir Dick (Chairman, British
    Aerospace)
    approval of agent 170
Eveleigh, Mr Justice 84
Exaro News 175
Export Credits Guarantee Department
    (ECGD) 27, 70, 164
    knowledge of commissions 111, 114,
        146, 166
Export-Import Bank (America) 76
exports 70, 110–11, 155
    licences 172

F-5 aircraft 85, 87
F-15 fighter jet 132
F-35 joint strike fighter 151, 181
F-110 engines 149
Fahd, Prince (Minister of Interior, later
    Crown Prince, then King, Saudi
    Arabia) 7, 132
    commissions 7, 107
    corruption allegations 130
    Scicon bid for Saudi Ministry of the
        Interior contract 94–5
Faisal bin Turki, Prince
    BAe benefits programme 139–41

Falle, Sir Sam (British High
    Commissioner to Nigeria) 101
Fanali, Diulio (Head of the Italian Air
    Force) 75
Far East 146
Farouknia (Genarmerie chief, Iran) 61
Feisal, King (of Saudi Arabia) 1, 5, 16,
    42–3, 132
    assassination 86, 89
    bans commissions on Saudi arms deals
        1968 16, 33, 35, 38, 40–2, 46, 54, 181
    budget decisions 3, 14
    concern about Panhard deal 33
    lobbied by Americans 12
    personal example 5–6
    relations with British Government 42,
        53–5
    sales to Saudi Arabian National Guard
        53
    warns Vickers about commissions 36
Finmeccanica 75
Fitzpatrick, Colin (British Defence
    Attaché, Jedda) 35–7
    report of commissions 35–7
Ford, Gerald (American President)
    proposals for international agreement
        against corruption 117
    proposals for new American law against
        corruption 117–18
    Task Force on Questionable Corporate
        Payments Abroad 78, 112, 117
Ford, Sir John (British Ambassador to
    Indonesia) 116
Foreign and Commonwealth Office 22,
    48–9, 52, 130
    internal history of relations with Iran
        57, 64, 71
    knowledge of corruption 25, 130
    see also Foreign Office
Foreign Corrupt Practices Act (America)
    72, 79, 90, 127–8, 149, 151
    becomes law 78, 122, 163, 182
    convictions secured under 149, 154,
        167, 172, 182
    sources xiii
Foreign Military Sales 85
Foreign Office *see* Foreign and
    Commonwealth Office
Foxley, Ian 177
France 19
    arms deals 11, 53, 82, 86, 94, 97, 107,
        130, 169

attitudes to proposed agreement
    against corruption in international
    trade 120, 122–3, 127
France, Sir Christopher (Permanent
    Secretary, Ministry of Defence) 143
Frangié, Suleiman (Lebanese President)
    27, 31
Freedom of Information Act 160
    use of to acquire documents xiii, 43–4,
        91
Fullerton, Bill (desk officer for Saudi
    Arabia, Foreign and Commonwealth
    Office) 49
Fustok, Mahmoud 108–9, 176
    payments to Charles Haughey 109
    see also Engineering and Trading
        Operations Company Beirut
Fustok, Mr N. 102–3, 105
    commissions 102
    see also British Leyland
Fustuq 43, 53, 55, 105, 176
    commissions 53, 108
    METICO 49, 176
    see also Millbank Technical Services
        (MTS)

G7 summit 120, 126
Gabr, Hassan 37
Gardiner, Peter (Managing Director,
    Travellers World) 138
    BAe benefits programme 139, 141–2,
        151–3
    legal advice 151–2
    personal papers xiii, 153
    Serious Fraud Office 153
Garlick, Helen (Assistant Director,
    Serious Fraud Office) 158–9, 163–4
Gaunt, Commander 24
General Electric Company 150
    conviction for corruption in Israel 149
    see also Associated Electrical Industries
        (AEI); Weinstock, Arnold
Ghanem, General (Commander-in-Chief,
    Lebanese Armed Forces) 27, 32
Gilby v *Information Commissioner*
    source of Chapter 3 documents xiii
Global Select 146
Goldsmith, Peter (Attorney General)
    155–62, 165
Government Communications
    Headquarters (GCHQ)
    documents xv
    reports 94

Government-to-Government contract
(American) *see* Foreign Military Sales
Government-to-Government contract
(British) 22, 48, 99
with Iran 61
with Lebanon 27
with Saudi Arabia 91, 106, 108, 131, 164
with Saudi Arabian National Guard 40,
42–3, 50, 106, 175, 177
GPT Special Project Management
Limited *see* Serious Fraud Office
investigation of GPT Special Project
Management Limited
Granada Television *see* British Petroleum
(BP)
Grand Mosque, Mecca 120, 129
Greece 93
Green, David (QC, Director, Serious
Fraud Office) 177
Greenwood, Allen (Chairman, British
Aircraft Corporation) 107
Gripen aircraft 169–70, 173–4
Guardian 98, 136, 159

Habre, Abdullah 25, 31
commissions 25–6, 30
see also Burnand, Peter
Hadsphaltic 176
Haifa bin Turki, Princess
BAe benefits programme 139–40
Harvard University study 180
Haughey, Charles *see* Fustok, Mahmoud
Hawk trainer aircraft 134, 159, 173–4
Hawker Hunter 33
Hawker Siddeley
Lebanese bribe request 33, 119
Haughton, Daniel (Chairman, Lockheed
Aircraft Corporation) 89
Healey, Denis
Chancellor 101
Defence Secretary 14–15, 19, 23, 43
proposals for international agreement
against corruption 124
Heath, retired Colonel Bernard
(salesman, Vickers) 37
Helms, Richard (American Ambassador
to Iran) 61
Henley, Sir Douglas (Comptroller and
Auditor General)
correspondence about BAC
commissions 108–9
Her Majesty's Revenue and Customs *see*
Inland Revenue (Britain)

High Court 157, 167
Hills, Roderick (Chairman, Securities
and Exchange Commission) 76–7
HIV/AIDS 180
Hlongwane, Fana 173–4
Hlongwane Consulting *see* Hlongwane,
Fana
Hobday, Glen (salesman, the British
Aircraft Corporation) 12–13
commission requests 13
Order of the British Empire 15
Holland *see* Netherlands, the
Home Office 154
House of Lords *see* Parliament
House of Representatives (America) 78
Hoveyda, Amir Abbas (Iranian Prime
Minister) 61, 64–5
Howarth, Gerald (Parliamentary Under
Secretary of State, Ministry of
Defence) 177–8
HSBC 175
Hubert, Harold (Director of Army Sales,
Defence Sales Organisation)
attitude to bribery 21–3, 26, 45
deal with Geoffrey Edwards 21
involvement in decisions about
commissions 27, 43, 45, 55
relations with Alamuddin, Sulayman
26, 47
relations with Chidiac 27
sales campaign in Lebanon 26–7, 32
sales to Saudi Arabian National Guard
43–5, 47, 52–5
use of agents 21, 22, 24
Hungary 169
Hussein, King (of Jordan) 23, 71

ICI 116
Indonesia 144, 146
Army 116, 143–6
Information Tribunal *see* Freedom of
Information Act
Inland Revenue (Britain) 111, 114, 155–6
see also Reporter, Shapoor
Inland Revenue Service (America) 77
International Hospitals Group 177
International Traffic in Arms Regulations
172
conviction secured under 172
Iran 22, 24, 38, 64, 71, 89, 154
British arms deals 60, 70, 97
corruption 71, 119

Islamic revolution 39, 67, 69–71, 129, 132
Ministry of War 38
1953 coup 56, 68
strategic importance 56, 70
Iraq 22
Islamic fundamentalists 120, 129
Israel 89, 132, 134
bribery 149
Italy 74–5, 79, 90, 120
Air Force 74
June 1976 elections 75
see also British Petroleum (BP); Saudi Arabia

Jack, Michael (MP) 160
Japan 75, 79, 86, 90, 118, 120
Jenkins, Roy (Minister of Aviation) 14–15
Jersey 4, 16, 69, 90
Jet Provost training aircraft 7, 8, 80, 131
see also Strikemaster
jobs 70, 156, 160
Jones, Bill 97
Jones, Ronald 165
Jones, Tom (Chairman and Chief Executive, Northrop Corporation) 73
Jordan 22, 23, 48, 71
Joseph, Keith (MP) 101
Judd, Frank (Minister of State, Foreign and Commonwealth Office)
proposals for international agreement against corruption 124–5
Judicial Review
action against Serious Fraud Office 162, 174
disclosure of documents xiii, 163
Juliana, Queen 74

Kamouh, Antoine 81–2, 84, 90
commissions 81–2, 90
Keith, Sir Kenneth (Chairman, Rolls-Royce)
attempt to bribe Anwar Sadat 115
seeks advice about Kamal Adham 115–16
Kérékou, Mathieu (Beninese President) 172
Khalid bin Abdullah, Prince
commissions 88
Khalil, Abdul Rauf (Managing Director, Arabian Electronic Projects of Jedda) 94–5

Khashoggi, Adnan 44, 46, 49–50, 95
agent for Lockheed 12, 89
commissions 55, 86–7, 89–90
sales to Saudi Arabian National Guard 54–5
Triad Financial Establishment/International Marketing 85–7, 90
Kissinger, Henry (American Secretary of State) 64, 90
Kleinwort Benson 62, 66
see also Reporter, Shapoor
Kotchian, Carl (President, Lockheed Aircraft Corporation)
commissions 18
evidence at Church Committee hearings 74–5
kumshaw see bribe
Kuss, Henry (Pentagon arms salesman) 13, 19
Kuwait 89
'dirty tricks' by the Defence Sales Organisation (DSO) 96–8

Land Rovers 102, 176
Law Officers (British Government) 15
laws 15–16, 63, 72, 75–6, 78, 102, 114, 117–19, 121–2, 127–8, 142–3, 147, 150–1, 161–5, 173–4, 176, 181–3
British failure to bring in new bribery law 163
penalties for corporate corruption 184
see also Administration of Justice Act 1970; Anti-terrorism, Crime and Security Act 2001; Arms Export Control Act (America); Bribery Act 2010; Companies Act 1985; Criminal Justice Act 1987; Foreign Corrupt Practices Act (America); Prevention of Corruption Act 1906; Public Bodies Corrupt Practices Act 1889
Lebanon 22, 24–33, 40, 58, 93, 119
Lefebvre, Ovidio 75
Leigh, David 159
Leopard tank 58
Levene, Peter (Chief Executive, Alvis) 144–5
Levi, Edward (American Attorney General) 90
Liberal Democratic Party (Japan) 75
Libya 90
Liechtenstein 85, 148, 175
Lightning fighter jet 7, 8, 11, 80, 98, 131–2, 134

Little Whale Cay 177
Lockheed Aircraft Corporation 169, 181
    agent in Japan 18, 75
    agent in Turkey 18
    commissions 18, 73–5, 89, 91
    conviction for corruption in Egypt 149,
        182
    legal opinion 75–6
    problems for investigators xv
    rival to BAC in Saudi Arabia 9, 12
    scandal 72–5, 77, 79, 89, 91, 95, 99–101,
        130, 172, 182
    Special Review Committee xv, 77–8,
        103, 168
    Swiss bank account 18
    TriStar airliners 75, 95
Lockheed Martin *see* Lockheed Aircraft
    Corporation
Lowry, Michael *see* Moriarty Tribunal

Macmillan, Harold (British Prime
    Minister) 42
Madam Tutut *see* Rakhmana, Siti Mrs
Malaysia 116–17
Malik, Adam (Foreign Minister,
    Indonesia)
    commissions 116
Marconi 150
Marubeni Corporation 75
    commissions 75
    Okubo, Toshiharu 75Matthew, John
        (QC)
    legal opinion about commissions 62–3,
        164
Mbeki, Thabo (South African President)
    180
McCarthy, Donal (Head of Arabian
    Department, Foreign and
    Commonwealth Office) 49
    discussions about official involvement
        in bribery 36–7, 44–6
Memorandum of Understanding
    for Al Yamamah 134–5, 158–9, 164
        inadvertent disclosure of 159–60
    with Iran 67, 69
    with Kuwait 98
    with Saudi Arabia 106, 131, 157
    with Saudi Arabian National Guard 53,
        55, 106, 175
Mensdorff-Pouilly, Count Alfons 169–70
Merlin International Limited *see* Vithlani,
    Shailesh
METICO *see* Fustuq

Middle East 6, 11, 17–18, 23, 33, 38, 44,
    55, 90, 93, 99, 101, 111, 115, 122, 127,
    130–1, 150, 157, 167, 177
MiG-21 aircraft 169
Miki, Takeo (Japanese Prime Minister) 75
Military Industrial Complex, Isfahan, 60
Millbank Technical Services (MTS) 27, 60
    commissions 51–4, 62–3, 67, 91, 97,
        108, 164
    fees 59, 64–5, 67–8
    relations with Fustuq 53, 55, 108
    sales campaign in Lebanon 27–32
    sales to Iran 58–63, 70–1
    sales to Kuwait 97
    sales to Saudi Arabian National Guard
        45–6, 50–4, 71, 108
    use of agents 46, 51–2, 62–5, 67, 99
    see also Reporter, Shapoor
Ministerial Group on Improper Trade
    Practices 121, 125
Ministerial Group on Special
    Commissions and Similar Payments
    94, 110–12
Ministers *see* British Government
Ministry of Defence (British) 21, 26, 48,
    50–3, 59, 63–5, 67, 70, 105–6, 108–9,
    129, 142–3, 153, 164, 175–6, 177–8
    Saudi Armed Forces Project 159–60,
        177–8
    view of role of agents 4, 19
    see also Defence Sales Organisation
Ministry of Defence and Aviation (Saudi
    Arabia) *see* Saudi Arabia
Ministry of Justice 178
Ministry of War (Iran) 61
Mitchell, Sandy 165
Modise, Joe (South African Defence
    Minister) 173–4
Mohammed bin Saud, Prince (Minister
    of Defence, Saudi Arabia) 4
Montagu, Sir Nicholas (Head of the
    Inland Revenue) 155
Moriarty Tribunal (Irish) 109
Morris, Willie (British Ambassador to
    Saudi Arabia, later Egypt) 36, 132,
    137, 176, 179, 181
    discussions about official involvement
        in bribery 36–7, 38, 43–4, 48
    report of AEI/Edwards dispute 81, 83
    reports of bribery in Egypt 115
    reports of bribery in Saudi Arabia 38, 91
    sales to Saudi Arabian National Guard
        42–3, 49–50, 52–5

Mossadegh, Muhammad (Iranian Prime Minister) 56, 68
Mulley, Fred (Defence Secretary) 98

Nasser, General 3
Nasser, Major General Sherif (Commander-in-Chief, Jordanian Army) 23
National Archives and Records Administration
documents xiii
National Audit Office 143
knowledge of commissions 143
National Enterprise Board *see* Ryder, Lord
nationalised industries 92, 104-5
Near East Resources
agent for Defence Sales Organisation (DSO) 22
agent for Daimler 26
agent for Shorts 26
commissions 26, 44-5
see also Alvis; British Aircraft Corporation, the (BAC); Vickers
Netherlands, the 23, 74-5, 79, 90
Nigeria 100-1, 103
Nixon, Richard (American President) 73
Norris, Sir Eric (British High Commissioner, Malaysia) 116-17, 179
North Atlantic Treaty Organisation (NATO) 79, 132, 169
Northrop Corporation 55
attempt to hire Geoffrey Edwards 11
commissions 85-7, 89-91
relations with Triad 85-7, 89-90
rival to BAC in Saudi Arabia 9
sales to Saudi Arabia ('Peace Hawk') 85-6, 89, 95
scandal 73, 79, 85, 87-91, 101, 172
Northrop Grumman *see* Northrop Corporation
Nott, John (Trade Secretary) 125
knowledge of corruption 130
proposals for international agreement against corruption 126-7
Noura, Princess 152
BAe benefits programme 136, 139-41
Nurdin, Frank 97, 99, 121
see also Kuwait

Obasanjo, General Olusegun 101
OECD Ad Hoc Group on Illicit Payments 150

OECD Anti-Bribery Convention *see* OECD Convention on Combating Bribery of Foreign Public Officials in International Business Transactions
OECD Convention on Combating Bribery of Foreign Public Officials in International Business Transactions 149-50, 161-3, 183
definition of bribe ix
see also Serious Fraud Office investigation of BAE Systems
offshore financial system 184
Okubo, Toshiharu (Managing Director, Marubeni Corporation) *see* Marubeni Corporation
Old Bailey 155
Olver, Dick (Chairman, BAE Systems) 168
Oman 130
Randel case 63
see also Qaboos, Sultan
Onn, Datuk Hussein (Prime Minister, Malaysia) 117
Organisation for Economic Co-operation and Development (OECD) ix, 114, 126, 149-51, 153-4, 162-3, 165, 172, 174, 184
Working Group on Bribery 162-4, 183
Organization of the Petroleum Exporting Countries (OPEC) 57, 132
Owen, David (Foreign Secretary) 66, 68, 71

Page, Sir Frederick (Chairman, British Aerospace) 131
Pahlavi family 71
Pahlavi Foundation 64, 66, 71
Pahlavi, Mohammed Reza *see* Shah of Iran, the
Pahlavi, Reza 68
Palliser, Sir Michael (Permanent Secretary, Foreign and Commonwealth Office) 65-6, 68, 115-16
Panhard armoured cars 36, 44
scandal about Saudi deal 33
Park, Alex (Chief Executive, British Leyland) 102-3
Parkinson, Cecil (Minister of State for Trade)
proposals for international agreement against corruption 127

Parliament (British) 19, 64, 73, 94, 98,
    101, 103–5, 108, 112, 114, 117, 121,
    123, 126, 130, 142–3, 157, 160, 162,
    165, 167
Parliament (Dutch) 74
Parsons, Sir Anthony (British
    Ambassador to Iran) 62, 64, 65
Patey, William (British Ambassador to
    Saudi Arabia)
    evidence at Information Tribunal xiii,
    43
PC-9 basic training aircraft 134
Peace Hawk *see* Northrop Corporation
Pennway Investment Corporation *see*
    Adham, Kamal
Pentagon (American Department of
    Defense) 13, 19, 55, 85–6, 89, 167
People's Republic of South Yemen (PRSY)
    see Yemen
Persian Gulf 53, 56, 180
    British military withdrawal 53, 56
Petromin *see also* Saudi Arabia
Pharaoun, Ghaith 44
Pilatus 134
Poland 169
Popular Front for the Liberation of the
    Occupied Arabian Gulf 137
Pound, Stephen (MP) 177
Powell, Charles 134–5
Powell, Jonathan 157
Pownall, Orlando (QC) 152
Prest, Nicholas (Chairman and Chief
    Executive, Alvis) 144–6
Prevention of Corruption Act 1906 15–16,
    63, 125, 152, 154, 164–5, 169
    convictions secured under 154
Private Eye 175
Proxmire, Senator William 118
P.T. Surya Kepanjen (PTSK) 145
Public Accounts Committee 143
Public Bodies Corrupt Practices Act 1889
    152
Pym, Francis (Defence Secretary) 130

Qaboos, Sultan (of Oman) 129, 137
Qatar 53, 130

Racal
    Randel case 63, 68
    sales to Kuwait 97–8
Rakhmana, Siti Mrs 145–6
Randel, Lieutenant Colonel David
    receipt of money from Racal 63, 121

arrested and charged with corruption
    63
    trial 64–5, 97, 154, 176
Range Rovers 102
Rapier missile units 69
Reagan, Nancy 132
Reagan, Ronald (American President) 132
Red Diamond Trading Ltd 148–9, 171–2
    commissions 171–4
Redshaw, Leonard (Chairman, Vickers
    Shipbuilding Group)
    commissions 17–18
    negotiation of submarine deal with
    Saudi Arabia 16–18
Reema bin Bandar, Princess 141Rees,
    Merlyn
    proposals for international agreement
    against corruption 124
Reid, John (Defence Secretary) 155–6,
    161
Reporter, Ardeshirji 68
Reporter, Shapoor 58–60, 69
    agent for British Aerospace (BAe) 69
    agent for British arms companies 68
    agent for Millbank Technical Services
    59–60, 62–7
    agent for the British Aircraft
    Corporation (BAC) 69
    career with the Secret Intelligence
    Service (SIS) 58, 68
    fee 59–60, 62, 64–5, 66–8, 176
    investigation by the Inland Revenue 67,
    69
    investigation by intelligence services
    69
    relations with the Shah of Iran 58–60,
    64, 66–7, 69
Robbie, Jim (Director, Vickers) 35
Roe, R.G. (Managing Director, Millbank
    Technical Services) 59
Roeber, Joe
    discussion of arms trade corruption xi,
    179Rolls-Royce 115–16
Romania 154
Rosier, Sir Frederick (Director, British
    Aerospace) 132
Rowan, Sir Leslie (Chairman, Vickers)
    35–6
    sales visit to Saudi Arabia 35–6
Royal Engineers 109, 177
Royal Ordnance Factories 70–1
Royal Saudi Air Force (RSAF) 136–7,
    158–9

Ryder, Lord 101–3
report 102, 105, 114, 176
see also British Leyland

Saab 169–70, 173
Saad, Lily 32
Sa'ad, Shaikh (Kuwaiti Defence Minister)
banning of agents from arms deals 97–8
Saba, Dr Elias (Lebanese Minister of Defence)
banning of agents from arms deals 27–8
Sadat, Anwar (Egyptian President) 115
Said, Wafiq 132
Saladin armoured cars 41, 43–4, 46, 49, 51
Salam, Saeb (Lebanese Prime Minister) 25–7, 30
commissions 32
Salim, Yoesie 144–5Sampson, Anthony 90
discussion of arms trade corruption xi
Sampson, William 165
Sanson, Alec (salesman, the British Aircraft Corporation) 5–7
discussion of commission arrangements 6–7
SAS 120
Saud, ibn, founder and King (of Saudi Arabia) 1, 3, 40
Saud, King (of Saudi Arabia) 3, 40, 42
Saudi Arabia 38, 51, 53–4, 56, 71, 75, 81, 85–6, 89, 93–6, 105, 115, 129–32, 134, 137, 141, 154–8, 164–5
corruption 21, 24, 119, 130, 167, 180
Decree No. 1275 89, 103, 107, 181
intelligence co-operation with Britain 161–2, 165
Italian commission payments to Petromin 130
Ministry of Defence and Aviation 40, 86, 88
Ministry of Finance 34
Ministry of the Interior 47, 94–5
place to do business 3, 6, 41
police and security services 120, 165
Special Security Forces 120, 165
strategic importance 83
torture 165
use of agents 164
see also commissions
Saudi Arabian Air Defence Assistance Project (SADAP) *see* the British

Aircraft Corporation (BAC) and British Aerospace (BAe)
Saudi Arabian Air Defence (SAAD) scheme 8
commissions 13–15, 80–1
Consortium 80, 137
contracts signed 80–1
involvement of Airwork 8–9, 13, 80–1, 106, 137
involvement of Associated Electrical Industries (AEI) 8–9, 13, 80–1, 83, 87, 106
involvement of Geoffrey Edwards 8–15, 80–1, 106
involvement of the British Aircraft Corporation (BAC) 8–13, 80–2, 131
negotiation 9, 13
Saudi Arabian National Guard 38, 40, 58
arms deals 41–55, 106, 175–7
British Military Mission 42, 44, 120
Land Rover deal 102
Office of the Program Manager 55
SANGMED contract 177
see also Abdullah, Prince; Freedom of Information Act
Saudi Arabian National Guard Communications (SANGCOM) project *see* Cable & Wireless
Saudi Army 52, 176
see also Panhard armoured cars; Tounisi, General Makki; Vickers
Saudi Ministry of Finance *see* Saudi Arabia
Saudi Princes *see* Saudi Royal Family
Saudi Royal Family 1, 3–4, 80, 87, 119, 130, 134, 154, 161–2, 178
BAe benefits programme 138–9, 142
commissions 82, 84, 86, 88, 115, 134, 159
Council of Ministers 37–8, 52–3, 81, 89
decision-making 5, 53, 115
see also Abdullah, Prince; Abdul Aziz bin Abdullah, Prince; Abdul Rahman, Prince; Abeer bin Turki, Princess; Bandar bin Sultan, Prince; Fahd, Prince; Faisal bin Turki, Prince; Feisal, King; Haifa bin Turki, Princess; Khalid bin Abdullah, Prince; Mohammed bin Saud, Prince; Noura, Princess; Reema bin Bandar, Princess; Saud, ibn; Saud, King; Sudairi, Zaid; Sultan, Prince; Turki bin Faisal, Prince; Turki bin Nasser, Princes; Turki, Prince

Scicon 94–6
  commissions 94–6
Scorpion armoured fighting vehicles
  143–6
Secret Intelligence Service (SIS) 65, 68
  documents xv
  1953 coup in Iran with Central
    Intelligence Agency (CIA) 56, 68
  reports 94
  see also Reporter, Shapoor
'Section 2 notices' *see* Serious Fraud
  Office investigation of BAE Systems
Securities and Exchange Commission
  (SEC) 78, 106
  enforcement of securities laws 76, 79,
    91
  Historical Society xiii
  Lockheed scandal 77, 90
  Northrop scandal 73
  voluntary disclosure programme 76–7,
    94–6, 111
securities laws 76
Senate (America) 110
Serious Fraud Office (SFO) xiv, 154–5, 174
  see also Garlick, Helen; Wardle, Robert
Serious Fraud Office investigation of BAE
  Systems 147, 149, 153, 154–8, 160–7,
    169–71, 173–4
  conviction 170–2, 183
  duration xiv
Serious Fraud Office investigation of GPT
  Special Project Management Limited
    174–5, 177–8
Shah of Iran, the 38–9, 55, 57–8, 64, 69
  'fund' 59, 65–7, 71
  1953 coup in Iran 56, 65, 68
  policy on corruption 24, 61, 68
  problems faced by his regime 64, 67,
    120
  Randel case 63, 65, 154
  relations with British Government
    56–60, 65, 69, 120, 176
  see also Reporter, Shapoor
Shaw, Sir Michael (MP, Deputy
  Chairman, Public Accounts
  Committee) 143
Sheldon, Robert (MP, Chairman, Public
  Accounts Committee) 143
Shell 116
Shorts *see* Near East Resources
Siemens Plessey Electronic Systems 170
  commissions 170
  see also BAE Systems

Silkin, Sam (QC, Attorney General) 105
  discussions about corruption in
    international trade 114
  proposals for international agreement
    against corruption 121, 123–5
SIMEC International 108, 175–7
  commissions 106, 175
Smith, John (Trade Secretary)
  proposals for international agreement
    against corruption 123–4
Soekarno, Mr 144–5
Soewondho, Rini 145–6
Somerfield, Bryan 175–7
Sourakia 134
sources xii
  British Government xiv
  Caldecote papers 13
South Africa 147, 154, 173–4, 180
South Korea 146
Soviet Union 19, 56, 169
Special Review Committee *see* Lockheed
  Aircraft Corporation
State Department 12
  fines BAE Systems 172, 183
  views of Northrop scandal 87–8
  study of anti-corruption laws 72
  see also Arms Export Control Act
Steel, David (Chairman, British
  Petroleum) 92
Steele, Lionel (International Sales
  Manager, Alvis) 145
Stokes, Sir Donald 21, 59
  review of British arms exports 19
Stonehouse, John (Parliamentary
  Secretary, Ministry of Aviation)
    14–15
Stormer vehicles 144, 146
Strathcona, Lord (British Defence
  Minister)
  proposals for international agreement
    against corruption 127
Straw, Jack (Foreign Secretary) 156, 161
Strikemaster aircraft 131, 134
'Sudairi Seven' 40
  see also Abdul Rahman, Prince; Fahd,
    Prince; Sultan, Prince
Sudairi, Zaid 35
Suffield, Sir Lester (Head of Defence
  Sales) 132
  evidence at Randel trial 64–5
  involvement in decisions about
    commissions 28, 50, 60, 66, 97–9,
    106

sales campaign in Lebanon 27–8, 32
sales to Iran 58, 62, 66
sales to Kuwait 97–9
sales to Saudi Arabia 38, 106
sales to Saudi Arabian National Guard
  48, 50, 52–3, 106, 175
view of Shapoor Reporter 62, 64, 66
Suharto, Mrs Tien 116–17
Suharto, President (Indonesia) 116, 144–6
Sultan, Prince (Minister of Defence,
  Saudi Arabia) 4, 12, 40, 80, 136, 166
  Al Yamamah 132, 134, 159
  British perceptions of 91
  Lockheed scandal 91
  negotiation of Saudi Arabian Air
    Defence (SAAD) scheme 14–15, 81
  Northrop scandal 86–8, 90
  receipt of assurances about Geoffrey
    Edwards 5
  sales to Saudi Arabian National Guard
    53–4
  see also Sudairi, Zaid
Sunday Times see British Petroleum (BP)
Sunderland (shipbuilders) *see* Nigeria
Swan Hunter *see* Nigeria
Switzerland 113–14, 116, 148, 157, 170
  bank accounts 18, 52, 85, 93–4, 103,
    111, 113–15, 157, 162, 164, 167

Tanaka, Kakuei (Japanese Prime
  Minister) 75
  commissions 75
Tanassi, Mario (Italian Defence Minister)
  75
Tanzania 154, 170–2, 183
Task Force on Questionable Corporate
  Payments Abroad *see* Ford, Gerald
Tebbit, Sir Kevin (Permanent Secretary,
  Ministry of Defence) 155–6
Thailand 116
Thatcher, Margaret (British Prime
  Minister) 125, 130–1, 150
  Al Yamamah 134, 159
  knowledge of corruption 130
The Corner House 162
The National Archives 158, 160
Thomson Houston 32
Thunderbird missile system 5
  commissions 6–7, 15
  negotiation of Saudi deal 5–8, 15
Titan Corporation 172
  'social payments' 172

Tornado aircraft 131–2, 134, 156–7, 159,
  166
Touche Ross & Co 108
Toufanian, General Hassan (Chief of
  Military Industrial Organisation and
  Procurement, Iranian Ministry of
  War) 58–60, 65, 67
Tounisi, General Makki (Director of
  Operations, Saudi Army)
  commissions 35–6
Trace International 179
Trade Promotion Coordinating
  Committee 179
Trades Union Congress 113
Transparency International 182
Travel Company, the 138
Travellers World 138, 153
  BAe benefits programme 138–42,
    151–3, 163, 167, 178
Treasury, HM 111, 114, 184
  attitude towards agents 22, 99, 111
Treasury Solicitor's Department 97
Triad Financial Establishment *see*
  Khashoggi, Adnan
Triad International Marketing *see*
  Khashoggi, Adnan
TriStar airliners *see* Lockheed Aircraft
  Corporation
Turkey 93
Turki bin Faisal, Prince (Head of Saudi
  Intelligence) 132
Turki bin Nasser, Prince 136, 138
  BAe benefits programme 136–43,
    151–2, 163–4
Turki, Prince (Deputy Minister of
  Defence and Aviation, Saudi Arabia)
  87
Turner, Damian 153
Turner, Mike (Chief Executive, BAE
  Systems) 168
Twal, Shehadah 23
  commissions 24

UN Convention against Corruption
  definition of bribe ix
  effects of grand corruption xi
UN Economic and Social Council
  (ECOSOC) 110, 117, 121, 123, 127
UN General Assembly 127
  Resolution 3514 110, 117
UN Security Council Resolution 1373 165
Uniglobe Aktiengesellschaft (Uniglobe)
  148

Unilever 116
United Arab Emirates 130
US Agency for International
    Development 76

Varley, Eric (Industry Secretary) 100, 105
    attitudes to corruption in international
        trade 101, 103–4
    proposals for international agreement
        against corruption 121, 124
Venezuela 22
Vickers 16
    Archive xiii
    commissions 17–18, 35–7, 45, 91
    negotiation of submarine deal with
        Saudi Arabia 16–18
    negotiation of tank deal with Saudi
        Arabian Army 34–7, 45
    use of Near East Resources as agent in
        Lebanon 26, 31
Vigilant anti-tank weapons 7, 48
Vinnell Corporation 55
Vithlani, Shailesh 170–2
    commissions 170–2

Walker, Leslie 165
Wardle, Robert (Director, Serious Fraud
    Office) 153, 156–7, 161–2, 166–7
Watergate scandal 72–3
Weinstock, Arnold (Managing Director of
    General Electric Company) 83–4
West Germany 58, 111, 114, 120, 131
Weston, John (Chief Executive, BAE
    Systems) 150–1, 167

Wikileaks website 163
William Brandt's Sons and Company Ltd
    25–7, 30–1
Wilson, Harold (British Prime Minister)
    14–15, 56
Wilson, Peter (Managing Director, BAE
    International Programmes) 153
Wilton, John (British Ambassador to
    Kuwait, later Saudi Arabia) 95–6,
    115, 176
Wingetac
    commissions 17
    negotiation of submarine deal with
        Saudi Arabia 17–18
Winship, Tony 137–8, 152
    BAe benefits programme 137–42,
        151–2
Winterbottom, Lord (British Defence
    Minister) 52
Woolf Committee 168
Woolf, Lord 167–8
Working Group 117–18, 120–5
Wright, Paul (British Ambassador to
    Lebanon)
    involvement in decisions about
        commissions 28, 31–2
Wright, Sir Denis (British Ambassador to
    Iran) 58
Wright, Sir Patrick (British Ambassador
    to Saudi Arabia) 159

Yar'adua, Brigadier Shehu Musa
    bribe 101
Yemen 3, 137